Jacques Ellul and the Bible

Jacques Ellul and the Bible

Towards a Hermeneutic of Freedom

Edited by
Jacob Marques Rollison

James Clarke & Co

James Clarke & Co
P.O. Box 60
Cambridge
CB1 2NT
United Kingdom

www.jamesclarke.co
publishing@jamesclarke.co

Paperback ISBN: 978 0 227 17794 5
PDF ISBN: 978 0 227 17806 5

British Library Cataloguing in Publication Data
A record is available from the British Library

First published by Pickwick Publishing, 2020

This edition published by James Clarke & Co, 2022,
by arrangement with Wipf and Stock Publishers

Copyright © Jacob Marques Rollison, 2022

All rights reserved. No part of this edition may be reproduced, stored electronically or in any retrieval system, or transmitted in any form or by any means, electronic, mechanical, photocopying, recording, or otherwise, without prior written permission from the Publisher (permissions@jamesclarke.co).

Contents

List of Contributors | vii

Acknowledgments | xiii

Introduction: A Hermeneutic of Freedom?—*Jacob Marques Rollison* | 1

Part I: Approaching the Biblical Text

CHAPTER 1: Jacques Ellul's View of Scripture—*David W. Gill* | 17

CHAPTER 2: The Authority of the Bible—*Jacques Ellul; translated by Anne-Marie Andreasson Hogg* | 29

CHAPTER 3: The Bible and Christian Action—*Jacques Ellul; translated by Lisa Richmond* | 41

CHAPTER 4: Scriptural Ethics: On the Meaning and Use of the Analogy of Faith—*Frédéric Rognon; translated by Jacob Marques Rollison* | 48

CHAPTER 5: Meaning and Its "Interplay" with Freedom in the Bible—*Jacques Ellul; translated by Anne-Marie Andreasson Hogg* | 61

Part II: Revisiting Ellul's Readings of the Bible

CHAPTER 6: Jacques Ellul as a Theological Exegete of the Old Testament—*John Goldingay* | 75

CHAPTER 7: What's in a Name? Jacques Ellul's Reading of Naming in Genesis 1–3—*Michael Morelli* | 82

CHAPTER 8: Jacques Ellul and Exodus: A Summary and Review
—*G. P. Wagenfuhr* | 95

CHAPTER 9: Ellul on Job: The Freedom of Waiting
—*Amy J. Erickson* | 111

CHAPTER 10: Ellul as a Reader of Ecclesiastes
—*Anthony J. Petrotta* | 118

CHAPTER 11: The Figure of Jonah in Ellul's Life and Work—*Jean-Sébastien Ingrand; translated by Jacob Marques Rollison* | 126

CHAPTER 12: Reading 2 Kings with Jacques Ellul—*Chris Friesen* | 142

CHAPTER 13: A Short, Complementary Note on Romans 13:1
—*Jacques Ellul; translated by Jacob Marques Rollison* | 152

CHAPTER 14: Review of André Chouraqui's Translation of the Bible
—*Jacques Ellul; translated by Lisa Richmond* | 155

Part III: Ellul and the Bible Today: Contemporary Dialogue

CHAPTER 15: Darwin and the Bible—*Jacques Ellul; translated by Matthew T. Prior* | 165

CHAPTER 16: Giving under God's Gaze: Figures of the Gift in the Bible and in the Work of Jacques Ellul—*Patrick Chastenet; translated by Christian Roy* | 168

CHAPTER 17: Nature and Scripture in Bernard Charbonneau's *The Green Light*—*Christian Roy* | 189

CHAPTER 18: Review of Ellul, *On Being Rich and Poor: Christianity in a Time of Economic Globalization*
—*Brian Brock* | 201

CHAPTER 19: Hope and Abandonment in the Bible
—*Elisabetta Ribet* | 204

CHAPTER 20: Ellul on Scripture and Idolatry
—*Andrew Goddard* | 212

CHAPTER 21: The Tower of Babel and the Hymn of Kenosis: Counterpoint Texts for Ellul—*Ted Lewis* | 218

CHAPTER 22: Ellul's Apocalyptic Understanding of Scripture in *Money and Power*—*Declan Kelly* | 234

Contributors

Anne-Marie Andreasson Hogg is Professor of Scandinavian Studies at North Park University in Chicago. She holds a PhD in Linguistics from the University of Illinois at Urbana-Champaign. She has translated many books, including several works by Jacques Ellul such as *An Unjust God?* (Cascade, 2012) and *If You are the Son of God* (Cascade, 2014). She is a member of the Association of Swedish Teachers and Researchers in America and the Society for the Advancement of Scandinavian Study.

Brian Brock is Professor of Moral and Practical Theology at the University of Aberdeen (Scotland). He earned his DPhil from King's College, London (UK). He is an editor of the theology and technology blog *Second Nature* and has published widely on the ethics of technology. His publications include *Christian Ethics in a Technological Age* (Eerdmans, 2010), *Captive to Christ, Open to the World: On Doing Christian Ethics in Public* (Cascade, 2014). He edited with John Swinton *Theology, Disability and the New Genetics: Why Science Needs the Church* (T. & T. Clark, 2007), and *A Graceful Embrace: Theological Reflections on Adopting Children* (Brill, 2018).

Patrick Chastenet is Professor of Political Science at the University of Bordeaux. He was Jacques Ellul's student assistant in the 1970s. He has published ten books on Ellul, including his recent *Introduction à Jacques Ellul* (La Découverte, 2019). He is the founding president of the Association Internationale Jacques Ellul, director of *Cahiers Jacques Ellul*, and a founding board member of the International Jacques Ellul Society. He has organized several international and multidisciplinary colloquia on Ellul's thought and legacy.

Chris Friesen pastors a Mennonite church near Saskatoon, Saskatchewan. His vocational life has included teaching and presence ministry in a northern aboriginal context, direction of an outreach program for inner-city children, curriculum writing for youth and young adults, leadership in a disability agency, and a decade-plus of recording, performing, and touring with his eight-member family band. He holds an MA in Theology from Mennonite Brethren Biblical Seminary in Fresno, California (now Fresno Pacific Biblical Seminary), where his thesis-as-novel, supervised by Mark Baker, surveyed Jesus's language of doom from hermeneutical and existential standpoints. He begins doctoral studies at Wycliffe College (University of Toronto) in fall 2020, proposing to bring into dialogue the soteriology of Jacques Ellul and Lesslie Newbigin.

David W. Gill earned his PhD with a doctoral dissertation on "The Word of God in the Ethics of Jacques Ellul" (University of Southern California, 1979; subsequently published by Scarecrow Press, 1984). He is the author of many articles, reviews, and book introductions on Jacques Ellul and co-editor of *Political Illusion and Reality: Engaging the Prophetic Insights of Jacques Ellul* (Wipf & Stock, 2018). Over his forty-year career as a university and seminary professor, he taught many courses and gave many public lectures on Ellul's thought. He served on the founding editorial team of *The Ellul Forum* from 1988 onward and he is founding president of the International Jacques Ellul Society (2000) and a founding member of the council of the Association Internationale Jacques Ellul.

Amy J. Erickson currently resides in Texas, where she teaches theology at Texas Lutheran University. She holds a PhD in Divinity from the University of Aberdeen (Scotland), granted for a thesis blending creative theological interpretation of scripture with theological-ethical analysis. She is the author of *Ephraim Radner, Hosean Wilderness, and the Church in the Post-Christendom West* (Brill, 2020).

Andrew Goddard is Senior Research Fellow at the Kirby Laing Institute for Christian Ethics in Cambridge, where he formerly served as Associate Director. He is Assistant Minister at St James the Less Church in London. He teaches for Fuller Theological Seminary, Pasadena and Westminster Theological Centre. He previously taught Christian Ethics at Wycliffe Hall, Oxford and then at Trinity College, Bristol. He has written on a number of areas in ethics and on Anglicanism and is currently researching and writing a book about Christian sexual ethics. He is also an Honorary Canon of Winchester Cathedral.

CONTRIBUTORS

John Goldingay lives with his wife Kathleen in Oxford, United Kingdom. He was formerly Principal of St John's Theological College, Nottingham, UK, then David Allan Hubbard Professor of Old Testament at Fuller Theological Seminary, Pasadena; he continues to teach online for Fuller. He has written a number of books and commentaries on the Old Testament.

Jean-Sébastien Ingrand is a pastor with the *Union des Églises protestantes d'Alsace et de Lorraine* (UEPAL) in France. He currently occupies a unique post within the French church tasked with investigating climatic and environmental justice. He has pursued theological studies in Heidelberg, Geneva, and Paris, and has also studied at *l'École biblique et archéologique française* in Jerusalem. Formerly director of the *Médiathèque Protestante* in Strasbourg, he is a passionate reader and collector of rare and antique books.

Declan Kelly recently completed a PhD in Systematic Theology at the University of Aberdeen. His thesis explored an apocalyptic reading of Karl Barth's soteriology. He continues to reside in Aberdeen and is currently working on an Introduction to Karl Barth for T. & T. Clark's "Theology and Religion Online".

Ted Lewis is Communications Consultant at the Center for Restorative Justice & Peacemaking at the University of Minnesota, providing training and consultation work for restorative justice programs nationwide. Ted also serves on the board of the National Association for Community and Restorative Justice. Since 2004, he has worked as an Acquisitions Editor for Wipf and Stock Publishers where he oversees the Jacques Ellul Legacy Series. He holds an MA in Religious Studies (University of Minnesota) focused on the sociology of religious-based conflicts and wrote his thesis on "Idolatry and Iconoclasm in Ancient Israel." In February 2017 he was appointed the first Executive Director of the IJES. He lives in Duluth, Minnesota.

Jacob Marques Rollison is an independent scholar living in Strasbourg, France. He holds a PhD in theological ethics from the University of Aberdeen. He is co-author of *Jacques Ellul* in the Cascade Companions series, as well as *A New Reading of Jacques Ellul: Presence and Communication in the Postmodern World* (Lexington Books, 2020). He has recently translated Ellul's two-volume *To Will &To Do: An Introduction to Christian Ethics* (Cascade). He is on the board of directors of the International Jacques Ellul Society.

Michael Morelli is Assistant Dean of Undergraduate Studies and Assistant Professor of Theology, Culture & Ethics at Northwest Seminary and College in Vancouver, British Columbia. He recently completed his doctorate at the University of Aberdeen (Scotland) which focuses on theology, ethics, and technology in the work of Jacques Ellul and Paul Virilio. Michael studies theological ethics, meaning he is fascinated by the ways God's truth confronts and changes the realities that make up our existence. He worked in local church ministry prior to his return to the theological academy and he continues to serve the church in a lay capacity. He also publishes and presents on a variety of topics within the fields of theology, morality, culture, politics, and technology.

Anthony J. Petrotta is Rector of St. Francis of Assisi Episcopal Church (Wilsonville, OR) and long-time adjunct professor of Old Testament for Fuller Theological Seminary. He is a graduate of Fuller Seminary (M.A.) and the University of Sheffield (UK) (PhD). He is co-author of the *Pocket Dictionary of Biblical Studies* (InterVarsity Press, 2002) and author of many articles and reviews.

Matthew T. Prior is an ordained minister in the Church of England and Tutor and Lecturer in Ethics at St. Mellitus College, London. He holds a PhD from the University of Bristol for a thesis on Jacques Ellul's theological engagement with technology. He is the author of *Confronting Technology: The Theology of Jacques Ellul* (Wipf & Stock, 2020). He is a member of the International Jacques Ellul Society

Elisabetta Ribet obtained a PhD in Theology from the University of Strasbourg for her thesis "La provocation de l'espérance. Perspectives théologiques actuelles dans l'oeuvre de Jacques Ellul" directed by Prof. Frédéric Rognon. Formerly a pastor of the Waldensian and Methodist Church in Italy, she has lived and worked in Strasbourg since 2014. She presently works on the formation of Chaplains and Pastors for the *Union des Eglises-Protestantes d'Alsace et de Lorraine* and teaches at the Protestant Faculty of Theology in Strasbourg.

Lisa Richmond is Vice President of Research at the Cardus Religious Freedom Institute in Hamilton, Ontario. She is the editor of *The Ellul Forum* and translator of Ellul's *Presence in the Modern World* (Cascade, 2016). She is nearing completion of her PhD at Université Paul-Valéry, Montpellier III (France) in seventeenth-century French literature.

Frédéric Rognon is Professor of Philosophy at the Faculty of Protestant Theology at the University of Strasbourg (France), President of the Justice and Prison Chaplaincy Comission of *the Fédération Protestante de France*, and Editor of the journal *Foi & Vie*. Among his published works are *Jacques Ellul: Une pensée en dialogue* (Geneva: Labor et Fides, 2007, 2013) and *Générations Ellul: Soixante héritiers de la pensée de Jacques Ellul* (Geneva: Labor et Fides, 2012).

Christian Roy (PhD McGill 1993) is a Montreal-based cultural historian, art and film critic, and multilingual translator. He has recently completed translations of Bernard Charbonneau's *The Green Light* (Bloomsbury, 2018) and Jacques Ellul's *Theology and Technique* (Wipf & Stock, forthcoming). His research focuses on the Personalist intellectual tradition, especially its pre-war roots in France. He is also the author of *Traditional Festivals. A Multicultural Encyclopedia* (ABC-Clio, 2005).

G. P. Wagenfuhr is Theology Coordinator of ECO: A Covenant Order of Evangelical Presbyterians. He has written numerous books and articles, many on Jacques Ellul. He holds a PhD from the University of Bristol for a thesis written on Jacques Ellul and his vision of Christianity. He and his wife reside in Cañon City, CO where they are developing a renewed vision of church as a plausible revelation of the kingdom of God. His latest book, *Plundering Eden: A Subversive Christian Theology of Creation and Ecology* (Cascade, 2020) offers a unique perspective on ecology influenced by Ellul's thought and method.

Acknowledgments

THIS VOLUME WOULD NOT exist without the important (and largely volunteer) work done by the leadership of the *International Jacques Ellul Society*. Thanks to all IJES members for supporting the society's mission and work. I would especially like to thank David Gill, President; Ted Lewis, Executive Director; and Lisa Richmond, editor of the Ellul Forum, for their support and encouragement. We are also grateful for ongoing the ongoing friendship and support of Patrick Chastenet and everyone else at our sister society, *l'Association Internationale Jacques Ellul*. Thanks are due to all contributing authors for their careful work and cordial correspondence. Thanks are due to Lisa Richmond, Anne-Marie Andreasson Hogg, Christian Roy, and Matthew Prior for their translation work.

Thanks are due, of course, to the Ellul family, for their ongoing support and friendship and their support of the society. Specifically, they are to be thanked for permitting the inclusion of the six translated articles by Jacques Ellul, including two unpublished texts. Thanks to Jean-Philippe Qadri for providing access to these materials. Likewise, thanks to the various publications permitting translations of previously published materials: thanks to Nathalie Leenhardt and *Réforme* for allowing the translation of "Darwin and the Bible"; thanks to Caroline Meffre and *Revue des Deux Mondes* for allowing the translation of Ellul's review of *La Bible: Traduction d'André Chouraqui*; thanks to Frédéric Rognon and *Foi et Vie* for allowing the translation of Ellul's *Petite note complémentaire sur romains 13:1*; thanks to Gallimard for allowing our translation of *Le sens et le jeu de la liberté dans la Bible*. Thanks to Pieter Lalleman and the *European Journal of Theology* and to Brian Brock for allowing us to reprint his review of *On Being Rich and Poor*. Thanks to Lisa Richmond at *The Ellul Forum* to allow us to include the articles from issue 36, and to their respective authors for kindly revisiting these articles.

Insofar as I bear a certain responsibility for this volume as its editor, I would like to dedicate my contribution to my sister Sarah, along with all other medical staff working to alleviate the suffering caused in the COVID-19 pandemic sweeping the globe as I finish work on this book, with deep gratitude for their important work.

JMR

Introduction

A Hermeneutic of Freedom?

Jacob Marques Rollison

Among the everyday activities performed by the modern individual, few are both as elementary and complex as reading. On one level, reading is completely self-evident. Children read in elementary school; adults read instructions, recipes, road signs, music. The quality of these readings is discernable by what they produce: the child says "cat," the food is tasty, or the music is harmonious (of course, assuming the letters "c-a-t," a well-conceived recipe, and a harmonious composition!). But what makes for a "good" reading once the scope is broadened to include more complex literary, historical, mythological, poetic, or philosophical writings? Is there a guaranteed method to produce good interpretations?

These questions are more complex when these various genres intertwine within a single work; even further complexity emerges when a tradition and community hear all genres in this one work as moments in divine-human dialogue. Precisely this kind of interpretive questioning describes the reflections of the Judeo-Christian tradition on the Biblical text. In the Christian community, reading has always been tied up with living; interpretation inevitably shapes life. And when interpretation is so inextricably ethical, an ethics of interpretation can prove useful. Here, the modern disciplines of biblical studies, hermeneutics, and theological interpretation of scripture step in, offering voluminous resources to accompany ethical reflection on scripture.

Yet for all the helpful tools that hermeneutic studies might give us, hermeneutics has its limits. It can never assume responsibility for our readings. However its tools might refine ethical thinking, they can never give an account for our lives and actions. Hermeneutics can interrogate our "how," but cannot dispense with our "why." When one raises the profound and contested subject of human freedom, recourse to hermeneutic method to justify one's actions serves as an excuse, an evasion; the challenge of freedom can only be taken up by a person, not a method. What, then, could a phrase like "hermeneutics of freedom" mean?

In the life and work of the twentieth-century French thinker Jacques Ellul (1912–1994), we have a lived example of one who wrestled at length with the meaning of free biblical interpretation. The essays in this volume present evidence of the stimulating, provocative, and fresh encouragement which readers of the Bible find in Jacques Ellul. While diversely grappling with Ellul's interpretations, the voices collected here resound in unison: Ellul forces us to reconsider our readings of (indeed, our *listening to*) scripture. Furthermore, despite his disappearance more than a quarter of a century ago, this volume marks an important moment in a very contemporary conversation, proving that we have by no means exhausted Ellul's potential to fruitfully upset and reconfigure the way we relate to Christianity's most influential text. Ellul's increasingly evident current relevance only further underscores his belief that the Word of God as attested by this text is living and present here and now.

Before describing the content of the contributions contained herein, I would like to draw on Ellul's volumes of theological ethics to comment on the concrete ways in which his approach might be considered a *hermeneutics of freedom*.

I. A Free and Prophetic Scriptural Hermeneutic

a. Situating Ellul's Ethical Works and Interpretation of Scripture

Allowing Ellul to rework our scriptural approach might involve revisiting our approach to Ellul himself. This volume is produced not only by veteran Ellul readers, but also by a new generation of scholarly interest in Ellul. The new eyes of the reader approaching Ellul for the first time should be welcomed by seasoned readers as an invitation to revisit what have become accepted approaches to his corpus.

While Ellul's multifaceted work has often been described as a dialectic between *theology* and *sociology*, it is more precise to describe this duality as a project of *theological ethics* in dialogue with an *historical-institutional* approach to social reality.¹ Ellul's project is ultimately a project of prophetic communication, involving both an address to his reader designed to interrogate contemporary life with biblical revelation, and a call to lived response in free dialogue with God as revealed in Jesus Christ. Seeing his work this way explains the substantial and central place in his corpus occupied by his five published volumes of theological ethics.²

To facilitate this communication, alongside his vast theological-ethical corpus Ellul wrote numerous volumes presenting theological interpretation of scripture. These volumes include both what might be dubbed "existential commentaries"—combining careful study of a given biblical book or theme with Ellul's intense, personal meditations on what this book or that theme means for readers *today*—and several volumes made from recordings of bible studies led by Ellul in his home in the 1970s.³ The present volume thus focuses on this theological-interpretive component of Ellul's work.

Arguably the most crucial ethical theme in Ellul's works (as in those of his lifelong friend and dialogue partner Bernard Charbonneau) is *freedom*. Ellul planned a four-part ethics including an introduction (*To Will & To Do*) followed by one part corresponding to each element of the apostle Paul's trio of faith, hope, and love: an *Ethics of Holiness* (faith), an *Ethics of Freedom* (hope), and an *Ethics of Relationship* (love). Based on his diagnosis of western society in the late twentieth century as fundamentally lacking hope, Ellul began with the *Ethics of Freedom*, guided by the feeling that this was the most urgent element for our time. Throughout his work, Ellul refuses to consider freedom metaphysically, viewing such an approach as foreign to Judeo-Christian thought. Instead, Ellul aimed to consider human freedom as lived in contemporary society—taking seriously all the concrete pressures and determinations of human action which such action involves—and to confront this freedom with his readings of the Bible. The result is a profoundly countercultural freedom whose biblical contours jarringly frustrate the political discourse situating much modern discussion of freedom. I will not try to describe the unabashedly Christological approach characterizing Ellul's fundamentally biblical theology here (as David Gill and others do a fine job

---

1. For more on this, see my introduction to Ellul, *To Will & To Do*, vol. 1, or at length, my *A New Reading of Jacques Ellul*.

2. Ellul, *To Will & To Do*, 2 vols.; *Éthique de la liberté*, 3 vols. Additionally, Ellul's 1000+ page manuscript of *Éthique de la sainteté* has yet to appear in French or English.

3. The first category includes works such as Ellul, *Judgement of Jonah*; *Politics of God and the Politics of Man*; *Meaning of the City*; and *Reason for Being*. The second category includes the two volumes compiled, edited, and translated by Willem H. Vanderburg, *On Freedom, Love, and Power*, and *On Being Rich and Poor*, as well as *Mort et espérance de la résurrection*.

in Part I of this volume). Instead, I would like to focus on how Ellul situates freedom in relation to his ethical interpretation of scripture.

b. Prophetically Proclaiming the Law of Freedom

One of Ellul's major ethical contentions is that the Protestant tradition has an underdeveloped approach to scriptural ethics.[4] Ellul tries to counter this deficiency in his ethical studies, and especially in his two-volume introduction to Christian Ethics, *To Will & To Do*. This means that Ellul's theological ethics offers not just biblically oriented thought about living but includes a built-in ethics of reading the Bible as well.

In volume one of *To Will & To Do*, he very clearly indicates the *biblical* foundations and distinctly Protestant contours of his ethical approach. In his thinking, biblical injunctions are not to be made into a law equally imposable upon Christians and non-Christians but are only valid by faith *in Christ*. We cannot arrive at the "good" via any casuistry, nor establish absolute criteria for good action. The good is the will of God, not the will of humanity; any good we might set up ourselves is thus in competition with God's good. Christian ethics is thus impossible, as such a declaration would necessarily be out of line with God's own declared good. However, as the church is a sociological group like any other, Christians spontaneously produce morality as a social bond. It would therefore be better that such morality be consciously created precisely to protect against temptations to absolutize it. Christian ethics are thus profoundly relative but not unimportant; they are thus *impossible*, but *necessary*.

He continues this discussion in the recently discovered second volume of *To Will & To Do*. Therein, Ellul develops the *analogy of faith* (or *rule of faith*) as a Spirit-guided and specifically ethical hermeneutic approach to the Bible. (This is treated at length by Frédéric Rognon in chapter four of the present work.) He notes that Paul discusses this volume specifically in relation to the prophet; developing theological ethics, then, is the specifically communicative function of the *prophet*.

Ellul often remarks how in the Old Testament, the prophets essentially lived out the freedom of the Word, calling Israel back to the spirit and letter of the covenant established with God throughout their history as a people. But he notes that the prophets did not simply repeat the Mosaic law, but selected elements of it and translated them into their own time and context. He thus writes:

---

4. See Ellul, *To Will & To Do*, 1:223.

> We must do concerning these texts exactly what the prophets accomplished in relation to the law of Moses; but this is only possible in the objectivity of an analogy of faith, in relation to the objectivity of the text; that is why there is no veritable contradiction between what is said by the prophets and the Pentateuch. Of course, on specific points, there are contradictions of form, of expression, of institution, but never of inspiration, because of the unity of the Spirit.[5]

In volume two of *To Will & To Do*, Ellul discusses what it means that Christ "fulfills" the law. Because Christians must take the Bible seriously in its entirety, the legal texts of the Old Testament cannot be ignored. But what is the relation between these Old Testament laws and contemporary Christian ethics?

Freedom enters precisely at this juncture. In *The Ethics of Freedom*, Ellul insists that freedom is the central, primary element in Paul's theology, calling it a "superstructure of revelation." He insists that Paul is not simply expressing a personal preference but is carrying forward the heart of Jewish thinking. For Paul, we know God as our Liberator, and our freedom is unthinkable apart from God's own presence.[6] (G.P. Wagenfuhr discusses this at length regarding the book and theme of "exodus" in chapter eight.) Moreover, in volume two of *Éthique de la liberté*, Ellul discusses the theme of "the law of liberty" as developed in the Epistle of James. Ellul sees this law of freedom not simply as an element in New Testament ethics; rather:

> There is thus no longer any question of putting multiple commandments into practice, of a morality; but the only requirement which God imposes on us is henceforth to behave as free men. And this becomes a *duty*. Our only duty is lived freedom. And James strengthens this affirmation by speaking of the law. This is truly a transposition of the entire law.[7]

The New Testament "law of freedom," therefore, *is* the entirety of the Old Testament law when refracted through the fulfilling work of Christ. Certainly, there is more to say. For example, Ellul insists that this law of freedom is none other than the command to love, an additional step which we cannot develop at length here. Likewise, Ellul spends multiple volumes clarifying this freedom precisely to avoid Christians' making it into a "value," which leaves it a malleable and abstract notion which we attach to almost whatever we please.

---

5. Ellul, *To Will & To Do*, 2: forthcoming from Cascade.
6. Ellul, *Ethics of Freedom*, 94–100, esp. 96.
7. Ellul, *Éthique de la liberté*, 2:14 (my translation).

But this is enough to highlight that for Ellul, there is no Christian ethic which is not rooted in and oriented by the law of freedom.

Therefore, Ellul's prophetic-communicative project functions just like an Old Testament prophet: he cries out to the entirety of a society who has forgotten (or never truly known) God's promises and God's ways, admonishing them to return to the injunctions of God's law. However, in the post-Christ context, this fulfilled law is none other than the law of freedom. Thus, Ellul's careful theological-scriptural interpretation of freedom as the central ethical element in both the Old and New Testaments of the Bible translates into a theological-ethical injunction to live in freedom. This, then, is the primary content we can assign to Ellul's *hermeneutic of freedom*: it is a hermeneutic in which freedom is the central ethical element, permitting us to see the unity of the scriptural whole and the work of God in the world around us.

A recurring critique of Protestant Christians in Ellul's time is that they have deeply misunderstood biblical ethics and thus failed to live out this freedom. As Ellul nuances it, this critique seems to apply quite well also to our own time. On the one hand, unnuanced readings of scriptural ethics often ignore the law's mediation via freedom in Paul's writings, tending to solidify his ethical proposals into an absolute morality, effectively creating a new law. Ellul even complains that in our day Christianity is largely seen *only* as a morality. This critique might arguably be applied today, for example, to much of anglophone evangelicalism worldwide, and markedly in North America. On the other hand, Ellul faults less "conservative" readings for a different version of the same fault: guided by a concern to appear in step with the times, some Christians reject this absolute morality in the name of embodying "principles" such as love; or being "present" to the modern world, accompanying it in its projects; or assigning ethics primarily political, rather than scriptural contours.[8] Ellul's critiques of these readings are even more acerbic: he sees them as a failure to take the whole of scripture seriously, and as ignoring the specific backdrop of New Testament's focus on grace, instead eliminating the ethically productive tension caused by Paul's injunction to non-conformity (in one of Ellul's most oft-cited ethical verses, Rom 12:2). It is thus that Ellul can say that we

> . . . make a pretext of grace and freedom to neglect the law and live on a lower level than the commandments . . . Freedom from the law opens the door to cupidity and hardness of heart,

---

8. Ellul critiques Niebuhr as representing the first of these options in *To Will & To Do*; he critiques French Barthians as wholly misconstruing "presence" in *False Presence of the Kingdom*; and he critiques liberation theologians for subordinating theological considerations to politics in general or to Marxist theory in particular, in *Jesus and Marx* and *Violence*.

so that I can ignore the poor and cheat my employees and have no scruples about murder or divorce. What is unleashed here is animal freedom, the autonomy of sin . . . I would rather see Christians use phylacteries and keep the Sabbath in Jewish style than see them as they are, abusing grace and freedom, not even going beyond minimal demands, living as they like . . . Puritans and literalists were far more serious than we who make a comedy of freedom, a pretext of grace, a mere emotion of faith, and the crassest social conformity of the Christian life.[9]

These critiques, too, seem currently relevant.[10] In short, we might suggest (adapting William Stringfellow's provocative phrase) that Ellul's hermeneutic of freedom is "too biblical for most Christians."[11]

c. Reading Freely

As the essays in this volume amply demonstrate, Ellul is a stimulating scriptural guide precisely because he reflects this freedom back into his reading of the text from which it springs. Just as Scripture nourishes Ellul's understanding of freedom, his freedom to variously adopt, adapt, or reject a range of hermeneutic methods and approaches is one of the most remarkable and palpable characteristics of his biblical approach.

Ellul explicitly formulates this hermeneutics of freedom. In *The Ethics of Freedom*, a section on "Freedom in Relation to Revelation" specifies three dimensions of specifically Christian freedom with regards to divine revelation: first, freedom of interpretation; second, freedom of deviation; and third, freedom of research.[12]

My interest here is in freedom of interpretation. Regarding this freedom, Ellul writes:

> . . . one of the things that disturbs me about modern hermeneutics is its complete subjection to the modern cultural background with its fashions and fads and scientific façade and

---

9. Ellul, *Ethics of Freedom*, 151.

10. For example, a 2011 sociological study of French Protestants noted a marked "desire to appear as modern, in phase with French society at the beginning of the twenty-first century" as a defining characteristic of French Protestant celebrations, specifically adapting its Calvinist heritage to give off an "image of a happy and optimistic modern Protestantism . . . " (Encrevé, "Les protestants français," 98, 102).

11. This remark appears in Stringfellow's endorsement on the front cover of the Eerdmans edition of *Meaning of the City*.

12. Ellul, *Ethics of Freedom*, 161–84, esp. 162.

> ideology. I find not the slightest sign of freedom here nor even the most modest approach to truth ... The very basis of hermeneutics is thus to be sought elsewhere, and in my view it lies in the act which God performs to liberate us ... The very freedom that God himself gives us means that we have to act as free men in relation to the text that objectifies God's word.[13]

In our western anglophone culture influenced by an analytical philosophical tradition and geared towards objective approaches to truth (themselves often problematic derivations from legitimate natural science), "truth" is often heard as equivalent to "absolute." When Christianity is forced into this mold, the person of Truth is translated into propositions; knowing truth shifts from a complicated relation to a divine person, to a correspondence to correct intellectual-objective methodology. Ellul rejects the scientism backing such interpretive schematics. But that does not mean, as some may be wont to think, that he succumbs to a "postmodern" relativity in which all truth is equal. Instead, for Ellul, truth was never reducible to its intellectual content, but was always a question of *life*. His rejection of fixed and closed hermeneutical method reopens the space for a lived relation to the text, opening the way for the biblical reader to rigorously seek the relation between the Word of God and their own life.

Ellul not only theorizes this hermeneutic freedom, but observably exercises it as well. We might see its manifestations, for example, in his dialogue with historical-critical methods,[14] his moderated use of structuralist method,[15] the liberty he takes with experimental, partial, and biased interpretative schematics,[16] or his adaptation of certain elements of Marxist thought (without ever fully accepting the possibility of a Marxist-style "materialist reading of the gospels").[17] We might also note that he feels no pressure to

---

13. Ellul, *Ethics of Freedom*, 162–63.

14. In numerous commentaries, Ellul begins by summarizing elements of historical-critical commentary which he employs in his interpretations—just before he notes how such methods generally flout the possibility of seeing a unified intention and meaning both within a given biblical book and across the biblical canon as a whole. Cf. Ellul, *Judgement of Jonah*; *Reason for Being*.

15. Ellul polemicizes against structuralist method in *Meaning of the City*, yet partially employs this method in his commentary on the book of revelation. Ellul, *Apocalypse*, 15.

16. For example, Ellul's *Humiliation of the Word* productively applies what Ellul admits is an oversimplified and biased distinction between seeing/images/reality and hearing/spoken language/truth. Ellul, *Humiliation of the Word*, 1–4.

17. The dialectical method employed in Ellul, *Apocalypse* is clearly partially modeled on Marxist historical dialectics; yet Ellul's *Jesus and Marx* is a sustained polemic against two concrete attempts at (and the very possibility of) a "materialist" reading

assert *complete* understanding. Even his "concluding" biblical commentary on Ecclesiastes explicitly sets entire verses aside without claiming to explain or understand them.[18] As part of Ellul's admittedly "naïve" interpretive approach, this is particularly encouraging for the non-specialist who feels the full weight of their ignorance when confronted with the expansive scholarly literature on any given biblical book or topic.[19] Finally, we might note that Ellul feels free to change his interpretations over time.[20]

In short, Ellul shakes up the assumptions which restrict our scriptural approaches, *whatever they might be*. He does not teach a method; he models a freedom which he hopes to pass on. His goal is neither to modernize an ancient text, nor to be "relevant" to society, nor to justify any human actions. To adherents of a fixed reading—whether the faithful tenants of literalist approaches, or to the technicians of the historical-critical apparatus, both of whom claim a certain kind of mastery of biblical meaning—Ellul's interrogative probing reopens the question of what the text might communicate about the living God, here and now. He strips biblical readers of methodical weaponry, puts their backs against the wall, and positions them to hear the still, small voice of love, which frees slaves, shatters illusions, and demolishes domination, bringing the prophetic question startlingly into the present: "Is not my word like fire, says the Lord, and like a hammer that breaks a rock in pieces?" (Jer 23:29)

Understandably, the prophetic challenges Ellul poses to entrenched reading habits are often unsettling and uncomfortable. However, may neither the thoughtful Christian wary of the risks to their theological understanding implied by Ellul's interpretive freedom, nor the rigorous scholar suspicious of the accessibility of Ellul's "naïve" approach, write Ellul off as belonging to another camp. The "negative," questioning power of the prophetic word he proclaims is intended to edify, to encourage faithful and liberated reading, and to result in a loving ethical practice.[21] And if he so challenges our biblical-hermeneutic approach that we are left confused, uncertain as to how we are to understand the Bible at all, I can do no better than to repeat his own response when this question was posed by an

---

of the Gospels.

18. Ellul, *Reason for Being*, 143n8.

19. On "naïve," see Ellul, *Apocalypse*, 12.

20. This is particularly notable in Ellul's approach to law, which changed continually, and in Ellul's approach to the theological concept of "recapitulation." Cf. Goddard, *Living the Word, Resisting the World*, ch. 6; Marques Rollison, *New Reading of Jacques Ellul*, ch. 5.

21. On "negative," see Ellul, *Humiliation of the Word*, 268; on edification, encouragement, and love, see *To Will & To Do*, vol. 2, ch. 3; *Ethics of Freedom*, 167.

attendee of the Bible studies which Ellul hosted in his home: "We can read our Bibles because of grace, and that is all."[22]

II. The Contours of This Conversation

This volume marks both a helpful survey of Ellul's biblical engagement and an important moment in the reception thereof. The chapters in this volume constitute four types of contributions. The first group presents expanded versions of papers initially presented at the biannual conference of the International Jacques Ellul Society (IJES) at Regent College in Vancouver in July 2018, whose guiding theme was "Ellul and the Bible."[23] In the intervening two years since this conference, versions of some of these papers have also reappeared in *The Ellul Forum*. A second group of chapters present new translations of Ellul's own writings, two of which make their first published appearance in these translations.[24] A third category includes papers written on other occasions which were expanded, reedited, revisited, or simply reprinted here.[25] Some of these were printed elsewhere (mostly, though not exclusively, in *The Ellul Forum*), while others make their published debut in these pages. A final category includes totally new contributions written in response to a call for submissions to this volume.[26] As it gathers the best contributions both from the many years of discussion in *The Ellul Forum* and elsewhere, pairs them with the best of recent multi-generational scholarship, and even includes previously untranslated and unpublished articles from Ellul himself, this volume thus aims to cover most of the width, breadth, and depth of its chosen subject.[27]

Indeed, the range of contributing voices is worth noting. Contributing authors and translators can be grouped in several ways. First, the volume places established authorities in Ellul studies (such as Patrick Chastenet, David Gill, Andrew Goddard, Ted Lewis, Frédéric Rognon, and Christian Roy) and seasoned Ellul translators (such as Anne-Marie Andreasson Hogg, Lisa Richmond and once again, Christian Roy) alongside

22. Ellul, *On Being Rich and Poor*, 168.

23. See chs. 1, 4, 8, 17, and 19.

24. See chs. 2, 3, 5, 13, 14, and 15. Chs. 2 and 3 appear here for the first time in any language, while the others appear here for the first time in English.

25. See chs. 10, 11, 12, 16, 18, 20, and 21.

26. See chs. 6, 7, 9, 16, and 22.

27. There is a notable exception to this goal of full coverage: the present volume lacks a specific treatment of Ellul's reading of Revelation. This is not an oversight; treatments of Ellul's *Apocalypse* are being held in reserve for publication in a future volume.

a new generation of emerging scholars and translators who specialize in Ellul's thought (such as Michael Morelli, Elisabetta Ribet, Matthew T. Prior, G.P. Wagenfuhr, and myself). Three other notable categories include established biblical scholars and theologians (such as Brian Brock and John Goldingay) and emerging theologians (such as Amy J. Erickson and Declan Kelly) whose research is not especially Ellul-driven, and pastoral practitioners manifesting no small Ellulian engagement themselves (such as Chris Friesen, Jean-Sébastien Ingrand, and Anthony Petrotta).

Furthermore, these contributions stem from recent "hotspots" in Ellul's *theological* reception. Historically, several cities have stood out as prominent reception hubs of Ellul's thought, including Bordeaux in France, and in North America, Berkeley, CA and Wheaton, IL in the United States, and Vancouver, BC in Canada. These hubs are still mostly represented in the present volume. However, this volume also reflects that Aberdeen, Scotland, and Strasbourg, France have been particularly strong hubs in recent years.

Summary of Contents

This volume is divided into three parts. David Gill's chapter opens part one, "Approaching the Biblical Text," by sketching the broad lines of Ellul's relation to the biblical text. The two following chapters present new translations of previously unpublished articles by Ellul which offer general commentary on his ethically driven biblical readings (and prefigure later developments in volume two of *To Will & To Do*). The first article, translated by Anne-Marie Andreasson Hogg, is a prepared lesson clearly delineating Ellul's understanding of how scriptural authority differs for Christians and non-Christians. For the former, he shows how Christian ethics can neither ignore, nor divide, nor directly apply the Old Testament law. For the non-Christian, Ellul notes how the universal Noahic covenant gives Christians a biblical basis for thinking through Christ's lordship over all things (a theme developed in Ellul's studies of Amos).[28] The second article, translated by Lisa Richmond, continues the ethical-institutional focus and gives a rare and early mention of Ellul's approach to the "analogy of faith." In chapter four, Frédéric Rognon develops this last element at length, situating it in its historical context and demonstrating it with detailed examples. Section one closes with a third article from Ellul (also translated by Anne-Marie Andreasson Hogg) concerning "Meaning and its Interplay with Freedom in the Bible," deriving from Ellul's contribution to a conference of Jewish intellectuals. Ellul finds that God values and respects human freedom, which

---

28. See Ellul, *On Being Rich and Poor*, 16–17.

interacts with an absence of an objective meaning to the Bible and to human history as a whole; instead, the meaning which God grants to human history involves human interpretation and decision, and humans can only perceive this meaning retrospectively.

Part two, "Revisiting Ellul's Readings of the Bible," aims to survey the major textual components of Ellul's biblical engagement. John Goldingay opens the section with a favorable and critical evaluation of Ellul as an exegete of the Old Testament, focusing on Ellul's studies of 2 Kings, Jonah, and Ecclesiastes. The next seven chapters focus on Ellul's specific engagement with a given theme in a biblical book. Michael Morelli highlights the gravity which Ellul's readings of Genesis place on the act of naming. G.P. Wagenfuhr focuses on Ellul's approach to the biblical book (and *theme*) of Exodus, highlighting the centrality of God as liberator in Ellul's readings. Amy J. Erickson highlights Ellul's figural reading of Elihu in his approach to the book of Job, emphasizing Job's wrestling with fear and the present value of waiting along with God. Anthony Petrotta explores, probes, and reconsiders Ellul as an insightful reader of Ecclesiastes. Jean-Sébastien Ingrand peruses the prophetic and personal elements of Ellul's sustained engagement with Jonah. And Chris Friesen fruitfully revisits his careful personal wrestling with Ellul's interpretations of 2 Kings. Part two closes with two more Ellul articles. The first of these articles, translated by Jacob Marques Rollison, demonstrates how Ellul continually reconsiders his interpretations, re-evaluating them in light of new contextual knowledge, here with reference to Romans 13:1. The second article, translated by Lisa Richmond, presents Ellul's review of a translation of the Bible by André Chouraqui, a renowned Hebrew scholar and translator who powerfully influenced Ellul's biblical interpretations.[29]

Part three presents additional topics and recent interventions involving Ellul as a biblical reader. The section opens with Matthew T. Prior's translation

---

29. Indeed, the inside front cover of several books in Chouraqui's biblical translations contain the following endorsement from Ellul, who (after comparing this translation's influence to that of Luther's translations) writes: "We are swept away in a current, a text which moves, evokes, awakens—a text which either leaves the reader discouraged, or provokes them to a new dimension, to a conversion of the intelligence (and the heart!): and I think that [this element] itself is the biblical text, its mark as a bearer of a revelation, which no translation until the present day had rendered palpable with so much strength, and perhaps, so much truth" (my translation). Chouraqui notes that Ellul was an early reader of his translation of the book of Revelation. Ellul further wrote a preface to Chouraqui's biblical study of the Psalms. The two thinkers corresponded at length, and Chouraqui read through Ellul's 1977 article "Impressions d'Israël," making suggestions which proved valuable to Ellul. See Ellul, *Israel, Chance de civilization*, 14n1. Willem Vanderburg in particular has picked up on the powerful influence of Chouraqui's translations; cf. Vanderburg, *Secular Nations Under New Gods*, 89.

of Ellul's short but poignant article on "Darwin and the Bible," which clarifies the types of questions involved in relating the Genesis accounts with questions concerning the material origins of the universe. Patrick Chastenet follows this with an Ellulian meditation on giving and gifts, mixing extensive biblical analysis with sociological considerations. Christian Roy considers the relation between nature and scripture in *The Green Light*, a profound work by Ellul's lifelong dialogue partner and friend Bernard Charbonneau which examines nature, freedom, and the ecological movement. Reprints of essays by Brian Brock and Andrew Goddard expand the conversation, with Brock examining Ellul's readings of Amos and James and Goddard explicating how the Bible desacralizes idols in Ellul's thought. Elisabetta Ribet parses the biblical terminology for hope and abandonment, drawing on material from her recent doctoral work on Ellul's *Hope in Time of Abandonment*. Ted Lewis expands on Ellul's pairing of the Genesis Tower of Babel narrative with the kenosis hymn in the second chapter of Philippians. Finally, Declan Kelly closes the volume, drawing out distinctly apocalyptic contours of Ellul's desacralizing hermeneutic in *Money and Power*.

In the diversity of readers and readings presented in this volume, the clear note sounded in Ellul's call to hermeneutic freedom reverberates in echo some twenty-five years after his death. We can only hope that the same note of freedom is discernable through the scholarly rigor and personal wrestling which these chapters manifest. If so, these polyphonic texts can be heard as renewing the call and inviting further voices to join the conversation, taking up the challenge to read—and live—in freedom.

Works Cited

Ellul, Jacques. *Apocalypse: The Book of Revelation*. Translated by George W. Schreiner. New York: Seabury, 1977.

———. *The Ethics of Freedom*. Translated by Geoffrey W. Bromiley. Grand Rapids: Eerdmans, 1976.

———. *Éthique de la liberté*. 3 vols. Geneva: Labor et Fides, 2019.

———. *False Presence of the Kingdom*. Translated by C. Edward Hopkin. New York: Seabury, 1972.

———. *Hope in Time of Abandonment*. Translated by C. Edward Hopkin. New York: Seabury, 1973.

———. *The Humiliation of the Word*. Translated by Joyce Main Hanks. Grand Rapids: Eerdmans, 1985.

———. *Israel, Chance de civilization. Articles de journaux et de revues, 1967–1992*. Paris: Editions Première Partie, 2008.

———. *Jesus and Marx: From Gospel to Ideology*. Translated by Joyce Main Hanks. Grand Rapids: Eerdmans, 1988.

———. *The Judgment of Jonah*. Translated by Geoffrey W. Bromiley. Grand Rapids: Eerdmans, 1971.

———. *The Meaning of the City*. Translated by Dennis Pardee. Grand Rapids: Eerdmans, 1970.

———. *Mort et espérance de la résurrection. Conférences inédites de Jacques Ellul*. Lyon: Éditions Olivétan, 2016.

———. *On Being Rich and Poor: Christianity in a Time of Economic Globalization*. Compiled, edited, and translated by Willem H. Vanderburg. Toronto: University of Toronto Press, 2014.

———. *On Freedom, Love, and Power*. Compiled, edited, and translated by Willem H. Vanderburg. Toronto: University of Toronto Press, 2010.

———. *The Politics of God and the Politics of Man*. Translated by Geoffrey W. Bromiley. Grand Rapids: Eerdmans, 1972.

———. *Reason for Being: A Meditation on Ecclesiastes*. Translated by Joyce Main Hanks. Grand Rapids: Eerdmans, 1990.

———. *Violence: Reflections from a Christian Perspective*. Translated by Cecilia Gaul. London: SCM, 1970.

———. *To Will & To Do: An Introduction to Christian Ethics*. Translated by Jacob Marques Rollison. 2 vols. Eugene, OR: Cascade, 2020.

Encrevé, André. "Les protestants français au miroir du cinquième centenaire de la naissance de Jean Calvin." In *La nouvelle France protestante. Essor et recomposition au XXIe siècle*. Fath, Sébastien, and Willaime, Jean-Paul, dirs. Geneva: Labor et Fides, 2011.

Goddard, Andrew. *Living the Word, Resisting the World. The Life and Thought of Jacques Ellul*. Paternoster Biblical and Theological Monographs. Carlisle: Paternoster, 2002.

Marques Rollison, Jacob. *A New Reading of Jacques Ellul: Presence and Communication in the Postmodern World*. Lanham, MD: Lexington, 2020.

Vanderburg, Willem H. *Secular Nations Under New Gods: Christianity's Subversion by Technology and Politics*. Toronto: University of Toronto Press, 2018.

Part I

Approaching the Biblical Text

CHAPTER 1

Jacques Ellul's View of Scripture

David W. Gill

JACQUES ELLUL (1912–1994) is best known for his sociological analysis of technique and the technological society. But simultaneous with his career as sociologist and historian, Ellul was an active and productive lay theologian, ethicist, and biblical commentator. In fact, in terms of both quantity and impact, Ellul's theological writings were the equal of his sociological corpus. It is not unusual to find students of his sociology who are relatively unfamiliar with his theological and biblical works (just as there are readers of his theological works who more or less ignore his sociological work).[1]

If anything is clear from Ellul, however, both the sociological and theological are intended to be read in a kind of dialectical counterpoint—much as his hero Soren Kierkegaard deliberately wrote his philosophical and theological works in a dialectical relationship. Ellul's sociological works intend to describe and analyze the reality of the world and its history, especially as dominated by technique. His theological works intend to describe the truth of a transcendent God who cares about and intervenes in the reality of the world to bring freedom in the face of its necessity and closure, life in the presence of the forces of death. This is a grand and ambitious agenda, of course, and requires a certain openness and faith for its full appreciation.

For Ellul, the relation of this truth with our reality is mediated by the Bible with Jesus Christ at its interpretive center. In traditional Christian

1. This essay has its roots in my PhD dissertation at the University of Southern California, *The Word of God in the Ethics of Jacques Ellul* (1979), subsequently published by Scarecrow Press. There is a significant though partial overlap between this essay and Gill, "Jacques Ellul's View of Scripture." An abbreviated version of this paper was delivered at the 2018 conference of the International Jacques Ellul Society at Regent College in Vancouver, British Columbia, Canada.

fashion Ellul sees Jesus as the living, incarnate God—at the center of God's written Word in the Scriptures of the Old and New Testaments. How does he understand the character of this ancient collection of documents we call the Bible, and how does he move from ancient document to assertions of truth for our own time and place? Certainly, students of theology and biblical interpretation will find that Ellul holds much in common with mainstream scholarship and the faith community. At the same time, some of Ellul's approach to Scripture is outside the mainstream. Some of what he writes will be rejected for various reasons, some will be challenging and debatable, but some will bring brilliant, creative insight previously unrecognized.

At the opening of his *To Will & To Do: An Introduction to Christian Ethics,* Ellul boldly writes that

> . . . the criterion of my thought is biblical revelation; the content of my thought is biblical revelation; my point of departure is provided by biblical revelation; the method is the dialectic according to which biblical revelation is addressed to us; and the goal is the search for the significance of biblical revelation as it bears on Ethics.[2]

This declaration of the fundamental importance and authority of the Bible for his theological work is echoed over and over in Ellul's writings. Basic to this stance was the fact that at "around twenty-two years of age, I was . . . reading the Bible, and it happened that I was converted—with a certain 'brutality.'"[3] Not a sermon, not an ecclesiastical rite, not a mystical vision, but the individual reading of the Bible was decisive in Ellul's embrace of Christian faith. The reading and study of Scripture over the next sixty years were central to Ellul's thought, life, and work. While his indebtedness to the biblically-oriented theology of Karl Barth certainly also pushed Ellul in this direction, it is finally his own personal encounter with Scripture that undergirds his Bible-centeredness.

Ellul's commitment to the importance of Scripture comes through in all of his theological and ethical writings—which means about half of his massive literary production. His official, formal profession was as a historian and sociologist on the faculty at the University of Bordeaux. But Ellul could never quench his thirst or stifle his imagination when it came to the study of the Bible. He often comments on the character and interpretation of Scripture. He provides many samples of his biblical interpretation, including several published studies of specific books of the Bible such as Jonah, Genesis, Ecclesiastes, 2 Kings, and Revelation. His unpublished tape recordings and

---

2. Ellul, *To Will & To Do,* 1:18.
3. Ellul, "From Jacques Ellul," 5.

notes (usually from Bible studies he led at his parish church) have also been published in part. Several of Ellul's theological and ethical topical books are also replete with biblical studies, e.g., on the city, money, work, violence, the virtues of hope and faith, and several volumes on ethics.

Ellul insists on the relevance of the ancient Scriptures for today, rejecting what he sees as the pretentiousness of many modern critics. We have no reason for arrogance or superiority in relation to the ancients:

> No one has demonstrated that those values which one rejects—those ethical instructions, that social view, that anthropology—were *only* assumptions of a bygone civilization. After all, even if they are *also* to be credited to a form of traditional civilization, it is quite possible that they were *nevertheless* what God willed for man in the order of the fall, or in obedience to his will.[4]

The Bible, as Ellul understands it, is remarkably modern and alive. We must

> Neither cover it with the trappings of tradition and theology, of moralities and rites—making a mummy out of it—nor expurgate it, cut it to pieces and scatter it, like the *membra disjecta* of Orpheus—making an experimental corpse out of it. All that is necessary is to let the explosive power of the word act, just as it is.[5]

Historical criticism is entirely legitimate as long as (1) it is not an end in itself that fails to move toward understanding the word of God conveyed by the text; (2) it is not presented as an affirmation of the superiority of "man come of age" at the expense of earlier civilizations; and (3) it is not a means of denying the inspiration and revelation of Scripture. The problem is that "we can no longer read the Bible in simplicity of heart, because this theology begets suspicion . . . We are in the period of 'dilution,' of watering down the expression as well as the content of revelation."[6]

Biblical Text and Word of God

Like Karl Barth, Jacques Ellul differentiates the written text from the living Word of God. In almost the same breath, however, he argues that in practice they are virtually equivalent. The Holy Spirit activates and empowers the text in correspondence with our decision or stance of faith. The revelation in

---

4. Ellul, *False Presence of the Kingdom*, 56.
5. Ellul, *New Demons*, 224.
6. Ellul, "Mirror of These Ten Years," 203.

the biblical text is equivalent to the will of God. Ellul cites Barth's formulation of this irreducible difference and proximity between the Spirit of God and scripture as God's word:

> His commanding and its commanding, are not to be separated . . . If the Bible is the living speech of God only in so far as it attests it, the living speech of God cannot be other than that attested by the Bible . . . But at once the God who has spoken and acted in relation to them also becomes our God in virtue of their witness.[7]

In Jesus Christ the law (objective, universal) becomes commandment (personal, individual, concrete address).

> The summons of the commandment is contained in its entirety in the Bible. But it does not cease to be a word for being "written" (hence objectified). It does not become letter, nor does the commandment become law. The word inscribed in the Bible is always living, and is continually *spoken* to him who *reads*.[8]

Nevertheless, this recognition of God personally summoning us is a decision of faith and obedience. "The word read in the Bible cannot be heard as a personal commandment except by faith."[9] With such an attitude we can "know the constant surprise of the transition from Scripture to the living Word."[10] The equation works in the opposite direction as well: "all alleged revelation in the present" is always "submitted to the control of the revealed Word in the Bible."[11]

Scripture is, of course, a book written by people in the historical forms and modes common their ordinary affairs. This, Ellul argues, is typical of God's action in human history. God adopts human work and fills it with new significance. God intervenes by "appropriating" a particular cultural linguistic form. This appropriation is followed by "contradiction" in the sense that God's message is holy, new, and other. Finally, there is "expropriation": God seizes this linguistic form into his service.[12] Thus historical

---

7. Ellul, *To Will & To Do*, 1:35n1; citing Barth, CD II.2, §38, 706.

8. Ellul, *Prayer and Modern Man*, 104.

9. Ellul, *Prayer and Modern Man*, 116. See also Ellul's preface to Chouraqui, *Les Cantique des cantiques suivi des Psaumes*, xv. There he describes the Bible as "un livre qui, *pour les croyants*, contient la parole de Dieu. Dans ce livre, c'est Dieu qui parle" (italics mine) ["a book which, *for believers*, contains the word of God. In this book, it is God who speaks"].

10. Ellul, *Ethics of Freedom*, 125.

11. Ellul, *To Will & To Do*, 1:238.

12. Ellul, *Meaning of the City*, 176; *Ethics of Freedom*, 164. This same pattern—

narrative, myth, symbolism, prophecy, poetry, apocalyptic and other literary genres are used by God to convey his Word. In fact, Ellul argues, God uses the redactors, editors, and compilers of the Bible just as much as he uses the authors of the "original autographs." Biblical revelation has as much to do with the shape of the whole canon and the internal relation of the parts as it does with the original historical meaning of the individual texts.

Ellul periodically distances himself from what he calls the "biblical literalists" who represent "antiquated, outmodes, trivial attitudes."[13] Literalism, for example,

> . . . closes its ears almost to the point of *credo quia absurdum*. The danger here is that of attaching faith to a record rather than to Jesus Christ. For the true reality of the book is Jesus Christ and to divert our faith from him to facts which are not so significant in themselves can be a serious mistake.[14]

Oddly enough, Ellul's attack on much of contemporary biblical scholarship contains objections similar to those he has against literalism: that is, the biblical critic's passion for historical and literary dissection of the text leaves little more than a mass of isolated, dusty fragments. The relationship of the parts to the whole (which may not have been in the mind of the original authors) and the centrality of Jesus Christ as the Word of God are set aside in the debates about the origin and facticity of individual texts.

A Whole Centered on Jesus Christ

The heart of Ellul's view of Scripture is that it must be read and understood as a total unity, and this unity must be understood and interpreted in relation to Jesus Christ as the definitive Word of God. There is no such thing as "mere tale," "mere historical incident," etc., in Ellul's reading of Scripture. The original editors and canonizers jealously guarded entrance to the canon. Everything has a point and a meaning.

Thus, in the *Judgment of Jonah* (1946) Ellul argues that the (probably later) insertion of the "song of Jonah" was fully intentional and that, far from being a crude patchwork, the total unity of the book is clear. The book of Jonah is placed, moreover, in the prophetic section of the Old Testament, not the historical section, and its interpretation must proceed with that in

---

appropriation, contradiction, expropriation—is how God relates to the city, kingship, even warfare, in Ellul's view.

13. Ellul, *Hope in Time of Abandonment*, 138n.
14. Ellul, *Judgment of Jonah*, 10.

mind. As prophecy, Jonah "plainly declares God's will in a given situation."[15] The prophecy is simultaneously the word of God to Israel and an intimation of Christ. We know that Jonah is, among other things, a figure and type of Christ because Jesus himself used the story in this way and because the internal details of the story make sense as references to him.

Ellul disparages any interpretation of the text and its symbols by imposing secret keys or traditions on the text. Instead,

> We are to interpret them solely by the Bible itself. The consensus of the records of the ongoing thought which is revelation allows us to seize on what may be symbolic elements in it, but always with the realization that we must keep as much as possible to facts as facts, since revelation has always to be incarnated. Hence there can be no single method of interpretation. As the different books fall into different categories, so there must be different categories of interpretation, though always related to the unvarying central line: Jesus Christ.[16]

Thus Jonah must be taken as a "significative (and not just a chronological) totality. It has to be taken synthetically, with the internal connections which join the various parts."[17]

Ellul repeats his argument for the Christocentric unity of the Bible in *The Politics of God and the Politics of Man* (1966). "It is impossible to ignore the fact of the unity of revelation and its movement. Everything leads to Jesus Christ, just as everything comes from him."[18] Second Kings, the subject of this volume, is placed in the historical section of the canon. It is a historical description of the intervention of God, especially in human politics. The connection with Jesus Christ turns on the interpretation of Elijah and Elisha as figures of John the Baptist and Jesus Christ. The superabundance of miracles in 2 Kings, as in the Gospels, is an indication of the unbounded presence of God's Spirit.[19] Though the problems are political the subject is prophecy and revelation, not just principles, ethics, and political procedures. Second Kings is concerned with the intervention of the prophet between God's decision and human action. As in his other biblical studies, Ellul takes several passing shots at critical historians and exegetes for failing to get at this more fundamental unity and meaning of the text.[20]

15. Ellul, *Judgment of Jonah*, 11.
16. Ellul, *Judgment of Jonah*, 46.
17. Ellul, *Judgment of Jonah*, 101.
18. Ellul, *Politics of God and the Politics of Man*, 9.
19. Ellul, *Politics of God and the Politics of Man*, 11.
20. Ellul, *Politics of God and the Politics of Man*, 80.

Ellul's Genesis-to-Revelation study of *The Meaning of the City* (1970) also "takes the biblical text as it is found today, in its entirety."[21] Of course, historical and critical studies can be helpful, especially in preventing gross errors. Ellul himself engages in some detailed critical study of Hebrew words for "city" (just as in his earlier *Theological Foundation of Law* (1946) he engaged in critical study of the biblical terms for justice, law, and righteousness).[22] But the compiling of the individual books and the formation of the canon as a whole are essential for a true grasp of the biblical "meaning of the city." "This is why an inclusive reading of the text appears indispensable to me."[23] Ellul's inclusive style of interpretation yields an impressive result when dealing with the major themes in the biblical story of Babylon, Jerusalem, and their sister cities. The Ellulian method may be less convincing when in the final section of the study he speculates on some of the symbols of the Apocalypse.[24]

Indeed, a fourth example of Ellul's understanding of Scripture is his book *Apocalypse: The Book of Revelation* (1975). The now-familiar themes appear again: the Apocalypse must be related to Jesus Christ. Its symbolism is not to be feared, even though in the past it has often provoked "delirium."[25] The Apocalypse must be read with respect for the genre of apocalyptic literature. The Apocalypse has a unity with a specific form and an internal movement. The French subtitle of the book is actually "architecture in movement." Perceiving its meaning requires "comprehension of the structure."[26] The meaning does not reside in the antiquity of the parts but in the total final product as it now stands. The knowledge of the original cultural and political milieu only partially clarifies the meaning, for the relation of the book to its milieu involves as much tension (contradiction) as it does harmony (appropriation) both in form and content.[27]

Many commentaries on the Apocalypse are, in Ellul's view, weak because (1) they only study the text scientifically, abandoning the question of its meaning; (2) they view it exclusively in historical-cultural terms, forgetting its present and future significance; and (3) they fail to develop a method appropriate to the subject and thus fail to probe the dialectical and

---

21. Ellul, *Meaning of the City*, xvii.
22. Ellul, *Meaning of the City*, 9–10n; cf. Ellul, *Theological Foundation of Law*, 37, 88.
23. Ellul, *Meaning of the City*, xviii.
24. Ellul, *Meaning of the City*, 196.
25. Ellul, *Apocalypse*, 9–10.
26. Ellul, *Apocalypse*, 257.
27. Ellul, *Apocalypse*, 29, 137–38, 266–67n.

symbolic meaning.[28] In contrast to these studies Ellul wishes to "discern the specificity of the Apocalypse."[29] He argues that the Apocalypse is a distinctive kind of revelation in Scripture, an act of God which displays "an internal movement."[30] It is the "totalization of history in one moment" and the illumination of the meaning of human works and God's work from the standpoint of the End."[31]

The Interpretation of Scripture

The perspectives we find in these four substantial examples of Ellul's studies of Scripture are reinforced by all of his forays into Scripture, including what he introduces as his "final" work (though chronologically, it was not): *Reason for Being: A Meditation on Ecclesiastes* (1990); his fascinating study of Romans 9–11, *An Unjust God* (1991); and the biblical interpretations that play a central role in *Living Faith* (1980), *Hope in Time of Abandonment* (1972), and his books on ethics.[32] First, there is "the radical unity which the thought of the Bible exhibits from end to end, over and above the diversity of authorship, schools of thought, and literary forms."[33] Second, this unity is rooted in and centered on Jesus Christ, the incarnate Word. The interpretation of the Bible must be incarnational and Christocentric.[34] Third, while scientific and historical studies assist the study of Scripture, the revelation of God's Word in the text requires the action of the Holy Spirit and the existential faith commitment of the reader. Fourth, accurate interpretation insists that specific biblical literature always be understood in light of its genre as prophecy, history, apocalyptic, poetry, gospel, and so on.

A fifth point Ellul makes (in *Ethics of Freedom*) is about our freedom in relation to the Bible. Part of this is how the Bible brings freedom to its readers. It sets us free from the voices of this world by bringing the voice and truth of the "Wholly Other" God. Thus, freedom "implies more than knowing who Jesus Christ is. It also implies knowing the Scriptures."[35] This importance of knowing the Scriptures is illustrated by Jesus's own recourse to Scripture in his debates with Satan (Matt 4:1–11). But Ellul goes on to insist

28. Ellul, *Apocalypse*, 259.
29. Ellul, *Apocalypse*, 11.
30. Ellul, *Apocalypse*, 12.
31. Ellul, *Apocalypse*, 24, 156.
32. Ellul, *Reason for Being*; *Unjust God?*; *Living Faith*; *Hope in Time of Abandonment*.
33. Ellul, *Hope in Time of Abandonment*, 142; cf. *To Will & To Do*, 1:57.
34. Ellul, *Hope in Time of Abandonment*, 172.
35. Ellul, *Ethics of Freedom*, 87.

that readers of Scripture have a certain freedom in relation to the text. This includes freedom of *interpretation*. Interpretation must not be arbitrary, but no human interpretation can be fixed and definitive. Ellul often referred to a rabbinic saying that every text has "seventy layers of meaning." Our freedom also includes a freedom of *deviation*—a right to err, to be mistaken.

We have freedom of *research*—provided it is respectful of preceding research, and appropriate to literary genre, canonical context, the incarnate center Jesus Christ, and the fellowship and mission of the community of faith. The ultimate limit is that we must not raise the serpent's question in Eden "Yeah, has God said?" We are free to question which human author wrote which passage, what was borrowed and from where, and so on—but we must not question that God is behind and over the whole canon, all parts of which have a truth to tell. As tightly as Ellul says he wants to hew to Scripture this message on freedom is essential for us as readers. He certainly is free to explore and interpret Scripture in new ways that are sometimes puzzling!

A sixth characteristic of Ellul's biblical interpretation is the way he insists that we invite the Bible to question us. Peter and his colleagues asked Jesus many questions, but the questions Jesus asked were much more important: "Who do you say that I am?" "When the Son of Man comes, will he find faith on earth?" and so on. In the early chapters of Genesis, the decisive questions come from God: "Adam, where are you?" "What have you done?" "Who told you this?" "Where is your brother?" But it is not just the explicit questions cited by the text; it is the way biblical accounts of justice, work, money, the city, law, violence, sexuality, character, healing, leadership, community and a long list of other subjects—*by their very nature*—can raise questions about how we view those subjects today. "I fail to see the justification for accepting as legitimate all the questions about the revelation . . . while at the same time refusing to question those systems, methods, and conclusions from the point of view of the revelation."[36]

A seventh characteristic of Ellul's biblical interpretation is his focus on cross-cutting themes—patterns and messages—rather than working his way through the text verse-by-verse from start to finish in a linear way. We could say that he helps us see the forest, not just the trees. Or, in a metaphor he has applied to his sociology (but which applies equally here), he directs our attention to the "main currents" under the ocean surface, rather than the waves on the surface.[37] One major example of this is the city: Ellul tracks the stories of Babylon and Jerusalem from Genesis to Revelation in a dialectic that had never before been brought into view in such a vivid

---

36. Ellul, *Hope in Time of Abandonment*, 145.
37. Ellul, *Hope in Time of Abandonment*, 280–81.

and penetrating way. Just as impressive was his study of money as it cuts across the canon (1954).[38] In his unique study of Ecclesiastes, Ellul detects an amazing pattern, interplay, and flow of vanity-wisdom-God through the text and the three major parts of his book are organized around this triad.[39] In his study of Revelation, the French title gives a big hint: *Apocalypse: Architecture en mouvement* [*Apocalypse: Architecture in Movement*]. Ellul does not walk through the chapters from beginning to end as most commentaries do, nor does he merely follow the telescoping series of sevens. Rather he begins with the central "keystone" section, chapters 8 to 14, and branches out from there. It is an extraordinary challenge to our reading of the text. No reader of Ellul's biblical studies remains comfortably where they were before encountering Ellul's interpretations of one text or another. If we return to where we started, we return with renewed vision after Ellul's challenge. Even more likely, we now have some new and helpful insight—if not a radically transformed perspective.

Eighth, and finally, I believe Ellul's biblical studies need to be seen as a kind of "prophetic" approach. In *The Politics of God and the Politics of Man*, Ellul describes the biblical prophet: "Man chooses his own actions. But between this decision by man and God's action we find the prophet." The biblical prophet "announces and can bend or provoke," he "understands . . . in depth," he provides meaning, he "plays a role which is radical and decisive and yet also independent, ex-centric, and disinterested." The prophet is "absolutely the wholly other," "absolutely new and surprising," and "disturbs our ritual, morality, and piety." The prophet brings the Word of God to bear on "the actual concrete situation of man" but "does not bring any solution or engage in any action." He says, "listen to the Word of God and make your decision." The prophet opens up deadlocked situations by mediating the Word of God who is Wholly Other.[40]

While Ellul never presumed to call himself a prophet, consider what he says about his own work: "I refuse to construct a *system* of thought, or to offer up some pre-fabricated socio-political solutions. I want only to provide Christians with the means of thinking out *for themselves* the meaning of their involvement in the modern world."[41] "The purpose of my books is to provoke a reaction of personal reflection, and thus to oblige the reader to choose for himself a course of action."[42] Clearly, Ellul's vocation is prophet-

---

38. Ellul, *Meaning of the City*; *Money and Power*.
39. See Ellul, *Reason for Being*, 38, for his diagram.
40. Ellul, *Politics of God and the Politics of Man*, 20–21, 47, 50.
41. Ellul, "From Jacques Ellul," 6.
42. In Menninger, "Jacques Ellul," 241.

ic—not just instructional or pedagogical. He thinks (and sees) dialectically: truth is found in the interplay of opposites. Revelation is given in a dialectical way. The role of the prophet is not to smooth everything out and present a mediating synthesis. It is to challenge, to stir up, to push. Understanding Ellul's larger vocation as a prophet is a critical key to understanding and appreciating the way he uses the Bible.

Beyond these eight observations on Ellul's biblical interpretation it is also helpful to note his comparison of the Hebrew-Christian understanding of revelation and Scripture to the Islamic view of the Koran (and also of the Bible).[43] Ellul rejects any commonality of perspective justifying the claim to be similar "religions of the book." Still more broadly, from a view at least as sociological and philosophical as theological, Ellul writes at length about the central importance of the word in communication and the quest for truth, especially in *The Humiliation of the Word* (1981).[44] It is not just a theological point or an article of faith for Ellul that the *biblical* word is central and dominant, it is a much larger claim about human existence.

* * *

I have read (and re-read) most if not all of Ellul's biblical studies over the past fifty years since I discovered them. I was also lucky enough to attend several of his studies on Ecclesiastes during my 1984–1985 sabbatical in Bordeaux—and to meet with him every other Friday afternoon at his home to discuss our mutual interests, especially concerning ethics. For all the things I gratefully learned from him—and that list is huge—I still disagreed on several. Sometimes by letter but also sitting in his living room when I could get to Bordeaux, I (respectfully) argued with him about his attempt to distinguish Satan from the Devil, ethics from morality, and the kingdom of God from the Kingdom of heaven. I questioned his negative theology of work drawn from the creation stories in Genesis and his view of a universal salvation imposed on humanity, like it or not. He loved it! As he said and wrote more than once, he was not looking to make disciples but to provide people with the resources to think out for themselves the meaning of their lives. There is no need to agree with everything Ellul wrote about the Bible, or even to share his faith commitments, to find his biblical commentaries uniquely challenging and insightful.

---

43. Ellul, *Islam and Judeo-Christianity*, 31–39.
44. Ellul, *Humiliation of the Word*; see also "The Word," in *What I Believe*, 23–28.

Works Cited

Barth, Karl. *Church Dogmatics*. 14 vols. Translated by G. T. Thomson et al. Edinburgh: T. & T. Clark, 1936–77.

Ellul, Jacques. *Apocalypse: The Book of Revelation*. Translated by George W. Schreiner. New York: Seabury, 1977.

———. *The Ethics of Freedom*. Translated by Geoffrey W. Bromiley. Grand Rapids: Eerdmans, 1976.

———. *False Presence of the Kingdom*. Translated by C. Edward Hopkin. New York: Seabury, 1972.

———. "From Jacques Ellul." In *Introducing Jacques Ellul*, edited by James Y. Holloway, 5–6. Grand Rapids: Eerdmans, 1970.

———. *Hope in Time of Abandonment*. Translated by C. Edward Hopkin. New York: Seabury, 1973.

———. *The Humiliation of the Word*. Translated by Joyce Main Hanks. Grand Rapids: Eerdmans, 1985.

———. *Islam and Judeo-Christianity: A Critique of Their Commonality*. Translated by D. Bruce MacKay. Eugene, OR: Cascade, 2015.

———. *The Judgment of Jonah*. Translated by Geoffrey W. Bromiley. Grand Rapids: Eerdmans, 1971.

———. *Living Faith: Belief and Doubt in a Perilous World*. Translated by Peter Heinegg. San Francisco: Harper & Row, 1983.

———. *The Meaning of the City*. Translated by Dennis Pardee. Grand Rapids: Eerdmans, 1970.

———. "Mirror of These Ten Years." *Christian Century* 87 (1970) 200–204.

———. *Money and Power*. Translated by LaVonne Neff. Downers Grove, IL: InterVarsity, 1984.

———. *The New Demons*. Translated by C. Edward Hopkin. New York: Seabury, 1975.

———. *The Politics of God and the Politics of Man*. Translated by Geoffrey W. Bromiley. Grand Rapids: Eerdmans, 1972.

———. *Prayer and Modern Man*. Translated by C. Edward Hopkin. New York: Seabury, 1970.

———. "Préface." In *Les Cantique des cantiques suivi des Psaumes traduits et présentés par André Chouraqui*, xv–xix. Paris: PUF, 1970.

———. *Reason for Being: A Meditation on Ecclesiastes*. Translated by Joyce Main Hanks. Grand Rapids: Eerdmans, 1990.

———. *The Theological Foundation of Law*. Translated by Marguerite Wieser. New York: Seabury, 1969.

———. *To Will & To Do: An Introduction to Christian Ethics*. Translated by Jacob Marques Rollison. 2 vols. Eugene, OR: Cascade, 2020.

———. *An Unjust God? A Christian Theology of Israel in Light of Romans 9–11*. Translated by Anne-Marie Andreasson Hogg. Eugene, OR: Cascade, 2012.

———. *What I Believe*. Translated by Geoffrey W. Bromiley. Grand Rapids: Eerdmans, 1989.

Gill, David W. "Jacques Ellul's View of Scripture." *Journal of the Evangelical Theological Society* 25 (1982) 467–78.

———. *The Word of God in the Ethics of Jacques Ellul*. Scarecrow: ATLA Monograph 20. Metuchen, New Jersey, London: 1984.

Menninger, David C. "Jacques Ellul: A Tempered Profile." *Review of Politics* 37 (1975) 235–46.

CHAPTER 2

The Authority of the Bible

JACQUES ELLUL

TRANSLATED BY
ANNE-MARIE ANDREASSON HOGG

THE PREVIOUS LESSON LED us to some necessary questioning in our lives. Yet, we were faced with an extreme difficulty: in the name of what do we call ourselves into question?[1] What will be our guide in this examination? What can bring answers to our questioning? The presence of the cross of Jesus Christ is the decisive fact, but we still have to live out this encounter, and freedom cannot be a glum withdrawal into ourselves, or a perpetually paralyzing question. Nor is freedom the anarchy of the joy of living; rather, it is the Lord's answer to the question that He himself places in our life. As we heard this question in the presence of the Cross and received the answer in the Resurrection, it is again to the Lord that we must go to find the real question and the answer about our daily life, our moral and social life; and this is why we will talk about the Bible here.

We are not going to address the theological problem of the authority of the Bible. Let us only remember that this authority is based on inspiration by God who reveals himself through the Holy Spirit to those who write the sacred texts. These authors have no authority in themselves, but only in so far as God continues to reveal himself to humans through them.

---

1. This chapter is a translation of the fourth of ten lessons given by Jacques Ellul to the *Associations Professionnelles Protestantes* in Bordeaux, France. While the exact date of their delivery is uncertain, these lessons are thought to have taken place around 1946–1948. The original typescript is in the *Fond Jacques Ellul* housed in the library of Sciences Po Bordeaux. Special thanks to Jean-Philippe Qadri and the Ellul family for permitting and facilitating access to the original document.

Thus, it is the Holy Spirit who enlightens Scripture and gives it authority for the reader. Of course, it is obvious that this authority can only exist for faith. We cannot expect unbelievers to consider the Bible to be truth and an authority able to direct their lives.

Therefore, the authority of the Bible cannot be universal. It does not exist for natural man. It only exists for the believer. This is a very simple notion that is indispensable for the study of the authority of the Bible in moral and social questions. Furthermore, this authority is not based on *a reasonable truth* (it is not because biblical texts express truth can be demonstrated scientifically by history, by psychology or paleontology that they are authoritative). Nor is it based on *a moral truth* (it is not because they represent the pinnacle of human morality, or because they correspond to natural morality that they are authoritative). Neither is it based on *a religious truth* (it is not because they represent a refined, monotheistic religion etc. that they are authoritative).

Their authority rests on the action of God, on God himself as He acted in their creation and continues to act. What all these texts show us is precisely this: God acting in such and such a way. The authority of these texts concerning the eternal and historical action of God rests on the continuity of this action of God in the present. This is true in the context of the spiritual life, but it is equally true for moral life and for social and political life, which we will particularly look at here.

The problem of the authority of the Bible in these matters brings particular problems because we will be tempted, here more than elsewhere, either to consider the Bible as totally outdated (as it refers to a world which is no longer ours), or on the other hand, to looks for ready-made examples that we can simply apply. Both of these attitudes are incorrect. The first one tends to spiritualize the Bible, while the second tends to turn it into a moral code, a new law.

Next, we are faced with another question: what authority can the Bible have in present-day questions that are so new that the Biblical authors knew nothing about them? A general theological response will not do, the kind of response we see too often: "Nothing that pertains to humans escapes the sovereignty of God and of Jesus Christ, therefore social and political problems are also in his hands. Since he reveals His Truth in Scripture, Scripture is related to these problems." This response is far too general and we need to be more precise. I am not satisfied with the response that one finds too often among Barthians either: "Scripture reveals to us that Jesus Christ really is the Lord of all things and gives us no indication of a social ethics; so act as you deem best for the glory of God. Do this using your reason and your human technique without attempting to "Christianize" your action and God will forgive your mistakes." I believe such an attitude totally neglects one essential aspect of Revelation.

This is why we will try to be more precise in our description of the authority of Scripture with respect to social and political life.

I. Authority for Christians

As far as ethics is concerned, generally, the authority of the Bible cannot be the authority of a Code because the Christian is called to live in freedom—that is, to choose and make up his mind not according to an exterior rule but according to the will that God puts in him by grace. Life within grace presupposes on the one hand, that one take the revelation of God in Scripture totally seriously (also as far as ethics is concerned), and on the other hand, that one be completely freed from the obligations, duties, and constraints with which this very Scripture seems to weigh us down. In other words, we need to live these words of God according to freedom. This forces us to remember a certain number of very simple and well-known truths within the domain of ethics before we can move on to the problem of authority in political and social matters.

1. Jesus Christ fulfilled—he did not abolish—the law. At the same time, he affirms that not one iota will disappear from the law; therefore, it is still valid. This means that Jesus Christ took upon himself the totality of the law and fulfilled all its work, that it has become a living law and no longer a paper law. He brought this law to its perfection, and thus we understand why it cannot disappear: this law is now in effect linked to Jesus Christ is such a way that it has become himself. It cannot be changed because Jesus is the same yesterday, today and for all eternity. This law then becomes all the more constraining to us as it is the very face of our savior. So, to the extent to which we are called to share in his life in the body of Christ, we become immediately fulfillers of this law as he himself is. The hearts of stone that could not be broken without the hammer of the law, a rigid and harsh law, thus become the hearts of flesh full of the value and the necessity of the law. This law receives its authority for us from the action of the word of God in us as it unites us to Jesus Christ.

2. Consequently, the works of this law are not natural works, deriving from our situation as creatures. These works are neither preliminary to our salvation, nor meritorious. The pagan may accomplish the works of the law, but the law has no particular authority for that person. In

reality, the works accomplished according to the law are the fruit of faith, the consequence of our salvation, and the sign of the grace given us and of the fellowship we have with Jesus Christ.

Therefore, these works come *after* conversion, not before. They are not done out of obligation—Christ is the one who bore the obligation, the constraint, and the curse that is attached to the law and he has freed us from it; these works are an act of gratitude and thankfulness to God. This is the work of the one who has been liberated and serves the master with joy, affection, and thankfulness, no longer as a slave, but precisely because slavery is a thing of the past. This is the act of the person who fulfills the law because he knows that this law delights the savior and acts in order to please the savior, as a token of love and no longer out of fear or to deserve a reward.

3. Thus we are constantly faced with the choice of what might please God. The concrete reality of our actions is therefore not what counts, but the willingness to glorify God and to thank him. We may make a mistake in the action we choose, but God who knows the heart knows for whom we are doing this. There is therefore no more possible legalistic mechanism. There are no actions that would be automatically fitting and others that would be automatically condemned. This is why we may say here that this law has no authority. What it describes physically is not obligatory as it is, but on the other hand, we need to know that what these practical actions express is what God loves. Consequently, while we are free to do or not to do—it does not lead to our salvation, salvation is given to us—we need to consider things honestly. In other words, if we do not do what God loves, we need to know that we do not love God, that we have no true gratefulness for the gift of salvation, and that we are no longer witnesses to his work but are actually despising the grace given to us.

4. All this shows us that it is not the law itself as it is in the Bible, or the actual content of biblical instructions, that we should consider eternally binding. We should not expect literal obedience, as most commandments have no more meaning: what for modern city dwellers can be the meaning of the innumerable Old Testament instructions about cattle, the soil, weaving or cooking? Yet these laws are not simply cancelled, they are not without meaning and significance. We need to search for and find the spiritual reality to which these commandments point in their temporary form. We need a kind of translation work: that is, what contemporary form can we find for an unchangeable divine thought? The biblical form has no authority

in itself, just as the body of Esau or Elijah had no value in itself. To believe that the literal biblical command should be scrupulously followed is to repeat the error of worshipping the relics of the Saints. On the other hand, to believe that the development of time has cancelled these commandments is to remove the Holy Spirit who dictated them and who gave their substance.

5. Finally, this moral code that stems from Scripture and has no obligatory penal character remains for us essentially an indicative morality, a morality of judgment. In other words, its basic usefulness is in providing an indication of the direction in which we can act, of how we can incarnate our faith, of what action would be pleasing to God. Thus, as it is not constraining, it serves as an example and a model for the invention of Christian freedom. Furthermore, it should enable us to judge ourselves. If we act in freedom, we can always judge the actions of our freedom according to the criterion of this law. For God tells us explicitly that each one will be judged according to their own actions and that this judgment is based on the law that he reveals. Therefore, the law keeps its full authority for the time of judgment. So we are left with a sort of guide which does not leave us totally disoriented in the use of our freedom. But of course, we must accept that this guide will have authority to judge us, and I do not think that we really do take God's grace seriously if we do not take the totality of his Law seriously.

Once we leave the question of general ethics and venture into social and political issues, we come up more forcibly against the question of anachronism. In a way, one is ready to accept that human beings are still the same, that the moral teachings of the Bible are still valid, even if they sometimes have a strange appearance, but one is not at all ready to accept that the social law has any truth at all. Even Calvin maintained that the ceremonial law for instance had been completely repealed, as had the political and social law.

It is nevertheless necessary to remark that Jesus Christ makes no difference between the various parts of the law when he declares that he fulfills and does not repeal. It is also necessary to notice that the Old Testament has been transmitted to us as a unit, with no separation between the prophets and the law, or between social law and moral law etc. These divisions between various categories of laws (that is, between various domains of ethics) are something that we introduce with no other reason or justification than our own reasoning and will. Actually, we need to accept this unity because it is constantly asserted. Nothing allows us to remove parts of Scripture. We cannot remove Leviticus or Numbers, nor any other part of Scripture. If we have understood what the moral authority of Scripture is, we need to recognize that this authority is as biding in the social and political realm as in the realm of personal morality.

Apparently, we are faced with a greater difficulty. The social and political situation today is so far from that of the Jews in the sixth or seventh century B.C. that the two have practically nothing in common. What was said in those days does not mean anything for our times, even when words are the same. For instance, if we consider the matter of lending without interest, nothing allows us to continue following the rules that the Israelites had in this respect. We cannot believe that God would have given an eternal truth in this social matter, a truth that would be valid for all time.

Yet, we cannot believe that developments over time would completely negate God's will as it was expressed in those days. In other words, to resort to anachronism to reject this law means that we are doubting the very inspiration of Scripture, and therefore also doubting *its* authority and *our* faith in it.

A few observations will enable us to better understand the authority that the Bible also has in these areas.

1. The Bible never offers us a dogmatic teaching with respect to philosophy. It does not present any political or scientific theories; rather, it constantly shows us the intervention of God in history, a human and "normal" history within a sociological and economic society. In other words, Revelation is always linked to a particular contingency. It is never eternal and timeless; it is always situated within time and in a particular situation. Right from the start, it is actually the announcement of the incarnation of Jesus Christ. Just as God himself became incarnated in a contingent human flesh, he also linked his revelation to a given historical situation. This attitude which appears throughout the Bible—since it consists of little stories, legends, myths etc.—is made clear, certain and confirmed precisely by the incarnation of Jesus Christ which authenticates all the rest. It is exactly because God revealed himself in a given society that we may be assured, first of all, that He continues to work in our Society, and secondly, that his Revelation is also valid for our Society. If his revelation had been perfectly philosophical and abstract it would have been valid for *no* time and *no* society, and it would be a pure impossibility for us. This would have made things much easier. Because his revelation is historical, then it is also called to be part of our political and our economic world . . . not in its literal form, of course, but rather according to the model that is given us. The "how" of this translation will be addressed in subsequent lessons, but at this point it is important to understand that the political

and social authority of the Bible for today comes from the fact that the revelation had a visible authority at a certain point in History, and that this authority rests on the Incarnation of Jesus Christ.

2. Furthermore (and in connection with this), we see that God acts through his judgements. In fact, he does not present principles, he does not give eternal, abstract laws; he is a living God who intervenes in the world by his judgements. The law is simply the present expression of this judgement. This judgement is always new and always living. It is established not only for the history of Israel, but also for the history of our times, and therefore it produces for our present times and our present society a law that we can know.

The law given in the Bible is first of all an exemplary law for us. It provides us with the example of God's judgements for a society, of the transformations that he requires, and of the behavior that he expects of those who belong to him. Let us not forget that these are examples; they are not to be slavishly followed, but may be translated. This attitude is much more precise that the search for a so-called general inspiration that we so love to look for. In these matters, one must remain very suspicious of what men call the spirit.

This law is also for us a kind of demonstration of the criteria that God uses in his judgements. He shows us from life in the Bible how and why he judges. We can thus see what rule we may use to act in our civilization, and can see which criteria announce God's judgement and which enable our society to avoid this terrible and destructive judgement.

Finally, this notion of judgement always brings us back to Jesus Christ; for God laid on him the total weight of his judgement. At the end of the series of God's consecutive judgements, he was the one condemned. It is because we see him thus judged that we can know that all God's past judgements in the Bible and all God's judgements on our present civilization are equally true and equally valid for us. Jesus is the one who gives authority to all God's acts in the past. He makes these acts a present reality here and now in the political world as well.

3. It is obvious that this authority shows us a relationship between the living God and the political and social world. It certainly does not allow us to play the little game of "Christian solutions." For many, there would be a capitalist solution, a socialist solution, a communist solution etc. . . . and then a Christian solution to political problems. In reality, there is no Christian solution, and even less any Biblical solution.

The Bible is not a book of solutions to problems. Of course, this does not mean that the Christian attitude would be to refer to non-Christian solutions and to adopt them purely and simply. The Christian attitude is never to look for solutions to the problems of the world. The Bible offers us no means and no authority to do that. When a group of Christians or a church brings forth an economic system, it comes from their own thinking and from nowhere else. Consequently, this system has no authority based on Christ. It might be the work of nice people or good technicians, but it is not the answer that God expects as a result of the judgement he pronounces.[2]

4. When the Bible speaks to the social or political question, it is in fact always speaking to the problem of man. The Bible does not propose one type of society or institution and it does not speak *to* Society. It speaks to man and proposes only one type of man: Jesus Christ. The Bible's revelation is not given in order to reorganize society, but exclusively in order to save man. Thus, we are not called to establish a society according to the Bible. Furthermore, since we are at the core of the problem of authority, let us be clear and understand that the Scripture may have authority for a person or a group of persons, but never for an abstraction such as Society or the State.

The criticism of this clear and indisputable affirmation will of course be: "In the order of reforms, one must choose: either one starts with the institutions, which will be the frame for moral and social reforms, or one starts with people, which will lead to a transformation of institutions." This is often how the dilemma is presented. Usually one thinks that Christians will choose the second option. Realists will choose the first option since individual transformation has almost never led to political change. Some Christians (who are socialist or progressive) also choose the second option. I believe that the Bible completely challenges this merely scholastic dilemma.

When the Bible speaks about man, it never speaks of him as an entity or an abstraction. It speaks about a concrete person, exactly each one of us. It does not consider that person separated from others or from circumstances

---

2. Editor's note: We have omitted translating a short paragraph here in which Ellul concretely applies these considerations to his audience, the *Associations Professionnelles Protestantes*. In the 1940s Ellul, along with his friend and mentor Jean Bosc, were involved in the creation of this network aiming to "reflect on how to reconcile Christian commitment and professional practice in daily life." Bosc headed up the Paris hub, while Ellul helped lead the Bordeaux faction. See "Les APP avec Jean Bosc," https://www.jacques-ellul.org/terrain/les-app-avec-jean-bosc.

etc., but within relationships with society, because man cannot be imagined any other way. It considers him in relationship with the State, with institutions, with the Economy etc . . . . And it is within this relationship that it talks about the State, about institutions, about the Economy. The Bible does not present an ideal society. It is in terms of this man that society has value. Therefore, this relationship is what needs to change. It is not society in itself, it is not man either in himself that needs change, but "an individual in society." And this change happens through an action which also affects society, but which is never a reorganization of society.

This Biblical position leads us to three consequences:

First of all, when we read Scripture, we should not look for anything else than God's word addressed to us personally. That is all the authority of Scripture. This word of God calls us into question. For this is a question that God asks of us personally. We should not try to pull through by shifting the responsibility to the bad organization of Society, which is supposedly keeping us from being just, good . . . Now, this question about my life also concerns my political attitude, my economic relationships, my role in society, and through me, it is a question for the society in which I live.

Secondly, once we have heard the question from God and accepted the judgement of God on our life, then—and only then, not before—are we in a position to speak to the society to which we belong. We are not to judge institutions according to political or economic criteria coming from somewhere else, but to announce the judgement of God on these institutions as well as on all human endeavors. Of course, we should not announce this *in abstracto*, but rather in a concrete, relevant and exact way, which requires a true understanding of the world we live in.

Finally, we know that God does not leave his judgement without response, his response is grace. Therefore, we need *to show* what the love of God is in this society. We need to give much importance to this word: to show. We are not to talk about God's love, we are not to announce God's love to Society. The announcement can be for one individual, but not to the Society where this individual lives. What is asked of us is to show effectively, in actions, this love of God manifested in Jesus Christ. In actions . . . that is, in our life. Of course, this love presupposes a relationship. It is not a personal matter; it is a social matter. This love is demonstrated by a way of life, a behavior, relationships with the authorities, with economic powers and with the various groups to which we belong. These will be different from the behavior and the relationships that the world proposes and institutes. Attempting to establish Christian institutions is a utopia; but to establish specifically Christian relationships *also* with institutions— that is all that is required of us.

Now, the announcement of God's judgement and the demonstration of God's love, which presuppose a serious change within individuals, provoke *ipso facto* changes in the institutions of a country without the need for legislation, but simply by their presence. They do not change all institutions, and do not do so according to a predetermined plan, or in a striking way, but in very concrete terms. It is not necessary to be a Christian minister or a Christian banker to create change. Quite the contrary, each one of us changes society in concrete terms where we are. This is of course, as long as we are willing to do so.

Furthermore, as there is no plan, no transformation can appear to be decisive, definitive as far as faith is concerned, or even sufficient. What is required is an effort constantly undertaken and constantly renewed, without completion. This is what gives the tenth century its revolutionary aspect as I described *in Presence au Monde Moderne*. It is of course, much easier to build an apparently Christian theory and to follow maxims. I am afraid that the Bible lacks all authority when we use it in such a way.

II. Authority for Non-Christians

"If the Bible possesses any authority, it must have authority for all." We have often heard this assertion. We will not study the problem of the authority of Scripture for non-Christians in general as far as the social and political realms are concerned; this would run the risk of becoming too theoretical. We will only reiterate what Christians should never forget in this regard in their ethical actions in society.

1. The Bible as such has no meaning, no authority and no value for non-Christians. We absolutely cannot require that they take it seriously for what it is. They may be able to find an admirable morality, historical information, or remarkable poetry in the Bible and declare that they agree with it. In reality, this agreement hides the truth from them. Their admiration is for what is human and perishable, for what has no authority in the Bible. We cannot ask them to change their lives or to have a conversion of heart in the name of this. In all our relationships with non-Christians we need to start from the Bible's lack of authority from the natural point of view. Therefore, it is impossible to measure the actions of non-Christians with the measures applicable to Christians. In other words, Christian ethics is not applicable to non-Christians. The morality shown in Scripture is not natural. It is related to the person of Jesus Christ. It is precisely because of

this that it can be called "Christian." Therefore, the person who does not recognize Jesus Christ, does not need to recognize the validity of this morality. We cannot ask this person to apply it because it has no authority over that person.

2. Consequently, we cannot hope that the teachings on social and politic ethics will have any value for a non-Christian person. This must certainly warn us against the ideology of "a political system drawn from Scripture." Such a system would only apply in two hypothetical instances: a situation in which all people were Christians—but this is unthinkable on earth—or the case of a Christian party taking power and building this kind of society by force, which of course is not in line with a Christian ethic. There is no other solution. For if we tried to justify a certain principal of social ethic with human reasons, we would be in the domain of natural authority but not in the domain of revealed authority. Consequently, the principle thus demonstrated would no longer be Christian since it would be founded on something else than the person of Jesus Christ.

We must also recognize that the transformation of our relationships with society appears to be of little importance and incomprehensible to non-Christians. We should we not feel much pride or hope about this attitude. We have been warned ahead of time that non-Christians would only understand this attitude *after* their conversion (see 1 Pet 2:12, Matt 5:16). So we must not expect to find an authority for non-Christians in our attitude. The demonstration of the love of God which is asked of us can only be understood when the love of God has visited non-Christians. Therefore, our attitude towards society, towards economic powers, towards the State can be neither understood nor accepted as an example from the outside. Yet, it is efficacious within the reality of events.

3. Finally, this does not mean that non-Christians are left to their own devices or have no morality. Scripture shows us that there is a certain behavior established by God in the covenant with Noah, a covenant, which like all covenants, is confirmed in the New Covenant in the blood of Jesus Christ. Scripture also reminds us that non-Christians obey an order over which Jesus Christ is lord. Therefore, to a certain extent it is possible for them to live in the good, a good over which Jesus Christ is Lord. Yet, this dependence of non-Christians on Jesus Christ is mysterious and hidden. It is only barely revealed in the Bible by faith. It is completely unknown to pagans. This is why anything that comes from it is devoid of authority in their eyes. This is also why

all political, social or ethical systems vainly search for a foundation, a solidity, an authority in the natural resources of man, without ever finding one. The indisputable existence of this order for all humans, and yet the impossibility of understanding the reason for it (who is Christ, hidden to the natural eyes), explains the uncertainty and variability of human systems.

Now, the duty of Christians is precisely to announce God's judgements with respect to this indisputable order. Thus, they can enlighten non-Christians on what these judgements really are and enlighten them on the foundation and the reason for this mysterious order which sets its mark on humans, for good or evil in the midst of sin. We must never forget that one way or the other we are each personally concerned through our duty to be present in the midst of the pagan world.

CHAPTER 3

The Bible and Christian Action

Jacques Ellul

TRANSLATED BY
Lisa Richmond

Does the Bible have something to say about social and political issues?[1] Can it still inspire Christian action today in these two areas that are completely secularized? We believe so. But we must understand how, and this means that we must begin by raising the question of method. This will be the focus of this article.

To begin, let us set aside the methods of biblical hermeneutics that seem inadequate to us. These are:

1. *Literalism.* Literalism asserts the literal inspiration of the Bible and requires us to submit to the text's formal content. All its commandments, laws, and ordinances must be accepted as such and applied literally. The danger in this approach is *moralism*, or, if one prefers, puritanism, which has as its tendency the separation of the moral and social elements that the revelation bears witness to, from the person and role of Jesus Christ.

2. *Spiritualism.* This approach is the opposite of literalism. Its watchword is "The letter kills, but the spirit gives life" (2 Cor 3:6). By wrongly interpreting this famous text of St. Paul, the claim is that it is possible to extract from the biblical letter a certain spirit (e.g., love, righteousness) that alone is authoritative. [But if this is so,] we must ask ourselves

---

1. This chapter is a translation of "La Bible et l'action chrétienne," *Bulletin du Centre Protestant d'Études* 2 (1950) 4–8.

why God chose this big book that is the Bible as the instrument of his revelation. In not wanting to retain anything but the spirit, spiritualism ends up retaining nothing but a faith in which divine law becomes practically identical with the ideas and wishes of religious man.

Among the methods to set aside, let us further mention a certain *mistaken Barthianism* that believes itself able to preserve a social ethic, and on the other hand a certain *biblical rationalism* that claims to draw general and rational principles from God's commandments which instead are always specific and revealed.

We will now try to suggest a method that can enable us to avoid these various pitfalls. But first we must make this point clear: the Bible does not provide us with God's revelation ready-made, so to speak. This revelation is both evident and hidden in the document that bears witness to it. What does this mean, if not that we must probe the Scriptures and work hard to *hear* and *understand* what they want to tell us, today just like yesterday and tomorrow? When we do this we [typically] downplay the role of the intellect. This is false. We are called to love God also with all our mind. Mental effort is necessary. To lead us into all truth, the Holy Spirit wants to make use of our minds, and not only of our right sentiments, our piety, our heart. So we must apply mental effort to the biblical texts.

In the subject that we are concerned with, the Bible and Christian action, we come up against certain problems right away:

1. Most of the texts about social morality are found in the Old Testament, in the Law. Is this law with its numerous ordinances still valid?

2. The political and religious institutions that we encounter in the Bible concern a people with its own history, the people of Israel. Are the rules of social ethics that applied to it now defunct? Can we still find something usable in them? What is more, Israel was both a people and a church. Should we disregard the ordinances that concern the people and retain only the laws governing Israel as a church? But is it so easy to distinguish the two?

3. Finally, we must not conceal how difficult it is to interpret biblical texts relative to human conduct. We can very easily make errors by giving into the temptation of making it into a human system with a little "faith" added in. Here is where the little-known method of the analogy of faith should step in. But what do we mean by this? Is it an objective, valid, sure criterion? And how are we to use it?

These are precisely the three questions that we will now examine to illustrate the method that we are proposing.

I. *The Meaning and Use of the Law*

Is the law—which is to say, roughly, the ten commandments—still valid for the Christian? If so, what use should we make of it? The witness of the New Testament is clear on this point: Jesus Christ has come to *fulfill* the law. In him the law is fulfilled, not abolished. This means first that it is *accomplished*, complete, in its deep reality; what it announced has come. Its hidden and definitive meaning has appeared: it is a person and not a casuistry. And this signifies therefore that it is *authenticated*: since Jesus Christ has achieved it, we see that it is indeed the will of God, valid for all. From this point on it is guaranteed and maintained by the one who fills it with his grace and his demands.

To say that in Jesus Christ the law is fulfilled signifies that it has become more relative, humbler, more obedient, in the sense that it appears now just as the shadow of which Christ is the reality. If it remains, it is relative to the work of Jesus Christ. Let us try to describe from this point of view the law's meaning and role for Christians and pagans.

For Christians, the matter is clear: the law is no longer a duty. It is there to give *indications*, for we singularly lack imagination and boldness for action. Second, it acts as a *check* for the action that is performed in faith. It serves to verify to us if what we believe to be obedience is indeed an obedience. But at the same time, it still provides an explanation of Jesus Christ and of his work. It tells us what he is and what he has done for us (consider in particular the sacrificial laws of the Old Testament that "were the shadow of things to come").

As for the law's role for pagans, in order to understand this, we must remind ourselves that if the ten commandments were given to the people of Israel through Moses, in the meantime there has been the coming of Jesus Christ. From this point on, history is divided into two different parts. The civilizations before Jesus Christ are incommensurable with the civilizations that come after Jesus Christ. Just as with the Incarnation it becomes clear that salvation overruns the category of the people of Israel to become a matter for the entire world, so also the law's fulfillment in Christ gives to this law a universal character and reach. The role that the law had played in relation to the people of Israel, as the schoolmaster leading to Christ, it now plays for the world as a whole.

Here we must watch out for two common errors with regard to the world:

1. To believe that we are obliged to proclaim to the world only the law, apart from the Gospel. We must preach both.
2. Conversely, to believe that we can demand of the world the works of faith, which comes down to confusing the practice of the law with the works of the law. We always want to moralize people, setting faith aside. Yet we can ask them to fulfil the works of the law only if they have faith.

II. *Institutions*

The people of Israel that the Old Testament speaks of belong to history. As a sociological phenomenon, they are "over," "defunct." But we must not forget that they are the *people of God*, and for this reason we cannot start out by considering their institutions defunct. As the people of God, this people are the bearer of certain human, social, and political values. It is God who made the twelve primitive tribes into one united people. Its institutions enabled it to cohere, to maintain itself in the midst of the great empires of the day. It is possible to affirm therefore that the institutions of Israel are, roughly—and obviously we are referring here to what is fundamental, not episodic and sociological—those that are indispensable for a people to live, maintain itself, resist internal chaos and external pressures.

But the people of Israel were both a *people* and a *church*, and it is almost impossible to distinguish between the institutions that are of the people and those that are of the church. We can assert that beginning with Jesus Christ, it is not the Church only that succeeds Israel, but *the Church and the world*. The Church succeeds Israel as a church, and the world succeeds Israel as a people. We recover on the global level the two elements that are at the base of Israel's existence. The Church continues one of the Israel's functions, the world continues the other.

All of Israel's political and religious institutions have the same meaning theologically: they prophetically announce the sacrifice and the kingship of Jesus Christ. This means that by the fact of Jesus Christ's coming, the present-day institutions of the Church and of the world that have succeeded Israel have a *theological* value: they have a relationship with Jesus Christ, his kingship, and indirectly testify to it. Just as every explanation of political or social text in Israel must be based on Jesus Christ, every application of these same texts in the modern world must be centred in the assurance that Jesus Christ is the Lord of the world.

Finally, from the fact that Israel's institutions, in their very imperfection, announce that which is coming, it follows that all of the institutions of this world should also be studied from the perspective of salvation and the Kingdom of God; what gives them meaning, for the Christian, is their orientation to Christ's return.

III. *The Analogy of Faith*

We now arrive at the essential problem of method that I am trying to sketch out: that of *the interpretation of texts*. Our criterion in this will be the analogy of faith, according to Romans 12:6. The analogy of faith is concerned here with the gift of prophecy, which is to say, the present-day preaching, explanation, and application of the Bible's message and understanding. It is thus entirely appropriate to use this criterion in relation to texts about ethics. What does "according to the analogy of faith" mean? And first, what faith are we speaking of? The faith of the Church certainly, and the content of this faith that is expressed by certain articles, certain confessions, of faith. There is no opposition between the content of the faith (its objective aspect) and the very act of believing (its subjective aspect), because in each case we are discussing faith in Jesus Christ.

As for the term *analogy*, it means this: the measure or specific proportion between two magnitudes. The analogy of faith is the relationship that we establish between a given text and the objective content of the faith of the Church or the attitude of believers.

Why is this notion of analogy necessary? Because there is a *necessary* interpretation of the biblical text. There is no readymade revelation. We are always called to discern the revelation in the letter of the Bible, and we cannot do so except by establishing the relationship between our interpretation and the articles of faith that the Church recognizes. We must accomplish this work ourselves, today—taking into account, certainly, the interpretation of the Fathers and the Reformers, but without stopping there as though that interpretation were definitive. When we face the Bible, we must always take up the stance of faith's dangerous uncertainty, which requires us to work out again, for ourselves and for our day, what others have worked out before us and for their time.

What does it mean then to interpret the biblical text according to the analogy of faith? It means first that we must distinguish between the revelation's *form* and its *substance*. God conveys his message to us through sinful men, and we receive it through our understanding as sinful men. Yet this does not mean that the form is irrelevant (God chose precisely *this* form!). To speak to us, God chose a history and not a philosophy! The form is not indifferent. Our job is to seek out the relationship between the revelation's form and substance and discover how to express this same relationship today. Thus, the works of faith are, for a given age, a *form* that preserves its value *as a suggestion*. For example, we must not slavishly imitate the works of Abraham, Moses, Isaiah, Paul, etc. Instead, we must seek how we should act today, by the analogy of faith—that is, by discovering for ourselves the relationship between the message's form and its substance. We must therefore understand the social and political situation of the biblical era (for example, the Christian attitude toward slavery during the first several centuries), and at the same time understand the social and political situation of our own day, so that we can see how, where, and when the same expression of faith can be expressed today. But in doing so we always run the risk of falling away from the revelation itself, inventing things and lapsing into error. Whence the necessity of referring to the articles of the faith of the Church—or, if you prefer, to what one might call its general outline, the Bible's *permanent content*. This is what is meant secondly by recourse to the analogy of faith. What is this permanent content? Here is some of it:

- Salvation by faith, and not by works.
- The *Soli Deo Gloria*, the final end of all Christian ethics.
- The dignity of man (because God, to restore this man to dignity, chose to die for him).
- The state of tension in the Christian life, positioned between Jesus Christ and the Prince of this World.
- Finally and above all, *Jesus Christ* and his work.

The entire Bible announces and reveals Jesus Christ to us. Yet we must avoid lapsing into typology and allegory. We must show great intellectual integrity and not distort the texts. For the subject that we are concerned with, we will specify then this final content:

1. All of *the texts are prophetic* in the sense that they all concern the God's singular decision to become incarnate in the man Jesus. In the same way, our works and our lives are also prophetic, as a reflection of the incarnation and God's great work.
2. All of the texts are prophetic in another sense as well: they are concentrated on Jesus Christ who has come and will come again. They must

be situated in the perspective that moves from the cross to Christ's return. Our works and our lives also exist, then, within the perspective of this return. They are here to go before Jesus Christ, who is coming again (cf. the parable of the virgins).

3. Jesus Christ *is Savior*: it is in light of this truth that we must understand the Bible's moral texts and all our works. We have complete freedom to accomplish whatever works we want, because they are not what save us. But there is more: all our works, both good and bad, must be saved with us, including our theology! Jesus Christ is the Savior and not right action, which must also be pardoned in him.

4. Finally, Jesus Christ *is Lord*: none of our works escape this lordship. In essence, our works must demonstrate to the world that Jesus Christ's victory is won, is a reality. It is our job, then, to "invent" the works of faith that best demonstrate this victory. It is not possible to give recipes, to set up a casuistry of Christian action. The work of faith has a spontaneous, immediate, and unexpected character, and this is why it cannot be defined in advance. One must first be in faith to produce the works of faith.

─────── CHAPTER 4 ───────

Scriptural Ethics

On the Meaning and Use of the Analogy of Faith

Frédéric Rognon

TRANSLATED BY
Jacob Marques Rollison

As a diligent reader of the Bible, Jacques Ellul placed scriptural revelation at the heart of his work, and particularly of his ethical works. It is thus that he could write: "the criterion of my thought is biblical revelation; the content of my thought is biblical revelation; my point of departure is provided by biblical revelation; the method is the dialectic according to which biblical revelation is addressed to us; and the goal is the search for the significance of biblical revelation as it bears on Ethics."[1] Ellul's ethical thought is thus "scripturo-centric," conferring a singular status on the biblical text. How, then, did Ellul read the Bible? In what way is his reading original, singular, and capable of renewing current interpretations?

This chapter proposes to respond to these questions in four steps. First, Ellul's critique of exegesis will be described. Second, we will present the core principles of the Ellulian approach to the Bible. In a third step, we will focus on the method of reading *par excellence* recommended by the professor from Bordeaux, "the analogy of faith." Finally, we will conclude with four examples of biblical texts interpreted according to the analogy of faith.

---

1. Ellul, *To Will & To Do*, 1:18.

Critique of Exegesis

Ellul addresses both historical-critical exegesis and structural exegesis with spirited critiques. While he does not consider them to be false or pointless, since they are undoubtedly precise and useful to the nature of the study, "they do not permit us to take even one step towards the ultimate. They certainly offer great precision, but they have nothing to say on the subject of truth; they do not permit truth to be glimpsed, but in fact perhaps hide it."[2] Ellul thus invokes the tension between Reality and Truth—a recurring tension throughout Ellul's corpus—to disqualify scientific and technical exegetical methods. He particularly reproaches these methods for stripping the biblical text of any spiritual dimension, reducing it to nothing more than a text like any other (on the same level as a work of Homer or Plato). To treat the Bible like an inert object would be like a surgeon forgetting that the patients on whom she is operating is alive, performing a dissection or an autopsy instead of an operation that would save them.[3]

This accusation recalls Søren Kierkegaard's polemical and sarcastic gripe with those who pretend to read a love letter with an arsenal of dictionaries, concordances, and encyclopedias.[4] For the Bible is indeed a love letter sent by God to his readers, to touch their hearts and address the most intimate areas of their existence.

Ellul also criticizes the Marxist exegesis fashionable in the seventies, and notably that of Fernando Belo, who purported "to read Mark via Marx."[5] The professor from Bordeaux catalogues the innumerable historical errors that allow Belo to integrate the gospel into the Marxist schema,[6] particularly reproaching him for performing a materialist and political reduction of a text which, precisely, refuses any materialist interpretation of life.[7]

What alternative does Jacques Ellul proposes to these exegetical impasses?

---

2. Ellul, *Sans feu ni lieu*, 17. This citation from the book's preface only exists in the expanded 1975 French edition, published after the first 1970 English edition.

3. Cf. Ellul, *Éthique de la liberté*, 1:210.

4. Cf. Kierkegaard, "Pour un examen de conscience recommandé aux contemporains."

5. Cf. Belo, *Lecture matérialiste de l'évangile de Marc*, 18.

6. Cf. Ellul, *L'idéologie marxiste chrétienne*, 113–53.

7. Cf. Ellul, *L'idéologie marxiste chrétienne*, 148–50.

Core Principles of the Ellulian Approach to the Bible

If Ellul rejects the scientific approach to the Bible, he does so in favor of his own Kierkegaard-inspired meditation. This latter approach essentially considers biblical revelation as addressed to the very existence of the human subject. But in so doing, he inverts the contemporary perspective (notably in Protestant milieus) which consists in opening the Bible every time we seek a response to our questions (whether ethical, social, or existential). Ellul clearly does not conceive of the Bible as a recipe book, nor even as a book of responses to our questions. The Bible is not a book of responses, but a book of questions which God poses to the believing reader.[8] If we come to the Bible with questions, these latter will not receive an answer, but will instead be displaced, decentered; we will come away from the Bible with our questions renewed, and with new questions posed to us.[9] It is up to us to respond to these new questions—i.e., to be responsible, by fully assuming our responses.

The Bible is thus a book that points man to his freedom and responsibility. Faithfully reading is listening, since faith is revitalized in silence.[10] The Bible poses us three principal questions.[11] First, it poses a confessional question: "Who do you say that I am?"[12]; second, an ethical question: "What have you done with your brother?"[13]; and third, an existential question referring to our seeking: "Who are you looking for?"[14] We are thus interrogated, and invited to give a confessional, ethical, and an existential response, by our words and in our life. Cain, for his part, refuses to respond to the question of God and thus assume his "responsibilities."[15] In posing too many questions to the Bible or about the Bible, we forget to receive the questions which the

---

8. Cf. Ellul, *Éthique de la liberté*, 1:203; 2:164, 181–82; Ellul, *La foi au prix du doute*, 147–52; Ellul, "Karl Barth et nous," 7; Ellul, *La Genèse aujourd'hui*, 214; Ellul, *Mort et espérance de la résurrection*, 53; Ellul, *Les sources de l'éthique chrétienne*, 57–58; Comte, "Entretien avec Jacques Ellul," 2.

9. Cf. Ellul, *Éthique de la liberté*, 2:164; Ellul, *La Genèse aujourd'hui*, 214.

10. Cf. Ellul, *La foi au prix du doute*, 151–55.

11. Cf. Ellul, *La foi au prix du doute*, 135–37.

12. Matt 16:15; Mark 8:29; Luke 9:20. The range of Peter's responses could support Ellul's reading of the Bible as a book of questions. These responses may thus vary from one person to another, but also with one person according to their stage in life.

13. Cf. Gen 4:9–10a. More specifically, the text says, "The Lord said to Cain, 'Where is your brother Abel?' He replied, 'I do not know. Am I my brother's keeper?' Then he said, 'What have you done?'"

14. John 20:15.

15. Ellul, *Éthique de la liberté*, 2:181–82.

Bible itself poses to us.[16] Instead of posing questions to the Bible (as the believer ordinarily does), and instead of posing questions about the Bible (as the exegete does)—in both cases, starting with extra-biblical concerns, and in danger of instrumentalizing revelation—this sort of reading involves letting the Bible pose questions to the world and to believers. It is thus a matter of exercising as robust a freedom towards the assumptions of the world as towards revelation.[17]

"The Analogy of Faith"

But the privileged method that Ellul proposes to avoid both literalism and textual critique is that of the "analogy of faith." This expression comes from the apostle Paul, who employs it only once (making it a *hapax legomenon*) in the epistle to the Romans:[18] κατὰ τὴν ἀναλογίαν τῆς πίστεως in Greek, *fidei analogia* in Latin. It is found in a passage consecrated to the diverse gifts given to different people in the Church: prophecy, service, teaching, exhortation, generosity, guiding the community, and mercy.[19] The analogy of faith is linked to the gift of the prophet: "Since we have different gifts, according to the grace that has been accorded to us, let the one who has the gift of prophecy exercise it according to the analogy of faith."[20]

John Calvin borrowed this Pauline expression in his *Commentary on the Epistle to the Romans*[21] (in his exegesis of Romans 12:6) and at several points in the *Institutes of the Christian Religion*.[22] In his commentary, Calvin argues for a broad conception of prophecy, understood not as the gift of predicting the future, but as a right knowledge of Scripture and a capacity to expound it clearly. It thus involves seeking to align all doctrine taught from Scripture with the foundations of the faith.[23] In *Institutes of the Christian Religion*, Calvin first mentions the analogy of faith in the introduction, in his address to the king of France. Against his adversaries who accuse him of diverting the Word of God from its true meaning, the Reformer recalls this: "When St. Paul willed that all prophecy should be interpreted

---

16. Ellul, *Éthique de la liberté*, 1:203.
17. Ellul, *Éthique de la liberté*, 1:205.
18. Rom 12:6b.
19. Rom 12:4–8.
20. Rom 12:6.
21. Calvin, *Épître aux Romains*, 292–93.
22. Calvin, *Institution de la religion chrétienne*: "Au roi de France," xxx; book iv, ch. 15, §4, 1252; book iv, ch. 16, §8, 1256; book iv, ch. 17, §32, 1321.
23. Calvin, *Épître aux Romains*, 292–93.

according to the analogy and likeness of faith (Rom 12:6), he elaborated a most reliable rule for examining all interpretation of Scripture. If, then, our doctrine is examined according to this rule of faith, we have the victory in hand."[24] In the main body of his massive treatise, Calvin refers to the concept of the analogy of faith on the subjects of the baptism of children and the Lord's supper. Infant baptism is not explicitly affirmed in the Bible, but silence does not imply censure (otherwise, women would not be permitted to take communion). However, there is the question of the baptism of entire families; it is thus in conformity to the analogy of faith that we can lay biblical foundations for baptizing children.[25] By the same token, the Reformer defends his comprehension of the mystery of the holy supper based on the methodological principle of the analogy of faith.[26] According to Calvin, the analogy of faith thus consists in interpreting Scripture by Scripture, allowing Scripture to interpret itself, and to dig deeply into each text to bring it in line with the other texts of the Bible.

Ellul resembles Calvin in his understanding of this rule of reading, though he still slightly demarcates his own position. In the second part of *To Will & To Do*,[27] the professor from Bordeaux devotes long passages to the analogy of faith.[28] Following Karl Barth while polemically disagreeing with him, Ellul begins by clearly distinguishing the *analogia fidei* from the *analogia entis*, a foundational concept of natural theology in the style of Thomas Aquinas.[29] His critique of Barth consists in saying that the theologian from Basel ceded to the temptation that he denounced himself, that of resorting to the *analogia entis*. Ellul then distances himself from Calvin by limiting the analogy of faith to the exercise of prophecy *stricto sensu*, instead of making this rule into a general principle for interpreting all biblical texts.[30] However, he understands the prophet's mission as being properly ethical: for Ellul, prophecy consists of elaborating an ethic under the inspiration of the Spirit, and in guaranteeing its objectivity by confronting it with Scripture. "If, then, prophecy consists in this formulation of a morality *hic et nunc*, inspired by the Spirit of God on the basis of (and in relation to) holy Scripture, we see very well that the analogy of

---

24. Calvin, *Institution de la religion chrétienne*, xxx.

25. Calvin, *Institutes of the Christian Religion: 1541 French Edition*, 1252, 1256.

26. Calvin, *Institutes of the Christian Religion: 1541 French Edition*, 1321.

27. Ellul, *Les sources de l'éthique chrétienne*. At time of editing, this volume is forthcoming from Cascade as *To Will & To Do* vol. 2; references will thus give page numbers from the French edition.

28. Ellul, *Les sources de l'éthique chrétienne*, 287–311.

29. Ellul, *Les sources de l'éthique chrétienne*, 281–85.

30. Ellul, *Les sources de l'éthique chrétienne*, 292.

faith in question here effectively concerns interpreting biblical texts, and that it implies a guarantee of objectivity."[31] This does not prevent Ellul from implicitly positioning himself close to Calvin's broad conception by applying this method to numerous texts in which he believes he discerns an ethical intention: "There can be no formulation of a morality for Christians based on the profound understanding of the ethical texts except through the analogy of faith", he declares.[32] He defines the analogy as "a relation between elements of a different nature or magnitude"[33] but also as "understanding the *reason*"[34] for this relation. Interpreting Scripture thus consists in understanding the tension between biblical revelation and the contemporary morality of an era, in order to reproduce this same tension in our own milieu, without literally adopting a statement which is outmoded today. The work of salvation accomplished by Jesus Christ constitutes the objectivity of the heart itself of revelation. The whole Bible points to Jesus Christ, designating him as Lord and Savior. Consequently, Jesus Christ must be the constant in relation to which the analogy of faith must be established.[35] And if a passage of the biblical corpus seems to depart from the image and the face of the God of love that Jesus has revealed to us, it must be studied and worked upon, until one discerns the elements of this passage which cohere with this kernel of the revelation.

Examples of Applying the Method of the Analogy of Faith

We will examine four examples of difficult biblical texts which the method of the analogy of faith will clarify by hearing them in echo with other texts, forming a harmonious symphony. Our presentation of these texts relies on Ellul's commentary, but also by extends it beyond what Ellul wrote concerning these texts.

Qoheleth / Ecclesiastes

Ecclesiastes is Ellul's most beloved biblical book: "There is probably no other biblical text which I have searched so much, from which I have received so

---

31. Ellul, *Les sources de l'éthique chrétienne*, 293.
32. Ellul, *Les sources de l'éthique chrétienne*, 297.
33. Ellul, *Les sources de l'éthique chrétienne*, 297.
34. Ellul, *Les sources de l'éthique chrétienne*, 297.
35. Cf. Ellul, *Les sources de l'éthique chrétienne*, 308–11.

much—which has reached me and spoken to me so much."[36] He therefore consecrated a meditative work to Ecclesiastes: *Reason for Being*,[37] a book which he conceived as the conclusion of his work as a whole.[38] Our author affirms to have chosen a path for this study which inverts standard academic procedures, departing from the Hebrew text itself and not from commentaries.[39] Likewise, he refuses to consider the Bible as equal to any other literary text, since it is the bearer of revelation.[40] Whence Ellul's search for textual coherence beyond apparent contradictions: for example, between 'all is vanity (including wisdom)' and 'seek wisdom (because it comes from God).' And he orients this coherence within a dialectical movement between "Reality" and "Truth." The Reality is that all is vanity, and the Truth is that everything is a gift of God. Reality prevents the Truth from being an evasion; the Truth prevents Reality from being hopeless.[41]

All commentators of Ecclesiastes have been disconcerted by the absence of a logical plan and have generally sought to identify different authors and different editorial layers. But according to Ellul, the book's coherence does not come from a plan but from a weave, like a threading of reflections that become entangled, echoing one another. The dialectic between vanity and wisdom finds its end in God: wisdom makes the vanity of everything apparent; but wisdom is itself vanity; and yet vanity is overtaken by wisdom. And nevertheless, the book of Qoheleth does not end in this immanent circle because of the reference to God, which is central and decisive because it ties together the dispersed factors. The contradictions are not gross errors of forgetfulness, as the exegetes say, but one of the keys of the book: "The principle of non-contradiction is a principle of death. Contradiction is the condition of a communication."[42] The work of Kierkegaard was decisive for Ellul's discernment of the dialectical movement at the heart of the book of Ecclesiastes. And it is in similar reference to the Danish thinker that our author finally argues in favor of a subjective and intuitive approach: "above all, to let oneself be seized by the beauty of the text, to receive it first of all in

---

36. Ellul, *La raison d'être*, 11.
37. Ellul, *La raison d'être*.
38. Ellul, *La raison d'être*, 13–14.
39. Ellul, *La raison d'être*, 11. This remark betrays deep prejudices as to the exegetical methods taught and practiced in the faculties of theology.
40. Ellul, *La raison d'être*, 16–18.
41. Ellul, *La raison d'être*, 42.
42. Ellul, *La raison d'être*, 52.

emotion and silent listening as with music, and to allow one's sensitivity, one's imagination, to speak before wanting to analyze and 'understand.'"[43]

Ellul synthesizes his approach in a spiral schematic[44] which allows us to navigate the apparent contradictions of Ecclesiastes by following the movement of the text. We are not dealing with a book written by three authors—with the first sceptic and disabused, seeing in all things only vanity; the second rich with experiences, considering a wisdom without God as an art of living with realism and lucidity; and a third who confesses his faith in God. Ellul sees only one author, who starts from vanity (1:1–11), responds to it with wisdom (1:12–18), but falls back into vanity since wisdom itself is vanity (2:1–11). This vicious circle finds its opening in God (who appears for the first time in 2:24); it is "before God" that everything takes on meaning, because everything is a "gift of God" (3:10–17; 5:17–19); therefore, "fear God" (5:6). And God has the last word (12:10–13). This interpretation is indeed an application of the method of the analogy of faith, for God is the beginning, the center, and the end of the Bible, all converges toward him. Consequently, every text which seems to neglect him can be clarified if one digs deeper until, at last, one finds God therein.

The Parable of the Wedding Feast[45]

Our second example is that of the parable of the wedding party, which is a parable of the Kingdom.[46] Each of these "parables of the Kingdom," spread all along the Gospel of Matthew from chapter thirteen until chapter twenty-five, gives us an image of the Kingdom of heaven: "the Kingdom of heaven is like . . . " Like a man, a mustard seed, yeast, a hidden treasure, a merchant, a net, a king. Here, in our parable, the Kingdom of heaven is similar to a king. This king organizes a wedding feast for his son. Once the feast is put in place, he sends out his servants to call those who were invited. The invitees were thus aware of the invitation; they knew that the wedding feast was going to take place, and that they were invited. And yet, they make excuses and decline the invitation, too occupied in their fields and commerce. Furthermore, the invitees seize, insult, and kill the king's servants. The king takes his vengeance by making them perish. Then he tells his servants to go and invite everyone they can find, in the streets and the crossroads: the "wicked and good," the text specifies. Wicked and good: everyone is invited. This seems to be a first

---

43. Ellul, *La raison d'être*, 323.
44. Ellul, *La raison d'être*, 40.
45. Cf. Ellul, *On Freedom, Love, and Power*, 188–95.
46. Cf. Matt 22:1–14; Luke 14:16–24.

decisive element.⁴⁷ And the wedding hall is full of guests. Now, one man has not worn his garment for the wedding feast. Only one in the whole crowd: this is a second determining element.⁴⁸ The king asks him how he entered, and he remains silent. So the king says to his servants, "Bind him hand and foot, and throw him into the outer darkness, where there will be weeping and gnashing of teeth." The king behaves like a tyrant. Ought we to identify the king with God, as is often done? Must we see the indifferent guests as believers who are a bit too lukewarm, and the poorly dressed guest as the unbeliever, the incredulous one, the infidel, the one who does not live according to the gospel, as is often done? Must we therefore see in this parable a means of terrorizing bad believers by menacing them with hell, as it has often been understood? Is this the image of the Father that Jesus came to reveal, speaking directly to us, without the ambiguity of the parables?

Let us therefore reconsider the elements that constitute the point of the text: the wicked and the good share the feast; only one is thrown into the darkness, punished and tormented. Even the indifferent guests are not thrown into the darkness, where there is weeping and gnashing of teeth. They are killed, they are dead; but they are not submitted to these torments. We are told nothing about what happens to them after their death. Only one is condemned, expelled, tormented for all. Who is this one if not Christ himself? This man who is thrown out without a wedding garment—it is Jesus himself! This man who remains silent when interrogated and threatened—it is Jesus, who remained silent before Pilate! All the others are clothed in a wedding garment, the wicked and the good—everyone! For Jesus is the one who took our faults upon himself and was condemned for us, in our place! This is what the apostle Paul says to the Corinthians, in a text just as enigmatic and scandalous: "The one who knew no sin, God made him become sin for us, so that we could become in him the righteousness of God" (2 Cor 5:21). He did not become a sinner; he became sin! And he paid for us. He was cast into torment, weeping and gnashing of teeth: he "descended into hell," as the Creed says. All this was done for us. And this is in accordance with the whole of the gospel message, according to the analogy of faith.

We might say: But what a cruel God this is, who casts his son into torment! I believe that here, dear friends, the whole interest of believing in the Trinity comes into play. If we believe that God is Father, Son, and Holy Spirit; if Jesus Christ is none other than God, just as the Father is God and the Holy Spirit is God; then this is not a god who cruelly casts a man, *a fortiori* his son, into torment. Let us not be bound by a literal or allegorical

---

47. Cf. Ellul, *On Freedom, Love, and Power*, 191.
48. Cf. Ellul, *On Freedom, Love, and Power*, 191, 194.

reading of the parable, according to which a king expels a guest. The king does not represent the Father; he represents the Kingdom, since it is the Kingdom of heaven that is like a king. No, according to the trinitarian faith, it is God as Jesus Christ who gives himself fully for us: it is a gift of self and not the sacrifice of someone else. God gives himself fully to suffering and torment, to weeping and gnashing of teeth, so that we who are sinners may be freed, saved from these troubles. And this is in accordance with the whole of the gospel message, according to the analogy of faith.

And the parable ends thus: "For many are called, but few are chosen." Here again, this is a strange formula. The parable has just told us that the wedding hall was full of guests; yet the lesson of the parable consists in telling us that there many are called, but few chosen. We thus cannot reasonably identify the guests, who are innumerable, with the chosen, who are very few. Perhaps the guests are the called rather than the chosen . . . This final formula cannot signify that very few will be saved at the end of time.[49] Euphemistically, "few are chosen" can mean "none are chosen, not one chosen." This formula signifies thus that we are not worthy of being saved, not one among us, but that Jesus alone has paid the price so that we might be saved. This formula signifies the infinite love of the Father, without which we can do nothing by ourselves. And this, too, is in accordance with the whole of the gospel message, according to the analogy of faith.

The Parable of the Judgement[50]

Our third example is the parable of the Judgement. This text poses several problems. It seems to go against the idea of salvation by grace and to defend the idea of salvation by works. Moreover, it raises the question of hell:[51] those who will have accomplished works of mercy (the sheep) will be blessed and will enter the Kingdom, and those who have not accomplished these works (the goats) will be cursed and will go to eternal fire. For those who have given food to the hungry and drink to the thirsty, those who have welcomed the stranger, clothed the naked, visited the sick and the prisoner, have served Christ himself; therefore, they have the right to eternal life. But those who have not done all this have not served Christ; consequently, they will go to eternal punishment.

49. Cf. Ellul, *On Freedom, Love, and Power*, 193–95.
50. Cf. Matt 25:31–46.
51. Ellul points out that there is no question of hell except in the parables because these latter are not lessons of doctrinal teaching. Cf. Ellul, *Ce que je crois*, 257–58; *On Freedom, Love, and Power*, 157.

But there is a small detail here that has too often gone neglected. The sheep are all surprised to learn that they have served Christ in serving their neighbor; by the same token, the goats are all surprised to learn that they have not served Christ in not serving their neighbor. They only discover this after the fact. At the moment that they encounter their neighbor, they are thus unaware that Christ identified himself with the littlest person, that he was, literally, this little one. In other words, those who appear in Matthew twenty-five have not read Matthew twenty-five—and for good reason! And this effect of surprise is the first decisive element. For we thus see that the sheep have acted in this way, not in order to be saved, but because they let their hearts speak. The attitude of the sheep, like that of the goats, was not linked to salvation, but to the capacity or incapacity to love the neighbor in distress. It is the opening or closing of the heart that is in question here—quite simply, the opening or closing of the heart before the concrete situation and immediate needs of the littlest one there is.

In this same way, a second small detail, more decisive yet, must be brought to light. First of all, what the Son of Man really says to the goats is that "insofar as (εφ'οσον) you have not done this for one of these little ones, it is for me that you have not done it." It is a question of *one* of these little ones. This means that it suffices to neglect one little one, only one, to be damned! Even if you help ninety-nine little ones, if you leave one of the hundred aside without regarding her, you are damned! But this means that we are all damned, for we have all neglected our neighbor at least once. We are all condemnable. This is the logic of the Law of the First Testament: it suffices to have broken one of the 613 commandments of the Torah, all while having accomplished the other 612, to have sinned against the entire Torah. But now if we look at what is said of the sheep, we observe that the same thing—the same, but inverted—is said concerning the sheep: "Insofar as you have done this for *one* of these little ones, it is for me that you have done it." This means that it suffices to have served one little one, only one, to be saved! Now, we have all helped our neighbor at least once. Even one time! Thus, we are all saved! Or more precisely, we are all at once condemned and saved, or rather, condemnable and acquitted, for we are all, every woman and man among us, simultaneously goat and sheep. Each one of us is at once both goat and sheep.

It is here that we find the point of our text—in this paradoxical knot between what we have not done (even if only once) and what we have done (even if only once); in our condemnation—which we all merit—and our salvation—which none of us merit, but which is offered to all. And this paradox invites us to turn towards grace. Each one condemnable, we cannot live but by the grace of God. And in this, our text echoes the whole gospel, the epistles, and the entirety of the New Testament, according to the analogy of faith. For this parable is designed to lead us to commit ourselves into the hands of grace.

Men and Women[52]

Our fourth and final example concerns what the apostle Paul says about women and to women. We have a general image of Paul as a conservative phallocrat, which we illustrate by citing the famous formula "Wives, be submitted to your husbands!"[53] But how can we understand this injunction, which contradicts the liberating work of Christ for women—these first witnesses of the resurrection, i.e., the first witnesses of what is at the very heart of our faith[54] (which is absolutely unique among all religions), and which contradicts even the word of Paul that affirms that "there is neither man nor woman"?[55] How might we interpret this verse according to the analogy of faith? First, Paul does not say, "Wives, be submitted to your husbands!" We must return to the preceding verse, where we read "Be submitted to one another!"[56] And verse twenty-two continues, "In the same fashion, wives, towards your husbands!" Thus, wives are invited to do regarding their husbands what everyone does (including men!), one to another, at the heart of the Church. Then Paul addresses husbands, saying "Husbands, love your wives!"[57] employing the verb αγαπεῖν, which does not designate conjugal love but unconditional love—the love with which God loves us. And there is a further addendum to this addendum: "Husbands, love your wives as Christ loved the Church and gave himself for her!"[58] Thus, Paul asks of men something much more demanding than he asks of women: to be ready to give their life for their wife.[59] And this is in agreement, according to the analogy of faith, with what biblical revelation says about women and about relations between men and women, including Paul, who affirms in the first epistle to the Corinthians: "The body of the woman belongs to her husband."[60] This conforms completely to the mentality of the era; but he hastens to add, "and the body of the husband belongs to his wife."[61] This, on the contrary, is ab-

---

52. Cf. Ellul, *La subversion du christianisme*, 122–24.
53. Eph 5:22.
54. Cf. Ellul, *La subversion du christianisme*, 120.
55. Gal 3:28.
56. Eph 5:21.
57. Eph 5:25a.
58. Eph 5:25.
59. Cf. Ellul, *La subversion du christianisme*, 123.
60. 1 Cor 7:4a.
61. 1 Cor 7:4b.

solutely inconceivable, unheard of, revolutionary, subversive, both in Paul's time and today: complete equality between men and women, even in bed. The method of the analogy of faith allows us to see that Paul, far from being a frightful misogynist, is a man of the avant-garde.

Conclusion

Through these four examples (chosen from among many others), Jacques Ellul invites us to rediscover the Bible as a love letter from God to men, including in its most enigmatic aspects. Such is the potential for the renewal of traditional readings that the method of the analogy of faith offers us.

Works Cited

Belo, Fernando. *Lecture matérialiste de l'évangile de Marc. Récit, pratique, idéologie.* Paris: Le Cerf, 1974.

Calvin, Jean. *Commentaires de Jean Calvin sur le Nouveau Testament. Vol. 4: Épître aux Romains.* Aix-en-Provence/Fontenay-sous-bois: Éditions Kerygma/Éditions Farel, 1978.

———. *Institutes of the Christian Religion, 1541 French Edition: The First English Version.* Translated by Elsie Anne McKee. Grand Rapids: Eerdmans, 2009.

———. *Institution de la religion chrétienne.* Aix-en-Provence/Charols: Éditions Kerygma/Éditions Excelsis, 2009.

Comte, Gilbert. "Entretien avec Jacques Ellul, 'Je crois que nous sommes dans une période de silence de Dieu.'" *Le Monde* (November 8, 1977) 1–2.

Ellul, Jacques. *Ce que je crois.* Paris: Grasset, 1987.

———. *Éthique de la liberté.* 2 vols. Geneva: Labor et Fides, 2019.

———. "Karl Barth et nous." *Bulletin du Centre protestant d'études* 37 (1985) 5–12.

———. *La foi au prix du doute: "encore quarante jours . . ."* Paris: La Table Ronde, 2015.

———. *La Genèse aujourd'hui.* With François Tosquelles. Le Collier: Éditions de l'AREFPPI, 1987.

———. *La raison d'être. Méditation sur l'Ecclésiaste.* Paris: Éditions du Seuil, 1987.

———. *La subversion du christianisme.* Paris: La Table Ronde, 2011.

———. *Les sources de l'éthique chrétienne. Le Vouloir et le Faire, parties IV et V.* Introduction and notes by Frédéric Rognon. Geneva: Labor et Fides, 2018.

———. *L'idéologie marxiste chrétienne. Que fait-on de l'évangile?* Paris: La Table Ronde, 2006.

———. *Mort et espérance de la résurrection. Conférences inédites de Jacques Ellul.* Lyon: Éditions Olivétan, 2016.

———. *On Freedom, Love, and Power.* Compiled, edited, and translated by Willem H. Vanderburg. Toronto: University of Toronto Press, 2010.

———. *Sans feu ni lieu. Signification biblique de la Grande Ville.* Paris: La Table Ronde, 2003.

Kierkegaard, Søren. "Pour un examen de conscience recommandé aux contemporains." 1851. Œuvres Complètes, 18:83–87. Paris: Éditions de l'Orante, 1966.

CHAPTER 5

Meaning and Its "Interplay" with Freedom in the Bible

Jacques Ellul

TRANSLATED BY
Anne-Marie Andreasson Hogg

Right from the start, I have to acknowledge that I find myself in a difficult situation. You will soon see that with a different mode of expression and a totally different approach than the one used by professor Atlan, I will reiterate what you have already heard, yet with slight differences, and you will clearly see how I differ at a certain point.[1]

The general theme for this morning's session is "The Bible, Source of Meaning," and it is from this theme that I will explain the title of my talk, which you might find a little enigmatic: "Meaning and its Interplay with Freedom in the Bible." As a matter of fact, I take the word "source" very seriously, and I take it in its literal meaning, that of a source springing forth, of running water, living water. A source is not a faucet, it is not constrained to flow through a pipe. Living water comes through and out of a source: water that is free.

---

1. This chapter is a translation of "Le sens et le jeu de la liberté dans la Bible," which first appeared in a volume of proceedings from a conference of Jewish francophone intellectuals discussing the Bible: *La Bible au present: Actes du XXIIème Colloque des intellectuels juifs de langue française*, ed. Jean Halpérin and Georges Levitte (Paris: Gallimard, NRF, 1982), 89–104. The volume is presented in three sections: "signs," "interrogations," and a "Talmudic lesson" by Emmanuel Levinas. Ellul's is the second essay under "signs," appearing just after Henri Atlan, "Niveaux de signification et athéisme de l'écriture" [Levels of meaning and the atheism of scripture]. All footnotes in this chapter are the editor's insertions.

As far as the term "meaning" is concerned, we have innumerable possibilities; and therefore we have to explore many diverse directions. There can be no immediate or clear answers. It is only through some shortcuts and multiple roads that we will ultimately approach the Bible as "source of meaning."

There will be three different stages:

First of all, I would like to ask, "what do we read about meaning in the Bible?" Then we have to answer the question "Is the Bible in itself the meaning?" This will lead us to the question of the freedom of man and the freedom of God.

As I ponder what I read in the Bible about meaning, I am led rather naively to make four remarks.

The first is that certainly in any biblical narrative, the things and the events pertaining to life have no meaning in themselves. There is no meaning, no particular direction in nature. We cannot find any clear meaning in our lives. Rather, the biblical narratives tell us that we *assign* a meaning. Faced with a historical event, the prophet assigns a meaning to the event, and proclaims the meaning of this event, its significance and its direction. In the same way (and, I would say here, in the opposite direction, which shows the duality of direction) the friends of Job, for example, bring Job from suffering into trial and temptation by assigning a meaning to what is happening to him. This shows that each time we assign a meaning, we are necessarily asking a question about truth.

It is possible to assign a wrong meaning, and this is what Job's friends are doing. It is also what false prophets do. Yet, this wrong meaning is nevertheless satisfactory; at first glance, it is perfectly coherent and perfectly logical. Consequently, one does not discern an included sense in things; rather, one assigns a meaning. But what is this meaning? Is it right or wrong? Meaning therefore does not emanate from things; it can only emanate from the non-sense of the world. And I would say that it is because the world is non-sense that it is possible to assign a meaning.

If it were not so, meaning would be included in what is "the vanity of vanities," and that is not possible.

Second remark: within this line of reasoning, it is obvious that the biblical narrative does not assign a meaning to each thing or each event; everything is not the bearer of meaning. There are events that are given value in Scripture, and there is also a multitude of actions and realities, which while not being without importance, are nevertheless without significance. We should not attempt to find some significance at any cost.

As one reads the texts from the Prophets, for example, one must consider the countless historical events which are taking place around them and to which they attribute no importance, no meaning, no impact; they just let them go. There are of course other events which are assigned a meaning. There is thus no direct objective equivalence between the various elements of the world and the world of meaning.

My third remark, also quite naïve, is that the Bible does not formulate a *system of meaning*. It is not—and I will come back to this several times—a mechanism that enables us to assign a meaning or a certain coherence to everything that happens. Biblically speaking, there is no closed system of possible meanings. The Bible never establishes any automatic correspondences, it is never closed, rather it is—and we will return to this point—a source; it is never dogmatic, always pragmatic. From the biblical text emanates a meaning, meanings or a plurality of meanings with a precise direction, and always with the idea that the meaning will reveal itself to be right or wrong when it is put to the test of what one experiences.

Finally—and I believe this to be rather worrying—sometimes for us (and in contrast to what many Christian thinkers have attempted to do), the Bible does not reveal an overall meaning to history in general. That is, history is not directed towards a clear and definite goal. Even the heavenly Jerusalem is not a meaning. In the same way, there is no clear distinction between stages in history, and our history does not have a general meaning. History, just like a specific event or a thing, has no invariable significance or direction established in advance. Here is where we always need to keep in mind the fundamental difference between the Prophet and the soothsayer.

The soothsayer—let us remember the kind of insanity that seized the French this summer as they were reading Nostradamus—is the person who warns you in advance about the course of history.[2] The prophets never did that; quite the contrary. Prophets gave meaning, not a prediction. Furthermore, in order to establish and to assign this meaning either to an event or to history, everything depends on the relationship to the Creator, to the One who has spoken, who is the Almighty as well as the Liberator.

For we must never forget that the central point is the liberation of the Hebrews. He is the Liberator. Yet, this relationship to the almighty Creator and liberator is never a relationship that is fixed in advance; it always depends on what "is in that relationship." Therefore, the fundamental action within this relationship, the possibility of giving history a meaning lies within the series of covenants with Adam, Noah, Abraham and Moses. The Covenant punctuates the meaning of history, but we cannot draw any foreseeable consequences from it. It is not possible on the basis of these Covenants to have

---

2. Nostradamus was a sixteenth-century French astrologist whose poems, often taken as predicting the future, saw a popularized resurgence in the twentieth century.

a kind of futurology, a foresight of what is going to happen later; and neither is it possible to enclose all possible meanings within the Covenant. The Covenant is only—and that is a fundamental point—a guarantee that our history, which is accomplished by us, is also willed by us; it is our work; it is our history; it is not a destiny, nor the automatic progression of a succession of events. Yet, it does not lack the possibility of renewal—remember the *series* of Covenants; there is a renewal. Furthermore, this history is not insane; history is not sound and fury; history is not an absurd tale told by an idiot.[3] No. Biblically, it is quite the opposite, although we cannot ascribe a meaning (and certainly not a single meaning) to this history.

This characteristic of biblical meaning in history—a meaning which is certain, and yet at the same time never frozen—is marked through agents used by God, the God of Abraham, Isaac and Jacob. I am well aware of all the difficulties inherent in using this word, "God," a word so often misinterpreted, misunderstood, and transformed into an idol. Yet, we need to keep in mind the One who has spoken, the One who established the Covenant even if we cannot say anything about him.

So, in order to communicate (and yesterday we were told that in order to communicate the Torah, God used four stages), God finally chose the word as a means of conveying meaning, although it often involves vagueness and misunderstanding. Earlier we were told about the text, the margin and the spaces between words and letters; that is essential. This also applies to the word. You do not hear what I say, there is a certain vagueness, and you do not receive me "loud and clear." I say—or I claim to say—"something" but you receive this "something" (remember, we just heard about the receptor) through the lens of your culture, your experience; and consequently, you immediately interpret it. The word is not the equivalent of a mathematical language and the meaning plays out between what I say and what you hear. The meaning plays out between the words and the misunderstandings, and the pauses are as important as the words.

Speech has this peculiarity—and here is where we find the first breaking point [with Atlan's article]—that it dictates in the present but inevitably refers to a past. If we did not have a common past, we would not be able to speak together. The meaning is dependent on the experience we have of this past through speech, and it always remains an expectation of the future. Speech unfolds in time, yet it is always future.

---

3. As Wagenfuhr notes, Ellul frequently cited the lines from Shakespeare's *Macbeth* (5.5.26–28) which he cites here: cf. *Prayer and Modern Man*, 167; *Hope in Time of Abandonment*, 91; *Apocalypse*, 118; *Subversion of Christianity*, 147; *What I Believe*, 15; *Perspectives on our Age*, 86. List taken from Wagenfuhr, *Revelation and the Sacred Reconsidered*, 56.

But can we say that in itself, the Bible is what gives meaning? Does it ascribe meaning by itself? Is it a meaning in itself?

Earlier, we were shown the plurality of interpretations, which demonstrates that there is, rightly, no clear, simple, and obvious meaning. I believe that there is no objective meaning in the Bible, and this is what was missing in the four meanings, the four interpretations that were presented earlier. There is no objective meaning, nor can the meaning be objectified; there is no clear mechanism to take us from the signifier to the signified.

Quite the contrary, the Bible destroys the certainty—just as it destroys all kinds of idolatry—that there is a clear and simple mechanism to take us from the signifier to the signified, from "it must be said" to "we say this." The Bible never presents us with a code, neither in the judicial nor in the linguistic sense of the word. It forces us to consider each experienced situation as new, for History (and not only its text)—whether individual history or collective history—never repeats itself. This will bring us to three considerations.

First of all, each event can have a plurality of meanings, and the Bible never leads us to an obvious choice between them. There has been and still is within Protestantism an old habit of consulting the Bible as a kind of book of oracles. One opens the Bible at random and points to a word and that is "what God is telling me today." One cannot do this to a biblical text.

From this plurality of meanings, we have to choose the one that seems to be true before God. Job never stops contesting; he keeps on contesting the meaning of what is happening to him. It is not possible that the meaning attributed by his friends should be the correct one. Therefore, God must finally give the correct meaning; he must finally answer. In other words, Job challenges a whole set of meanings in order to finally obtain the one which will hold before God.

Yet, if the meaning that we attribute is true, we will only know this afterwards. In other words, I need to commit myself in order to discover a meaning in what I am experiencing, or a meaning in what is going on in the world. This is a meaning that I can identify because I have read a story in the Bible, but I am not able in advance to say that the meaning I am ascribing is true.

I remember this particular experience—and maybe I will shock some of you, as I am venturing outside of the domain of exegesis, which is a domain that you know much better than I do—I remember Elijah fleeing after his victory over the prophets of Baal. He has just apparently scored a victory, and yet here he is fleeing into the desert saying, "All is lost, I am left alone" at the very moment when he had apparently won the victory. And at that moment, you know the great Revelation, the earthquake, the fire, the wind, etc. "and God was not..." until the moment when there is this whisper that disappears and "God was there and Elijah prostrated himself." In reality, we are faced with the discovery of another meaning that Elijah could not see, and yet, it is in retrospect that Elijah can understand what has happened.

If we attempt to question the Bible to discover the future or the present meaning or a possible direction, we will only find a provocation and a designation—but never a meaning in itself.

A provocation that appears to have two orientations. First, as I have previously made clear, the Bible is never a book of recipes; it is never a book of already-organized answers; and it is not a computer (to see it that way could be a great temptation today). Rather, *God questions us* through it, and *we* are the ones responsible to provide find *the response*. It is a question when we see God asking Adam: "Where are you?" It is obvious that God knows, but Adam must answer, must be responsible. This is the question asked of Cain: "What have you done?" Obviously, God knows, but Cain needs to acknowledge his responsibility and needs to answer. This is also the question asked of Abraham: "Will you go as far as sacrificing?" This is the question asked of Job: "Do you love even if you get nothing in return? Can you be stripped of everything and still love?"

Thus, any commandment from God is in itself a question. And it is not only a question of obedience or refusal—what I am going *to do*—but it is a question about the meaning: who *I am* before God. I am made responsible by this Bible, that is, responsible to answer and responsible to give a meaning to my life before God.

But in a second sense, it is also a provocation, at a second level. A biblical text is not unambiguous; there is not one clear and simple meaning. I am questioned about the meaning that I will assign. I cannot avoid interpreting, and as I interpret, I have to commit myself. Again, we must remind ourselves that there is not *one* sole method of interpretation. When I ascribe a certain meaning to biblical texts, I am responsible before God for the meaning that I have given; and the meaning of the text will necessarily have consequences for the meaning I ascribe to my life. It is from the meaning that I ascribe to the text that I can give a meaning to my life, to events, to the history of my times and to the probable future.

And finally, the Bible is a designation. It is not withdrawn into itself, it does not turn back on itself, rather it refers back—and this is the true breaking point with what was said earlier—it refers back to the One who said this word, and the witness who speaks in this Bible. The prophet refers back to the One who speaks finally, and who is Himself the only meaning and who can assign this meaning in a way that may appear arbitrary to us.

It refers back to the One who spoke this word: The witness who speaks in this Bible refers only to this person.

I will mention two things among possible meanings. When Moses came down from Mount Sinai he had a veil across his face. The biblical text tells us why, but perhaps this veil means: "Do not look at me, but look at the One who is behind me." The important person is not Moses but the one who spoke to Moses. It is the same in Christian illustration. In the altarpiece of Grünewald, we see John the Baptist pointing to the crucified one and John the Baptist's finger is huge, totally disproportionate, in order to say precisely this: "I am not important, this one, the Other, is important."

Thus, the Bible remains the witness to the One who spoke. I do not believe we can separate the Bible from the One who speaks it, nor can we separate the text from the man who spoke it, from the prophet, for example, and certainly not from the Lord, the Holy One who here spoke decisively and finally.

I have to admit that I find it difficult to accept the recent position according to which the Torah is admirable; the Torah is what can save us, the Torah is the truth etc. As for the God of Abraham, Jacob and Isaac, we are not quite sure . . . it is not very important to believe in Him . . . and anyway we cannot affirm anything . . .

For my part, I cannot conceive that we might separate the one from the other. If the Torah exists, it is because the God of Abraham, Isaac and Jacob spoke, because He freed His people and because this event *occurred*. I believe the weight of the word is determined by who spoke it. The word does not contain a truth in itself; there are no texts that contain a meaning in themselves. This is the great error of structuralist linguistics, for example, which maintains: "The text has no history, the text has no references; it has no author; the text is just there." You look at the texts, and that is all; and then you search for structures and how they function with reference to each other. As far as I am concerned, I do not think it is possible to separate the text from the one who was in it. And it is because I believe in this particular God, and in no other, that I can receive His word as an irreplaceable meaning. For it is this God who finally grants meaning to what I say or to what I experience, who will recognize the validity of the history that I live and who also assures me that there is always an overflow of meaning.

The skill of the exegete does not discover new meanings, it is because of the overflow of meaning in the Lord who has spoken that we can always find, discover a new meaning.

And we are thus led to the interplay between the freedom of God and the freedom of man. I believe that the sovereign freedom of the Lord who speaks does not encroach upon the freedom of man, does not prevent the freedom of man. We must obviously get out of the absurd nineteenth-century dilemma in which one claimed to imprison biblical faith: "Either God is omnipotent, and man can do nothing, or man can accomplish something, but then God is not omnipotent." In my opinion, this is an absurd dilemma. Quite the contrary, it is when man is separated from God that he is subject to all sociological, political, economic, and other determinisms, and that he is subjected to fate in the guise of independence and autonomy.

The person with whom God makes a covenant becomes free thereby because God is the liberator, and there is no other freedom that this. This is included in God's choice, the fact that God chose the word. There is a constant interplay between the freedom of God and the freedom of man. This is a freedom willed by God so that man may respond—but respond by assigning a meaning to life.

If there is no freedom for man, if there is no liberation of man, then there is no response, no possible interpretation. If there is no covenant with God, there is no meaning.

Thus, we can see that God's freedom and man's freedom are closely implicated in each other and, biblically, we see the interplay of meaning and freedom constantly.

The word spoken to us by the God who gives meaning is also an order, a command and a promise. But the commandment never constitutes a limitation on freedom.

This is another constant misinterpretation (outside of Israel and outside of the authentic Christian way) as commandments are interpreted as the negative form of a permanent ban—and thus a limitation on freedom. Quite the contrary, they are the limits that enable life; within these commandments, it is possible to live; if you overstep these commandments, it is no longer possible to live; there is no longer any possible freedom; there is only death.

The order of love, which is the order of the commandment, always includes a promise and a choice for us. A promise, because God includes the future of what He is going to do within the commandment that he gives us. In order to find the meaning, we accept to live under this promise, in the promise which will assuredly be given; but we should not forget that for God a thousand years are as a day. We cannot fix the date, but we can know precisely as we read this Scripture that any promise given by God has always been kept and fulfilled.

The Bible shows us these fulfilments and goes from fulfilment to fulfilment. There is always a new development of a new promise. In these fulfilments, the meaning appears in a dazzling way, and we can continue to believe in the promises that we hold—for God has never broken his promise, and we can discover a hidden meaning in our history, a meaning hidden under and in this promise.

Yet at the same time, there is a choice. Any biblical word forces us to choose: "I set before you life and good, death and evil." Any prophetic word also implies a choice: "If you do this, says the prophet, this is what will happen." In other words, the prophet reveals to us that if we do not hear the word of God, a mechanism will operate, the mechanism of fate, the force of things.

This is what I find to be revealed throughout the prophetic writings. If we go outside of the commandment, we will fall into the interplay of mechanisms, of fate known to the ancient world and which we now discover in various forms everywhere in society.

We are terribly impressed by the system. We live in systems, and these systems work. Yes, but this only has any weight and any force insofar as we do not listen to the prophetic word. "If you do this, this is what will happen . . . so do not do this, do what the word of God tells you."

And even in the Bible, the words that seem to be words about a resolution or a decision by God are also words that force us to choose. How many times do we not read: "God decided in his heart" and further on "God repented." Remember the story of Jonah: God decided to destroy Nineveh, and God did not do it.

The choice we need to make is at the same time the choice between meaning and non-sense. Either we ascribe value to this good, to life, to the promise, to the word—and then everything is illuminated by meaning; or we challenge this word, and then everything becomes non-sense.

But in this choice, which *depends on us*, we are not alone. We are absolutely not talking about the false liberty that was described in the Middle Ages, the liberty of Buridan's donkey who is placed between two bales of hay of the same value and same appearance. He is placed exactly between them and can go to the one or to the other; he can choose anything. That is not the freedom of the God who liberates.

For when we are told, "I set before you life and good, death and evil," yet this is not the end. "Choose the good" follows. Also, in the word addressed to Cain: "Sin is crouching at your door," the word does not end there: "You must rule over it" follows.

In other words, we are not left alone before this choice between meaning and non-sense, between obedience and disobedience; we are not left alone in our inability and in our fragility. For God is with us: "My word is with you so that you may choose life"; "I set before you good and evil, life and death, choose the good"; "my word is with you, Cain, so that you may rule over sin."

At that very moment meaning springs forth as a light in the meeting between this word and our word, between this promise and our free obedience, between this love and our love.

This, finally, is where meaning resides, and not in some kind of direct impetus that would come from the Lord. This is why biblically speaking, there is never any arbitrary or absurd meaning, even in the most incredible story. God is not arbitrary and our human adventures, whatever they may be, have meaning and truth because of the love of God. The book of Job, which I have already quoted twice, seems to me the great attestation that there is nothing absurd in human history.

I will conclude by saying that in multiple ways, the Bible is an inevitable and irrepressible source of meaning. How can we then avoid going one step further? Is it the only source of meaning?

We are tempted to fall into apologetics, and this seems sterile to me. We can only go further with prudence, and I will only say two things.

First of all, we are inevitably led back to a personal decision. I do not claim to be objective, but nothing I know of literature, philosophy, or religious texts ever presents this complex, historical, and existential interplay that I have tried to describe. Nowhere do we find this relationship between the one who speaks and the one who listens and who will also speak later, between the one who presents the meaning in a totally original way (first at the beginning and then later in a different way), the one who will bring man to this way that I think is the best and truest. This is an assessment, a testimony; it is not a reason.

What might be a reason is the fact that the question we are raising here, "the Bible, source of meaning," is the very question of meaning stemming from the Bible and only from the Bible. Nowhere else has this question of meaning even been mentioned.

This leads us to understand that when the question of meaning is being considered in the whole world today, as is happening in all cultures and among all intellectuals whatever their origin, it is clear that the question of meaning is the most important one; and I maintain that this question of meaning has been transmitted from the Bible.

We no longer know this—we do not know that it is there that humans were asked about meaning for the first time. This is not a question for intellectuals only; it is really the radical and decisive question for our times, times suffering above all from the lack of meaning.

If modern man is anguished and if he is afraid, it is because there is no more meaning. He can find no meaning in anything—not in history, not in philosophy, not in the past; and apparently there is not even any future.

The question itself stems from the Bible and is asked of the whole world, Jews and Christians alike. This is the question, and it is asked because the Bible asked it; and no one else ever did anywhere else.

Furthermore, this Bible enables us to know that there is a future ahead of us; and we thus can be bearers of meaning to the world around us. We need to remain *witnesses* to the fact that the possibility of a final meaning always remains open to us.

Works Cited

Wagenfuhr, Gregory. "Revelation and the Sacred Reconsidered." PhD diss., University of Bristol, 2013.

Part II

Revisiting Ellul's Readings of the Bible

CHAPTER 6

Jacques Ellul as a Theological Exegete of the Old Testament

JOHN GOLDINGAY

JACQUES ELLUL WAS UNEXCELLED in the twentieth century in his creative theological use of the Old Testament, in works such as *Violence* and *The Meaning of the City*. He was also unexcelled as a theological exegete of the Old Testament text—that is, someone who from time to time focused on expounding particular works within the Old Testament. I here consider three such expositions from different stages in his life: *The Politics of God and the Politics of Man* (on 2 Kings), *The Judgment of Jonah*, and *Reason for Being* (on Ecclesiastes).

The Politics of God and the Politics of Man

The Politics of God and the Politics of Man (Eerdmans, 1972; French original, 1966) is my favorite Ellul book. Fifty years ago, there was nothing to read on the theological significance of 2 Kings; indeed, it was hard to imagine that it had any theological significance. Even Calvin didn't produce a commentary on 2 Kings. Then along came Ellul with his magnificent observation that "this Second Book of Kings is characterized by two aspects of revelation. The first is political in the narrow sense; the problems in most of the texts are political."[1] The second is that "more than anything else . . . it displays concretely the play of what Karl Barth has called the free determination of man in the free decision of God. We are constantly in the presence of the relation

---

1. Ellul, *Politics of God and the Politics of Man*, 13.

between man's action and God's" (his work and the translation belong, of course, to the days before gender-inclusive language).[2]

Second Kings thus implies an approach to a conundrum that has been important in Western thinking: how can we say both that God is sovereign and that human beings make real decisions? It's one of those questions that is answered (or rather discussed) more effectively by narrative theology than by systematic theology. The latter properly focuses on analysis, logic and unequivocal statement. Without giving the impression that they see this question as a conundrum, the Scriptures themselves approach it in a narrative way. In 2 Kings,

> we see man deciding on a great number of actions freely and alone. Many of them fail. They are nonsensical. They misfire. They are lost in the sand. But some succeed. And when this occurs, these deliberate acts which men do for their own reasons and according to their own calculations are the very ones which accomplish just what God had decided and was expecting (even though the men often do not know this or are not aware of it at first). These acts enter into God's design and bring about exactly the new situation which God planned.[3]

In expounding this theme Ellul talks the reader through a number of the stories in 2 Kings, some involving Israelite and Judahite kings, some involving foreign kings and leaders. The first one he covers concerns Naaman. What an extraordinary story it is, about the way Yahweh heals a man who is a military warrior and a victor over Israel, who ends up "a man who is no longer gnawed away by leprosy physically, a man who, resting in the peace of God, ceases to be gnawed away by the idolatry of the state which divides and corrupts the innermost depths of man."[4] About Joram, Ellul comments, "It is never possible to see what act of man does in fact fulfil the will of God . . . But what we need to know now is that it is man and he alone, and for his own motives, who manifests willy nilly the hand which gives and takes away, which slays and makes alive."[5] Then there is a foreign king, Hazael: "the glory of Hazael will be quickly tarnished. The Word of God which launched him will be spoken no more when he invokes it."[6] About Jehu: "Even when the king is faithful and leads the people to God,

---

2. Ellul, *Politics of God and the Politics of Man*, 15.
3. Ellul, *Politics of God and the Politics of Man*, 17.
4. Ellul, *Politics of God and the Politics of Man*, 40.
5. Ellul, *Politics of God and the Politics of Man*, 70.
6. Ellul, *Politics of God and the Politics of Man*, 88.

everything is still false and ambiguous. Thus God makes the big decision."[7] The implication of Ahaz's story: "The adulteration of the church by power, e.g., its social conformity in the Middle Ages, corresponds precisely to the action described here, namely, that of Ahaz. Our only guarantee of efficacy is the achievement of nonconformity."[8] To another foreign leader, the Assyrian Rabshakeh, who defies and scorns Yahweh, the only proper response is silence. In the same historical and narrative context, about Hezekiah: "At issue is God's honor. We observe that the miracle of God corresponds to the direct insult addressed by man to God. We ourselves need not seek means to avenge God's honor. God alone avenges his honor. We should simply bow in fear and trembling before this incomprehensible expression of the dignity of his love."[9]

In a closing meditation on inutility, Ellul concludes: "in spite of God's respect and love for man, in spite of God's extreme humility in entering into man's projects in order that man may finally enter into his own design, in the long run one cannot but be seized by a profound sense of the inutility and vanity of human action."[10] Yet we can pray, and we can be wise, and we can preach.

The Judgment of Jonah

In light of the thrust of Ellul's exposition of these stories, it is surprising also to be told that they are all "set in the perspective of Jesus Christ . . . Everything leads to Jesus Christ, just as everything comes from him. Hence Jesus Christ is not absent from the somber adventure of the Second Book of Kings."[11] I do not really know what that declaration means, and I cannot see that Jesus makes much difference to the implications of the stories, which is why they speak so importantly in our Western context. But this statement by Ellul is evidently important to him, and it links with a central thrust of a much earlier work, *The Judgment of Jonah* (Eerdmans, 1971; French original 1952). It is to me a more problematic one. It almost begins by telling us that "the true reality of the book is Jesus Christ,"[12] to which I have to respond, "No it is not." Perhaps for Ellul it would be more-or-less enough to say "the

---

7. Ellul, *Politics of God and the Politics of Man*, 118.
8. Ellul, *Politics of God and the Politics of Man*, 141.
9. Ellul, *Politics of God and the Politics of Man*, 181.
10. Ellul, *Politics of God and the Politics of Man*, 190.
11. Ellul, *Politics of God and the Politics of Man*, 9.
12. Ellul, *Judgement of Jonah*, 10.

true reality of this book is the God and Father of Our Lord Jesus Christ"; I would be happy with that statement.

Ellul properly wants to put in their place two sorts of people: those who say that the book is about universalism rather than particularism, and those who think it is about being swallowed by a whale. No, says Ellul, it is about God and us, about God's relationship with us and ours with God, about the nature of election and the nature of grace and the nature of vocation. They were realities not because of who Jonah was and not for his sake, nor could they be halted or frustrated by his resistance. In a related statement that anticipates his exposition of 2 Kings, Ellul observes that God respects our freedom but makes us fulfill the role he assigns to us in spite of ourselves. The Jonah story is about someone who finds that "the man who flees from the word of God seals himself off in his solitude."[13] He goes through an adventure throughout which he is "alone in the face of God and in the face of death and in the face of Nineveh."[14] Except that he is unwittingly surrounded by a cloud of witnesses cheering him on. And so are we all.

Ellul also puts in their place people who think that the "psalm" in chapter 2 of Jonah was inserted into the book by an imbecile, which was a more dominant conviction when he wrote this book than it is now. Neither does he accept the view that the fish is a place of salvation for Jonah, which is still a dominant assumption (and I think a correct one). For Ellul, the fish is something more like the Old Testament sea monster. Inside the monster, Jonah is in Hell. In the course of his flight from God Jonah goes though Hell, but from there realizes that God accepts him. Jonah's story further shows how we hold the fate of our fellow human beings in our hands. Our situation is thus not a happy one for us, as God points out in Ezekiel 33. God could have saved Nineveh without Jonah, but he wants human beings to have a part in his work. "The Christian is not just the man who is saved by Christ; he is the man whom God uses for the salvation of others by Christ."[15] Further, "when it is said that God repents, it means that he suffers."[16] It is an implication of the verb *niham*, which means repent or relent or have a change of heart or "suffer grief" (as the Brown, Driver, Briggs Hebrew lexicon puts it). God takes on himself the wrongdoing of the Ninevites. One can certainly see here an assumption that casts light on what God is doing in Jesus.

---

13. Ellul, *Judgement of Jonah*, 29.
14. Ellul, *Judgement of Jonah*, 22.
15. Ellul, *Judgement of Jonah*, 89.
16. Ellul, *Judgement of Jonah*, 99.

Ellul often reminds me of Karl Barth and his exposition of the Old Testament in the *Church Dogmatics*, and Ellul does express appreciation (though also criticism) of Barth. He also reminds me of the less-well-known Swiss Old Testament theologian Wilhelm Vischer, Barth's pastor, to whom Barth and Ellul both refer with appreciation. Like Ellul, for me these two are a tad too Christological in their interpretation. But the fact that the God who was involved with Jonah was the God who came into the world in Jesus means that Ellul's reading Jesus into Jonah brings out more than it reads in. And in the end, I guess I would rather keep company with them than with the thin exegetes who see nothing of transhistorical significance in Jonah.

Reason for Being

In *Politics of God* Ellul also comments, "Everything is useless, and we are thus tempted to add: Everything, then, is vanity."[17] It is the starting point of the thinking of Ecclesiastes or Qohelet, and thus of *Reason for Being* (Eerdmans, 1990; French original 1987). Ellul planned *Reason for Being* as his last word, just in case he did not write any more books; he produced it when he was 75 years old. Before his death at 82 he did write some more, as he thought he might, but he sees *Reason for Being* as the summation of thinking he had been doing over his life, not least about Qohelet. Ellul calls his book a meditation, which is maybe an excuse for not being too structured or logically argued, like Qohelet itself.

He notes the paradox in writing a book about a book that warns about writing books. Like everything else, he recognizes, the book he writes falls under the judgment "all is vanity" (he reminds me of Thomas Aquinas allegedly declaring that everything he had written seemed like straw). But there is also in Qohelet the encouragement to do with all your energy what your hand finds to do, and this book is what Ellul's hand found to do. In a parallel with comments in *The Judgment of Jonah*, Ellul is deservedly rude about scholars who attribute different parts of Qohelet to different authors. In connection with Qohelet they do so on the basis of a lack of consistency between the views expressed within the book, as if the scholars had not realized that paradox or contradiction is an essential principle in Qohelet. What strange assumptions critics make, Ellul comments—as if one person cannot write things that are in sharp tension with each other; indeed, if a writer cannot do so, how could a compiler have put them together without noticing the problem? And if Qohelet is so impossibly contradictory, how is it that the compilers of the Scriptures accepted the book? Again,

---

17. Ellul, *Politics of God and the Politics of Man*, 196.

the trend of critical scholarship has maybe moved a little in Ellul's direction over the past thirty years. On the other hand, another aspect to his trenchant critique has more rather than less bite in the twenty-first century. How strange, he comments, that exegetes judge texts instead of seeking to interpret them! They write as if they feel a need to be combative towards them in light of the centuries of these works being regarded as sacred and authoritative, or (I would add) in light of the assumption that we obviously have the right perspective on the truth, on whose basis we can evaluate everything that has come before.

After the discursive introduction in which he makes these points, Ellul divides his book into three sections of eighty or ninety pages each. The first concerns Qohelet's key but controverted word *hebel*. As an equivalent, Ellul is happy with the word *vanité*, which naturally comes out in English as *vanity*. Alongside that not-very-illuminating word, he helpfully puts the words vapor, smoke, unsubstantiality, fragility, and evanescence. The great vanities, Qohelet declares, are power, money, work, happiness, and the good. In that introduction in which Ellul also tells us that we are going to get his own angle on Qohelet, not something that takes its framework of thinking from the work of Old Testament scholars, it is surprising that Ellul discusses the meaning of *hebel* in dialog with a series of such scholars. It is useful that they are mainly French, writers of whom readers in the United States or Britain will probably not have heard such as Chouraqui and Chopineau, as well as ones who are a little better known in the English-speaking world such as Lys, Neher, and Podechard. So here, at least, he does work in dialogue with other scholars, though this is not to say that he fails to incorporate his independent thinking—for instance, in his development of a link between *hebel* and Abel, whose name in Hebrew is *hebel*.

Wisdom is the second great theme in Qohelet that Ellul identifies. He comments that readers are less interested in wisdom than in vanity. With greater boldness than your average Old Testament scholar, he will make comments such as "I am utterly opposed to von Rad's opinion," which he sees as setting up a false antithesis between Qohelet and Proverbs (I think they seem very different because they have different starting points; they do not mean the same thing by wisdom).[18] In connection with wisdom, Ellul discusses irony, science, finitude, and death.

Ellul's third theme is God, who is mentioned over thirty times in Qohelet. It is no secular book. But it never uses the name Yahweh, which reminds us that the truth it expounds is not limited to the Jewish people. Nor does Qohelet pretend that we know more about God than we do. He does

18. Ellul, *Reason for Being*, 131.

affirm that God in Qohelet is the God who gives, who gives quest and desire for eternity, and gives enjoyment. He also gives judgment, though we can understand judgment as a gift only if we go back behind the understanding of justice in light of Roman law that we have inherited since postbiblical times. And he grants accessibility to him, even though it is an accessibility that needs to be combined with humility.

From time to time in this book, too, Ellul mentions Jesus, as one might expect, often to note that Jesus's teaching coheres with Qohelet's. The God Qohelet describes chose to be Jesus's God. "God has answered our desire for eternity in Jesus Christ."[19] But Ellul does not imply that Jesus is the answer to the question posed in Qohelet in a way that means Qohelet's questions are no longer questions for us. If anything, Qohelet's key insights about the ambiguity of power and wisdom stand with more force after Jesus.

It is possible to be a sophisticated Hebraist, Ellul comments, but a superficial thinker. Somehow Old Testament scholars forget why they got interested in the Old Testament books in the first place, and never come back to expounding what the books have to tell us about God. In contrast with them, that is why I have found Ellul illuminating, ever since I first came across his work on 2 Kings.

Works Cited

Ellul, Jacques. *The Judgment of Jonah*. Translated by Geoffrey W. Bromiley. Grand Rapids: Eerdmans, 1971.

———. *The Politics of God and the Politics of Man*. Translated by Geoffrey W. Bromiley. Grand Rapids: Eerdmans, 1972.

———. *Reason for Being: A Meditation on Ecclesiastes*. Translated by Joyce Main Hanks. Grand Rapids: Eerdmans, 1990.

---

19. Ellul, *Reason for Being*, 247.

CHAPTER 7

What's in a Name? Jacques Ellul's Reading of Naming in Genesis 1–3

MICHAEL MORELLI

How to Be a Good Reader of the Bible

A GOOD THEOLOGIAN IS a good reader of the Bible, and reading a good theologian shows you how to be a good reader of the Bible. Ellul didn't consider himself a theologian in the way the word commonly is used, but I think he is a good theologian insofar as he is a good reader of the Bible. Take his readings of the first three chapters of Genesis as an example. He reads these texts in ways which make you read and re-read not only what he wrote about them, but also read and re-read what is written in the texts he is writing about. That is a sign of a good theologian. He or she will cause you to read and re-read scripture in ways which materialize striking insights.

I want to examine Ellul's readings of naming in the first three chapters of Genesis for two reasons. First, I want to heighten attentiveness to biblical texts that tend to be read inattentively. Second, and related to the first reason, I want readers to take naming as seriously as Ellul does. In scene two of the second act of William Shakespeare's *Romeo and Juliet*, Juliet muses tragically with her lover Romeo as they converse in the Capulet's orchard:

> Tis but thy name that is my enemy; / Thou art thyself, though not a Montague. / What's Montague? It is nor hand nor foot, / Nor arm nor face, nor any other part / Belonging to a man. O be some other name! / What's in a name? That which we call a rose / By any other word would smell as sweet; / So Romeo would, were he not Romeo called, / Retain that dear perfection which

he owes / Without that title. Romeo, doff thy name, / And for thy name, which is no part of thee, / Take all myself.[1]

Indeed, what is in a name? To show how Ellul helps us respond to this question with his readings of naming in Genesis 1–3, I will open the next section with a sketch of his understanding of revelation and history to frame the exegetical sections that follow. In the first exegetical section, I will examine important aspects of Ellul's readings of God's speech in Genesis 1 to contextualize his readings of naming in Genesis 2 and 3. In the second exegetical section I will look at Gen 2:19, in which God asks Adam to name all the animals in creation. In the third exegetical section I will consider Ellul's readings of Gen 2:22, in which Adam names the woman who is created by God *Woman*. In the fourth exegetical section I will explore Ellul's readings of Gen 3:20, when Adam re-names the woman created by God *Eve*. In the fifth and final section I will offer concluding remarks about what Ellul thinks is in a name, and hopefully, provoke further reading of his commentary on Genesis 1–3, as well as, further reading of these biblical texts themselves.

Ellul's Understanding of the Bible

The first questions that arise for most modern readers about texts like Genesis 1–3 typically concern historicity. To what extent are these scriptures historical, and if they are historical, how? Ellul locates the answers to these questions within the larger question of how history and the present interact with revelation in and beyond biblical revelation. The answer to this much larger question is at once complex and simple. True revelation interacts with history and the present in potent and mysterious ways. In *Living Faith* Ellul writes:

> Revelation calls into question everything solid and taken for granted. It shakes the foundations of the most elaborate cultural edifice; it stirs up uncertainty. Indeed, it creates uncertainty—never the narrow-minded, rigid, unshakeable certitude of the person who believes the way a cow chews its cud. It seizes hold of everything that constitutes our humanity, our state and societies, our hierarchy of values, our morality and our religion, and puts it all in the crucible. It leaves us totally uncertain as we try to decide how to rediscover and rebuild a liveable world. And this uncertainty is all the more overwhelming because we can't rely on clear evidence from revelation itself.

---

1. Shakespeare, *Romeo and Juliet*, 107–8 (2.2.38–49).

> The revelation that arouses faith is never so univocal, so rational and incontestable that we can both fully comprehend it and maintain constant certitude. When revelation occurs, the one who receives it experiences a constant re-appropriation of the connotations, dimensions, and depths, the "levels" of that revelation. Once again we are full of uncertainty. The question is not "Will I still have faith tomorrow?" but rather "What will I make of this revelation tomorrow? How will I come to renew my understanding of it? What will come surging up into my conscious mind from the past/present revelation planted deep with me in the unconscious or whatever one wishes to call it?"[2]

If the question *did it happen?* was put to him about Genesis 1–3, Ellul would answer affirmatively. He would also add that it went down in a way which "calls into question everything solid and taken for granted."[3] *How, though?* the skeptic may still inquire. Such questions represent relatively reasonable lines of inquiry, but instead of saying too much about how in this section, the next sections will show how through its engagement with Ellul's readings of naming in Genesis 1–3. Here it is sufficient to say that Ellul takes history and historicity seriously when he exegetes a text.

Ellul is a versatile, provocative, and in many cases generous exegete. He is a cautious Barthian who favours "the freedom of research."[4] He is a sincere Kierkegaardian who thinks true truth can only be communicated indirectly.[5] In *The Meaning of the City* he writes, "Revelation provides us with both a means of understanding [a] problem and a synthesis of its aspects as found in the raw data of history and sociology. However, we must not expect perfect agreement, for the two realities are not on the same plane."[6] If history and the present are on a horizontal plane revelation comes down from a vertical plane to do something on the horizontal plane. In contrast to the descent of revelation, the horizontal plane does not ascend to revelation. Or, at least it should not try to. Otherwise, the people who live on the horizontal plane become like the builders of the Tower of Babel. Interesting, then, that the Babelian builders were the ones who wanted to "make a name" for themselves with a tower that ascended

---

2. Ellul, *Living Faith*, 144–45.

3. Ellul, *Living Faith*, 144–45. See also Ellul, *On Freedom, Love, and Power*, 25–29; 48–49; and 71–73 for a discussion of Scripture, revelation, history, and historicity as it relates to the first three chapters of Genesis.

4. See Ellul, *Ethics of Freedom*, 176–82 for a discussion of the freedom of research.

5. See Ellul, *Reason for Being*, 118–19 for a discussion of Kierkegaard's influence on Ellul's take on direct/indirect truth.

6. Ellul, *Meaning of the City*, 153.

to their envisioned place of revelation . . . [7] But back to revelation and history as Ellul describes it in *Meaning of The City*.

Ellul uses an apt metaphor to punctuate his point about the interaction of revelation, history, and the present as described above. The metaphor serves as a fitting conclusion to this section. He writes, "I cannot mistake the sun for the colors of the spectrum, nevertheless I could not know color but by the help of the sun. I could doubtlessly make a chemical analysis of the coloring agents, I could study all the physical or biological aspects of color, without ever having an inkling of living color, unless all these aspects are brought into play by the simple fact of light bringing out color."[8] For Ellul, revelation, including biblical revelation, is living light bringing true color out of history and the present; we need it to see history and the present for what they truly are and are not.[9] Let us now examine how Ellul's understanding of biblical revelation hits the horizontal plane with his reading of naming in the first three chapters of Genesis.

"Then God Said . . ."[10]

There is so much speaking in Genesis 1 that it is easy to miss how much and what kind of speaking there is. Ellul misses neither. He observes, "The first act of God is to speak: God says. It is by his Word that God brings things to being."[11] But "the word *word*, *dabar*, in Hebrew, is not *words*" in a conventional, modern sense.[12] Rather, "*Dabar* means at the same time the speech we know, words, language itself, etc., but also the power of action." It characterizes simultaneous "speech and action" to the extent that "what is said is done, what is done is said. It is rigorously coincidental, it coincides

---

7. Gen 11:4. All Bible translations in this chapter are from the New Revised Standard Version. See Ellul, *Living Faith*, 129–30 for further commentary on the Tower of Babel story—specifically, how the narrative reveals the going-up-ness of religion and the coming-down-ness of revelation. See also Ted Lewis's chapter in this volume.

8. Ellul, *Meaning of the City*, 153.

9. From my perspective, such passages sharpen Ellul's rather blunt prolegomena in *To Will & To Do*: "I confess, therefore, that in this study and this search, the criterion of my thought is biblical revelation; the content of my thought is biblical revelation; my point of departure is provided by biblical revelation; the method is the dialectic according to which biblical revelation is addressed to us; and the goal is the search for the significance of biblical revelation as it bears on Ethics."

10. Gen 1:3.

11. Ellul, *La Genèse aujourd'hui*, 30. Ellul's emphases and capitals. All translations are my own unless otherwise specified.

12. Ellul, *La Genèse aujourd'hui*, 30.

perfectly. Creation is, therefore, produced by the word alone, the mere fact that God says."[13] Putting this feature of the text in its historical context, Ellul points out that any portrayal of one God effortlessly creating the world and everything in it with words would flummox Israel's neighbours at the time this text was crafted. Most cosmologies at this point in history portrayed creation as the product of divine combat. Not so for Israel's cosmology and its one God revealed in Genesis 1.[14] Much more could be said on this and other facets of Ellul's readings of God's speech in Genesis, but it is necessary to move to his commentary on God's creation and blessing of the animals in Gen 1:22–25 to stay focused on the aims of this chapter. To that end, Ellul interprets Gen 1:22–25 as follows:

> God made animals and [there] is [a] difference between animals and the rest of creation. We are already walking towards man [. . .]. Animals, like humans, are blessed. And [God] blesses them by speaking to them, he blesses them by saying be fruitful. He speaks to them, but blessing is another complex Hebrew word, *bara*, which means three things: a good word, in the literal sense of blessing; [it] also means bringing salvation; and then [it] means kneeling. Thus, the relation is established: there is a good word which is said to the animals, there is a salvation which is promised to them, and the animals are in the love of God.[15]

God creates all the animals. God perceives all the animals as good. God kneels and anoints all the animals with fruitfulness. God reveals an overwhelming, even salvific, love for all the animals. God does not name all the animals. Why? The text does not answer this question directly. It does mention that God asks Adam to name all the animals in Gen 2:19–20. Ellul thinks these texts hints at the answer. He writes, "God's declaration in the first creation narrative [situating] Adam as lord of creation, corresponds precisely to Adam's naming of animals in the second narrative."[16] It shows that "since God creates and governs through his Word, and the

---

13. Ellul, *La Genèse aujourd'hui*, 30–31.

14. Ellul, *La Genèse aujourd'hui*, 31.

15. Ellul, *La Genèse aujourd'hui*, 41–42. Ellul cites the book of Jonah to substantiate the claim that God offers a word and a promise of salvation to the animals. Indeed, 3:6–10 and 4:11 show animals being included in God's salvific care for Nineveh, and it is noteworthy that the Ninevites include their animals in their repentant acts (cf. 3:6–10). Likewise, it is noteworthy that animals are "provided" and "appointed" by God in this book to challenge, teach, and soften the hardhearted Jonah—not only the well-known sea creature "provided" to swallow Jonah (cf. 1:17) but also the worm "appointed" to eat the bush that provides Jonah cover from the scorching heat (cf. 4:7).

16. Ellul, *Humiliation of the Word*, 48.

human being is in the image of God, called by God to subdue (govern) and have dominion (command), he can only do it by *the same means*; that is, the *word*. Humanity must fulfill its royal function in the midst of the animals through the word, and not through the violence of implements." As such, "The only power [here] is that of the word."[17] If, as revealed in Genesis 1 and 2, humanity was intended by God to be kings and queens of creation, humanity was intended to be kings and queens who gaze upon and speak to creation with a love like God's. Accordingly, Ellul thinks these parallels show that God does not name the animals because when God asks Adam to name the animals, God intends this responsibility to be the first formative means by which Adam will learn how to gaze upon and speak to creation in the way God lovingly does. This gaze and speech is nowhere near the power of God's gaze and speech. But still, Adam's speech is powerful, and it seems God is teaching Adam to have a gaze and speech that reflect the powerfully loving look and speech of God. How, then, will Adam employ this powerful gift and responsibility when the animals are brought before him to be named? What does Adam's naming of the animals do to the animals? What does Adam's naming of the animals do to Adam—or God, for that matter? The next section will examine Ellul's answers to these questions.

> So out of the ground the LORD God formed every animal of the field and every bird of the air, and brought them to the man to see what he would call them; and whatever the man called every living creature, that was its name. The man gave names to all cattle, and to the birds of the air, and to every animal of the field; but for the man there was not found a helper as his partner.[18]

Ellul frequently distinguishes between the kind of naming actually revealed in these texts and the kind of naming most modern readers assume is revealed. Though some may characterize Adam's naming as the establishment of a scientific taxonomy of kinds and species, Ellul emphasizes that a Hebrew reader would characterize this naming as the establishment of "a 'taxonomy' which is free." He says:

> God does not know what man is going to decide [for each name]. And I would say, God doesn't want to know. [It] leaves man free, man will say for himself what he calls such an animal. And God wants to see what he is going to call them. So man has the gift of speech and his speech is a true language since it determines reality[.] For the Hebrews, to give a name is to

---

17. Ellul, *Humiliation of the Word*, 48.
18. Gen 2:19–20.

define an existence, it is to define, I would almost say a destiny. So he will give the animals a name, which means his mastery over them, but a mastery which is spiritual. It corresponds to [man] dominating creation as God dominates it, that is to say in love, and by means of love, and there, by means of speech, purely and simply.[19]

Adam does not *classify* each creature with a name. He *commissions* each creature with a name. With God present and expectantly observing—apparently with no foreknowledge of the names to be given, implying that God is willing to be surprised—Adam anoints each creature with a name to bless it as it is on its way toward a free and fruitful future. While the texts in view here are protological, the way Ellul draws out their meaning shows how these texts near the borders of the eschatological. That is, Ellul helps us to see that the names which Adam gives to the animals commission each creature toward a *future* that God intended and intends to be free and fruitful.

Furthermore, the delicacy and vulnerability of this naming event must be observed. As Ellul puts it, "To give one's name [as it is here] is to reveal one's whole being, it is to place oneself at the disposal of those to whom one is speaking, it is to grant one's truth (and not reality.)"[20] The animals are exposed to Adam as they draw near and wait for a name, but Adam too is exposed as he draws near in order to discern a name for each animal. The vulnerability of each animal waiting to be named breeds a reflective and reflexive vulnerability in Adam as he closely and carefully contemplates each animal to name it. "When Adam gives a name to a plant" Ellul writes, this does not mean he will "call it cruciferous, because it presents such and such a sign, and the plants presenting the whole of these signs are of such family, etc. He attributes a destiny to be filled before God. Master for creation, by and for God, he presents it thus to God by naming it."[21] God is watching as Adam contemplates the animals and plants and God welcomes Adam's unforeseen anointing of each facet of God's creation with a name. Now we are bordering on the triadic, the triune! There are three parties present for the naming, not two, and this triad only heightens the delicacy and vulnerability of creation contemplated before God as Adam's names God's creatures. Eventually, the pinnacle of Adam's naming is reached when Adam names the woman who God creates. After

---

19. Ellul, *La Genèse aujourd'hui*, 119.

20. Ellul, *Théologie et Technique*, 152. For further discussion of the relationship between reality/image/sight and truth/word/hearing, see Ellul, *Humiliation of the Word*, 23–30.

21. Ellul, *Théologie et Technique*, 153.

Adam wakes up from a thick sleep induced by God, it seems Adam recites poem or sings a song as he sees and names the woman who was fetched and fashioned from his side while he slept.[22]

> And the rib that the LORD God had taken from the man he made into a woman and brought her to the man. Then the man said, 'This at last is bone of my bones / and flesh of my flesh;/ this one shall be called Woman, / for out of Man this one was taken.'[23]

Neither the form nor the content of Adam's speech is recorded in Genesis 2:19–20. There is only confirmation that Adam names the animals and that God recognizes the names. But then the form and the content of Adam's naming is rendered in Genesis 2:21–22. Adam wakes up. He sees the woman. He recognizes the woman. At last! No longer alone! Here she is! The man poetically unfolds the meaning folded into the name he gives to the woman: *Woman/ishshah* taken out of *ish/Man*.[24] The form and content of the names align marvelously, reflecting the marvelous alignment of the man and the woman. God approves. The man and the woman are naked and unashamed before each other and God.[25]

It is likewise revealing that the text does not show Adam being told that the woman was fashioned from his side. Rather, the text shows Adam recognizing that she was and immediately pronouncing her name: *Woman*. How does Adam recognize the woman was made from his side if he was not told that she was? Perhaps there is a stinging wound where the rib once was, and he relates the sting to the healing of loneliness he experiences when he first sees the woman made from his rib. Perhaps, as he learned to perceive the true reality of creatures and pronounce their names as shown in Gen 2:19–20, he was prepared to perceive the true reality of the woman before him. Perhaps. The text does answer the question. But Ellul describes Adam's recognition of the woman and proclamation of her name in the text in following way: "When Adam sees Eve he bursts into speech. He

22. Gen 2:21–22.

23. Gen 2:22.

24. Gen 2:18 reads, "Then the LORD God said, 'It is not good that the man should be alone; I will make him a helper as his partner." Ellul mentions in *La Genèse aujourd'hui* (121) that "[This] is the only thing that is not good in this creation, the only thing that is not good. Everything, as we have seen, was very good [cf. Gen 1:31], but there is one thing not good: the man alone." Essentially, he picks up a revealing textual parallel between God's recognition of all prelapsarian creation's goodness—"very good" in Gen 1:31—and a noticeable absence of goodness—"not good" in Gen 2:18—in prelapsarian creation when man is alone.

25. Gen 2:24–25.

speaks because of her and for her. She was flesh of his flesh, bone of his bone; and yet different: a dissimilar similar person."[26] The word "burst" is aptly employed here. Adam's burst into speech launches his readers right over the how of his recognition and immediately lands us upon the what. After what must have been a long, long duration of time spent contemplating and naming all the animals in creation—all the animals!—there is no time for the text to explain how Adam sees what he sees and knows what he knows when, for the first time, he gazes upon this woman. After all this time Adam has finally discovered the creature who is the dissimilar similar one who will remove his loneliness. He bursts into speech that froths with joy and admiration. He recognizes that she is the one who was made from the rib removed from his side; she is the one who has removed his loneliness. She is like him but not him. She is with him. The name *Woman* proclaimed here thus anoints an incredibly intimate moment of dissimilar similar people meeting and recognizing each other for the first time, and the loneliness which evaporates when such meetings happen. Is this not one of the many overwhelming virtues of love—to truly recognize a dissimilar similar person who removes your loneliness?

The moment recorded here is so intimate that Ellul uses the Hebrew word *Yada* to describe Adam's recognition rendered in the text. He describes it as a fertile moment that blooms into inexpressible pleasure and joy: "When Adam meets the woman, he suddenly becomes aware of himself." This is because "each of the two needs the other to know themselves. And when he recognizes her, there is the verb *Yada*." When "we want to talk about sexual union we say: 'The man has known a woman.' *Yada* has this meaning." But it is also "like [the meaning of the word] Eden[.] There is the sexual factor[.] Then *Yada* means to meet, to experience, to participate together. Man is himself only in this meeting, in this *Yada*, in this meeting with the woman."[27] The "Word *Eden* in Hebrew means delight. With a double sense of sexual communion and joy. And this is the place where man is put. He is put in this garden where he lives with pleasure."[28] In this garden filled with delight and joy the meeting of man and woman happens and they *know/Yada* each other with deep delight and joy. The woman is named *Woman* because Adam is aroused to delight and joy as he gazes upon her and without hesitation pronounces her name: *Woman/ishshah* taken out of *ish/Man*. If, then, *Woman* is named with such pleasure and joy by Adam,

---

26. Ellul, *Humiliation of the Word*, 12.
27. Ellul, *La Genèse aujourd'hui*, 121.
28. Ellul, *La Genèse aujourd'hui*, 111.

why would he rename Woman *Eve*? Ellul's reading of naming in Genesis 3 provides the heartrending answer.

> "The man named his wife Eve, because she was the mother of all living."[29]

After the Fall Adam sees Woman as a bearer of children rather than the bone of his bone and the flesh of his flesh. He renames her *Eve*. One passive line defining *Eve* replaces the four poetic lines of delight actively proclaiming the meaning of the name *Woman*. Ellul describes this post-Fall re-naming as follows: "It is only *after* the Fall, in the midst of the disorder of powers, that he names his wife *also*: 'Eve, because . . . ' (Gen 3:20). This is a reflection of the disorder of powers."[30] The problem is not that Adam recognizes Eve's capacity to bring human life into being. Rather, the problem is that by re-naming Woman *Eve*, he assigns a name that confines her to this one capacity rather than her many capacities as bone of his bone, flesh of his flesh, helper, and partner.[31] As for the post-Fall "disorder of powers" Ellul mentions in this quote, his descriptions of this disorder contextualize his claim that Adam's re-naming Woman *Eve* is constricting rather than liberating:

> The fall brings about a radical break—the *universum* which had been created has been shattered. (a) Adam is no longer in direct communion with God: he hides. The break between them is complete. Starting from this break between God and man, all other breaks follow—Adam and Eve separate. (Adam accuses his wife—what greater break could there be?) They are no longer one, but two. Man and the animals are separated (Eve accuses the serpent). They learn fear and shame: "Then the eyes of both were opened, and they knew that they were naked" (Gen 3:7). [The] relationship among the elements of creation is completely upset. Instead of unity and communion, there is now an "I" and a "You." There is the gaze of the Other, which is the gaze of a stranger imposed on me. Now I am under the scrutiny of the gaze of the Other, which is a look without love, without understanding and welcome, but only coldly observant (like science, which discerns the objective reality of things and which sees

---

29. Gen 3:20.

30. Ellul, *Humiliation of the Word*, 47.

31. Gen 2:20–24. Unfortunately, "helper" and "partner" in Gen 2:20 have been interpreted and applied in suspect, if not downright oppressive, ways. Just as Ellul does not interpret these words and the passages of which they are a part in such ways, neither do I. For examples, see Ellul, *La Genèse aujourd'hui*, 120–22 and Ellul, *Subversion of Christianity*, 75–79 for reflections of his remarkably high view of women, which, as it happens, he derives from Scripture.

that I am "other." This observation now transforms everything into an object, and the other has become an object for me). The mirror of creation is shattered. The *universum* is broken.³²

Along with all the other brutal consequences of the Fall described here, Adam experiences an epistemological snap wherein he no longer perceives and speaks to creation as he did before the Fall.³³ Eve's post-Fall birth is still fertile with hope even though it is painful. As her new name suggests, her childbearing will bring all post-Fall human life into being. Furthermore, post-Fall birth gains increasing significance as time passes—especially when another woman's womb brings the Son of God into earthly being to undo the Fall's tragic realities. The problem, then, is not Eve's childbearing (beyond its pain). The real problem portrayed in Gen 3:20 is the post-Fall patriarch's gaze landing upon a woman and identifying her as capable of only one thing: giving birth to babies. What happened to the poems this man used to recite and the songs he used to sing for his love, the dissimilar similar person who took away his loneliness? After the Fall those poems and songs seem to have evaporated and become faraway if not non-existent memories. Adam's re-naming Woman *Eve* consequently reflects what was forewarned by the curse spoken in Gen 3:16: "I will greatly increase your pangs in childbearing; / in pain you shall bring forth children, / yet your desire shall be for your husband, / and he shall rule over you." As Adam starts to dominate in post-Fall creation, he re-names Woman *Eve* and confines her to a singular function which does not anoint her on a way to a free and fruitful future. These are the tragic depths to which Adam's naming has fallen!

Just as the situation is not good for Woman who is re-named Eve after the Fall, so is it not good for all of the animals. Ellul writes:

> To grasp thoroughly the extraordinary difference in "Adam's" kind of dominion before and after the fall, it is enough to compare what God said to Adam and what he said to Noah. To Adam, he said, "Be fruitful and multiply, and fill the earth and subdue it; and have dominion over all the animals" (Gen 1:28). To Noah (after the flood and while they were trying to rediscover a just humanity before God), he said, "Be fruitful

---

32. Ellul, *Théologie et Technique*, 154–55.

33. Ellul, *Théologie et Technique*, 153–54. Note Ellul's use of the word "science" in this passage. Ellul is aware that the Greek root of the word *science* is *epistēmē*, which is also the Greek root of the word *epistemology*. See Ellul, *Reason for Being*, 51–58 for one of many Ellul's discussions of science as a way of knowing in the modern world. Such themes are important for Ellul's work as a whole, but there is not space to explore them here, though I do discuss them at length in my forthcoming book *Theology, Ethics, and Technology in the Work of Jacques Ellul and Paul Virilio*.

and multiply, and fill the earth. The fear of you and the dread of you shall be upon every beast of the earth . . . into your hands they are delivered" (Gen 9:1–2) [. . .]. Instead of ruling in communion and without means, now there is fear, the terror which the animals feel regarding the man who rules them by his technical means. The animals no longer come, but flee instead. They are no longer loved in thanksgiving for creation; they are no longer presented by Adam with praise to God; they are delivered into the hands of man. In the one instance, there is the word; in the other, the hands.[34]

Before the Fall, the animals willingly approach Adam and wait as he self-reflectively and self-reflexively anoints them with a name. After the Fall, the animals bolt away in fear and dread because they are hunted and delivered into the hands of men. Consequently, the pre-Fall "'taxonomy' which is free"—the freeing names Adam gives to the animals before the Fall—snaps shut like a trap. The rigid taxonomy of kinds and species so often studied, named, and instrumentalized by humanity begins to replace the free taxonomy imagined and proclaimed by Adam before the Fall.

With all of this in view, Ellul's contention that "the mirror of creation is shattered" after the Fall is confirmed. He helps us to see how and why Adam's post-Fall naming reflects this tragic shattering of creation's once ornate and revealing mirror.[35] But, as Ellul also points out, hope remains in creation and the name even after this brutal shattering. Such hope can be found in what Ellul calls the "work of the Word."[36]

So, What's in a Name?

Previous sections have shown at length how Ellul's readings of naming in Genesis 1 to 3 offer elaborate answers to Juliet Capulet's question "what's in a name?"[37] In this concluding section, the succinct answer which can be given to Juliet's question is that, according to Ellul and his readings of Genesis 1 to 3, there is much in a name—much to marvel at and much to fear. In short, there is incredible power in a name. As Ellul writes in *Humiliation of the Word*, "This work of the Word [i.e. God's Word] in a person is [taught] in the Bible

---

34. Ellul, *Théologie et Technique*, 154. Again, there are hints at other important themes in Ellul's work in this passage which I cannot explore here, but also explore at length in the book mentioned in the previous footnote.

35. Ellul, *Théologie et Technique*, 154–55.

36. Ellul, *Humiliation of the Word*, 37 (Ellul's capitalization).

37. Shakespeare, *Romeo and Juliet*, 107–8 (2.2.38–49).

through the importance given to the Name. The word or syllable that indicates a person is the person himself. Let not anyone speak to us in this connection of primitive ideas. A person's name is not so much a magic way of getting hold of him as it is the profound meaning of his being."[38] While it is of interest to me to explore how naming after the Fall could express the profound meaning of a person's being in the way Ellul describes it here, it is "the work of the Word in a person" which most concerns me here as I conclude.

My hope, dear reader, is that as we have examined Ellul's readings of naming in Genesis 1 to 3, you have experienced "the work of the Word"— God's Word—in yourself. I certainly have as these texts, and Ellul's readings of these texts, have worked me over and urged me to ponder, and ponder again, the power of a name. What names have I given to people, to creation? Have these names liberated or constricted, blessed or a cursed? What about names you have given to people and creation? Have they liberated or constricted, blessed or cursed? Such are some of the many questions a person begins to ask when they read, and re-read, Ellul's readings of scripture and the scriptures Ellul reads. As cited earlier, Ellul believes "revelation calls into question everything solid and taken for granted."[39] And this includes, of course, biblical revelation and its revelation of the power contained in a name.

Works Cited

Ellul, Jacques. *The Ethics of Freedom*. Translated by Geoffrey W. Bromiley. London: Mowbrays, 1976.
———. *The Humiliation of the Word*. Translated by Joyce Main Hanks. Grand Rapids: Eerdmans, 1985.
———. *La Genèse aujourd'hui*. Paris: Editions L'AREFPPI, 1987.
———. *Living Faith*. Translated by Peter Heinegg. San Francisco: Harper & Row, 1980.
———. *The Meaning of the City*. Translated by Denis Pardee. Eugene, OR: Wipf & Stock, 2011.
———. *On Freedom, Love, and Power*. Translated by Willem Vanderburg. Toronto: University of Toronto Press, 2010.
———. *Reason for Being: A Meditation on Ecclesiastes*. Translated by Joyce Main Hanks. Grand Rapids: Eerdmans, 1990.
———. *Théologie et Technique*. Edited by Yves Ellul and Frédéric Rognon. Geneva: Labor et Fides, 2014.
———. *To Will & To Do: An Introduction to Christian Ethics*. Translated by Jacob Marques Rollison. Eugene, OR: Cascade, 2020.
Shakespeare, William. *Romeo and Juliet*. The New Cambridge Shakespeare, edited by G. Blakemore Evans. Cambridge: Cambridge University Press, 2003.

---

38. Ellul, *Humiliation of the Word*, 37 (Ellul's capitalization).
39. Ellul, *Living Faith*, 144–45.

CHAPTER 8

Jacques Ellul and Exodus
A Summary and Review

G. P. WAGENFUHR

Ellul on Exodus

THE THEME OF EXODUS occupies an important place in the thought of Jacques Ellul: it forms the biblical foundation of his theology of freedom.[1] While a fair amount has been written on Ellul and freedom or liberation, I am not aware of a specific investigation into his view on exodus.

Rather than surveying the literature reference by reference, our analysis will proceed thematically. This is rather easy to do, because Ellul uses the concept of exodus consistently across many of his works. While I will reference the use of exodus in several of Ellul's writings, this chapter is not intended as a comprehensive study of the theme in the entirety of his vast corpus. Although *Ethics of Freedom* is his central work on freedom, and thus on exodus, Ellul makes unique claims in other works as well.

The Centrality of Exodus in Scripture

Exodus is a Greek word meaning a "way out." Generally, it refers to any major act of leaving. In the Bible it is specifically used to refer to the particular event of the Hebrew people leaving Egypt and going into the wilderness. By extension, it refers to any way out of a type of oppressive situation, like subjection to Rome by the Jewish people of the second temple period, or

---

1. This chapter was originally published in *The Ellul Forum* 64 (Fall 2019) 17–34. The version presented here has been lightly edited.

even as a general human condition like that of sin. Ellul argues that exodus is *the* central narrative of the Hebrew Scriptures.[2] It is a major part of Pauline theology, which does not contrast with but compliments the rest of the New Testament.[3] Jesus's whole work is seen as an exodus.[4] Interestingly in this regard, Ellul explores the Pauline and Johannine literature and compares them, but he does not make use of key passages of Luke in *Ethics of Freedom*. In his inaugural address in the synagogue of Nazareth, Jesus claims that he is the fulfilment of the year of the Lord's favor in which he will proclaim liberty to the captives (4:18–21), a surprising omission that would have significantly strengthened his position on the centrality of exodus and linked exodus with jubilee.

Ellul characteristically does not thoroughly defend the claim that exodus is the central biblical narrative, nor cite sources that would support this claim. Such a claim sounds far less radical after the thorough work of more recent biblical scholars such as N. T. Wright.[5]

God as Liberator

Just as exodus can refer to a specific event in the Bible or a generalized theme of leaving oppression, so too is God understood as the one who brings the people of God out of Egypt and the one who frees people from oppression in general.[6] God is known as liberator, for Ellul. He makes the bold claim that God is God only as our liberator.[7] This is not a claim about the nature of God so much as it is about God's relationship to a people bound by necessity and slavery. God is the God of Israel because of his liberating action, as in Exodus 20. Thus, God can be known only in the experience of liberation.

This point helps to explain an important shift in Ellul's thinking over the course of his writing. It can be understood as an important reason why Ellul's approach to the order or knowledge of sin shifts from his earlier writings to his later works. In an interview, he explains that he began with

2. Ellul, *Anarchy and Christianity*, 39; *Reason for Being*, 298.

3. Ellul, *Ethics of Freedom*, 94–98.

4. Ellul, *Living Faith*, 276.

5. See Wright, *New Testament and the People of God*; Wright, *Jesus and the Victory of God*; and Wright, *Resurrection and the Son of God*.

6. Examples of this abound in Scripture. The songs of Moses and Miriam (Exod 15), Hannah (1 Sam 2), and Mary (Luke 1:46–55) should be added to the long list of Psalms that convey this theme of the exaltation of the weak or lowly. Jesus's sermons about the kingdom of God/heaven likewise include the same kind of power reversals (Matt 5:1–12; Luke 6:20–49).

7. Ellul, *Ethics of Freedom*, 96.

a strong, Calvinist view of sin, before moving later in life to seeing sin less and less as an important category. Following Barth, Ellul sees that sin can only be recognized through the experience of liberation in Christ. The depth of sin is revealed only after one has been rescued from the sin itself. This means that the message of sin is itself a message predicated on the reality of liberation.[8]

Like any situation of normalcy, one requires critical distance to better understand the shape of a situation in which one formerly lived. Those who are fully integrated into their own contexts or *milieux* are therefore unable to understand the structures of their bondage. Sin cannot be understood except from the position of liberation. This means that liberation must come before the preaching of sin and repentance for such a message to be heard as plausible. This insight offers one avenue toward understanding the whole of Ellul's corpus. As one liberated in Christ, Ellul believes that he can perceive the structures of human bondage. Those things that are called "necessity," the sacral values and myths of a milieu, are the places where the work of Christ must be applied in thought and in action. Ellul does not address sin in many of his sociological works, e.g. *The Technological Society* or *Autopsy of Revolution*. Ellul first seeks to disorient those who are integrated into bondage, to introduce a spark of discontent, which may develop into a desire for liberation. It is then that the message of liberation in Christ becomes plausible. This theological method is one of Ellul's most important legacies.

Ellul makes the sovereignty of God dependent on God as liberator. In *The Subversion of Christianity*, he writes about Islam's influence on Christianity which he sees in the doctrine of providence. Islam holds to a very strong version of submission to the will of God. Ellul thinks that providence is

> . . . the very reverse of what we are told about the biblical God, who opens up freedom for us, who lets us make our own history, who goes with us on the more or less unheard-of adventures that we concoct. This God is not "providence" (which is never a biblical word). He is never the determinative cause or an irreducible conductor of events.[9]

God's sovereignty, although not expressed in providence,[10] is still necessary for liberation. "God has to be ours, and sovereign, if we are to be truly free. Israel is free only to the extent that its God is absolutely sovereign."[11] That is, God must be a higher authority than all others, or we fall back into

---

8. Ellul and Vanderburg, *Perspectives on Our Age*, 85.
9. Ellul, *Subversion of Christianity*, 107.
10. See also Ellul, *What I Believe*, ch. 12.
11. Ellul, *Ethics of Freedom*, 96–97.

slavery as the Israelites do. If God is not sovereign, he does not have the power to truly liberate. This deduction from the essence of God (sovereign) to his historical action (liberation) does not deeply interest Ellul, who would prefer to refer to God as revealed in Scripture rather than God as he must be based on logical outcomes of his divine essence. He maintains that the two perspectives—God does everything and humans do nothing, or humans do all things—are unbiblical.[12] He believes in a third option, that God has full sovereignty, and thus full potentiality, but does not use his power to override the will of humans. Instead God uses his power and authority to liberate people according to his will.

The Judeo-Christian God is unique in his revelation as the liberator. Ellul contrasts Yahweh with Ancient Near Eastern gods, who are not sovereign, so that human history is really just the "'fallout' of divine misadventures."[13] And he contrasts the God of the Bible with Allah of Islam, whose all-encompassing, unalterable will is his primary attribute.[14] Indeed, Ellul thinks that God as liberator is so crucial to the Bible that he sees God's first real self-revelation in his call to Moses from the burning bush to act on behalf of liberation.[15]

While God is clearly the liberator in the exodus, the great and final exodus comes in Christ, which has become a major theme of recent New Testament scholarship.[16] But whereas current scholarship often points toward the historical aspects in which Christ saw himself, and Paul saw Christ, as liberator (from Rome, from law), Ellul also emphasizes the current aspects of liberation in Christ. Christ frees us from politics, from being *in* politics, for example.[17] Jesus's incarnation and crucifixion is the final exodus, the banishment of death.[18]

Although Ellul consistently points to the necessity of the sovereignty of God for the reality of liberation, he also says that God cannot be understood

---

12. Ellul, *Subversion of Christianity*, 147–48.

13. Ellul, *Apocalypse*, 49.

14. Ellul, *Subversion of Christianity*, 107.

15. Ellul, *Humiliation of the Word*, 58.

16. See Wright, *Paul and the Faithfulness of God*. For example, "Paul is clear that, as with the Israelites of Exodus 3:13–15 and elsewhere, the events concerning Jesus and the spirit have constituted a fresh and full revelation of who the one God actually is" (657).

17. Ellul, *False Presence of the Kingdom*, 183. By "in politics" Ellul means that Christians are able to choose to join in the political arena but are not subject to it. Politics is "there *to get into* as a pure act of will . . ."

18. Ellul, *Living Faith*, 276.

as the master of the universe,[19] as Christ *Pantocrator*.[20] By this he means that God is better known through exodus than through Genesis, and that God revealed himself as Jesus. Jesus is localized, personal. God's love is expressed in direct personal ways, not in a universal sense. God is revealed in Christ on the cross, not in universal lordship.[21] This is a major aspect of Ellul's theological and ethical vision. God allows human freedom, but that does not make him any less sovereign.

The Historicity of the Exodus

The exodus is the great historical event in which God liberates Israel from Egypt. But for Ellul the exodus is not the only liberative event in the Bible. He points also to Abraham's call out of Ur as an exodus, and to the whole work of Jesus.[22] These are portrayed as historical acts of liberation. But as he is with many other points in the Old Testament, Ellul is less interested in establishing the historicity of the events than he is in reading the text as a revelation of the character of God. For Ellul, biblical history is not a bare catalogue of events but the revelation of God's meaning for human history.[23] Thus, whether or not the exodus of Moses happened as narrated in the book of Exodus does not interest Ellul, and he does not discuss it.

Although Ellul does not believe in a distinction between a Christ of faith and a Christ of history and has little time for Bultmannian demythologization,[24] he is nevertheless careful to distinguish the reality of the historical event from its enduring theological implications and spiritual realities. One might argue that exodus is a typological theme for Ellul. That is, the exodus of Moses is a type that gives structure to much of the rest of the biblical revelation. Ellul means this in some specific and some general ways.

Specifically, Ellul links the work of Christ with the Passover lamb. "The Word, the passage, the crossing, is the celebration of liberation. History can be read only in the light of this liberation."[25] For Ellul, humans must be liberated for God to be God, and all history leads to this liberation, which is its final product. We might say that for Ellul, the crucifixion of Jesus, the

---

19. Ellul and Chastenet, *Jacques Ellul on Religion, Technology, and Politics*, 103.
20. Ellul, *False Presence of the Kingdom*, 69.
21. Ellul, *Ethics of Freedom*, 85.
22. Ellul, *Living Faith*, 274.
23. Ellul, *Apocalypse*, 49. This entire book is dedicated to this thesis. See also Ellul, *Subversion of Christianity*, 147–49.
24. Ellul, *Ethics of Freedom*, 68–69.
25. Ellul, *Apocalypse*, 119.

paschal lamb, is *the* historic event, the point at which history definitively gains its meaning and purpose. Again, this liberation is only possible by recognition of the sovereignty of God in the Lamb.

From this point, Ellul can move to see exodus as a spiritual or existential reality. Ellul notes on a number of occasions that the Hebrew word for Egypt, *mitzraim*, means "twofold anguish," citing the Talmud as support for this interpretation.[26] This "twofold anguish" is oppression and death. Egypt is both physical oppression and spiritual finality in meaninglessness. The liberation of God cannot be limited to one or another in isolation. This hints, of course, at Ellul's ethics found in many of his theological works, such as in *Presence in the Modern World*. But this link between historical and existential reality is also clear in his concept of the principalities and powers, which has been elaborated at length.[27] He views the powers as having a reality dependent on humans, but this is still a reality that is oppressive. The exodus is liberation from the powers.[28] Pharaoh is not simply Pharaoh but a power of oppression, an embodiment of the prince of the world.

Threefold Exodus

In one of his few hints at the corporate aspect of liberation, Ellul explains that exodus has three aspects: God's self-revelation that brings a people into his mystery, liberation from oppression and idolatry, and the institution of a people by giving a law of liberty.[29] Each of these has a depth to them. God's self-revelation is liberative. This freedom from slavery to the necessary course of events and situations is what gives meaning to history, as written by the liberating God. Liberation from oppression includes both a spiritual and a material element inseparably. Ellul also notes here that liberation is from idolatry. This highlights another major theme in Ellul's work: his investigation into false belief. One could easily argue that much of Ellul's sociological work subtly points to the idolatry of various fields: *la technique, la politique*, propaganda, power and violence, money and economics, the state, and the city. Each of these represents a field in which humans aim to construct ultimate meaning, solutions, and security, but which are all false sources of meaning.[30] Again, God must be entirely sovereign if he is to be liberator, which means that all other powers must be submitted or dethroned. The

26. Ellul, *Reason for Being*, 39; Ellul and Vanderburg, *Perspectives on our Age*, 84.
27. See Dawn, "Concept of 'the Principalities and Powers.'"
28. Ellul, *Ethics of Freedom*, 133.
29. Ellul, *Ethics of Freedom*, 96.
30. Ellul, *Ethics of Freedom*, 97–98.

problem that lies at the heart of idolatry is the enthronement of anything else, the sacralization of the forces of necessity and determination.[31] Thus, Ellul says, "Spiritually the most destructive and deceptive act is that of making a virtue of necessity."[32] To claim that obeying necessity or adapting to contextual determinations is virtuous is an annihilation of any possible meaning, because it shows that humans are fully and only products of their environment. For Ellul, there is no meaning if there is no freedom. To believe that all things are predetermined or fate, an *amor fati*, like that of Nietzsche, is nothing but capitulation. Exodus thus begins with God's self-revelation, which opens humans up to the possibility of the alternative, to the destruction of the power of necessity. God is outside of contextual determinations or the realm of necessity, so that his self-revelation is a revelation of an alternative and thus the possibility of freedom. Exodus then liberates people from necessity and from the idolization of necessity. This is both a material and an imaginative liberation. Exodus is a liberation from myth, which is the formation of narratives of meaning that integrate people into an environment of determinisms. And liberation in Christ is freedom from alienation,[33] which is Ellul's best attempt at modernizing talk of sin. There is external alienation, in which a person is possessed by another or by a larger category like a corporation. Self-alienation is the defining of oneself in another. This is slavery, but it focuses on the dehumanizing aspect of redefinition of identity rather than simply the conditions of subjection.[34]

Finally, exodus leads to the giving of law, which we explore in the next section.

Freedom and Law

In the exodus, God liberates a people to the wilderness wherein he gives them his law. As a scholar of the history of institutions, Ellul is keenly aware of the realities of law. The giving of law is the grounds of freedom, "the charter of the liberty of the people of God."[35] For Ellul, ethics is the ground of freedom, not its inversion. The law of God is a law of liberty. It forms the basis for an expression of freedom by retaining the sovereignty of God. "The deeper meaning is that the law is the word of God. It is thus liberation. The

31. Ellul, *Ethics of Freedom*, 37–50.
32. Ellul, *Ethics of Freedom*, 45.
33. Ellul, *False Presence of the Kingdom*, 206.
34. Ellul, *Ethics of Freedom*, 24.
35. Ellul, *Ethics of Freedom*, 96.

aim of the commandment is to free, not to enslave."[36] Law forms the limits in which freedom is possible.[37] It is a schoolmaster of freedom. It is not the end of freedom but its foundation. There is a necessary tension between obedience and transgression, which is what enables freedom.[38]

Although the law is the basis of Israel's freedom, throughout Israel's (and humanity's) history, they constantly fall into new forms of bondage. Eventually, even the law of God becomes a bondage for Israel.[39] The very grounds of exodus thus can become a new bondage. This happens when the tension between obedience and transgression is resolved on one side or the other. Freedom occurs in a tension between slavish obedience and rebellion. Constant transgression of the law is itself a way that one defines oneself by the law. The purpose of the law of God is to help maintain a tension that enables the law to recede into the background as a foundation of liberty. When Israel elevates the law over the Spirit of God, the law becomes a slave master.[40] Put another way, when the law becomes an independent objective power, rather than an expression of the sovereignty of the liberating God, it enslaves. Thus, the first commandment of the Decalogue is the command to worship and serve Yahweh alone.

Bearing God's Revelation

Exodus is the ground of any human ability to bear the revelation of God to the world. Without living in the freedom of God there is no possibility of revealing God.[41] One brief paragraph in *The Ethics of Freedom* (96) provides a helpful window onto the whole theological framework of Ellul's thought. The role of Israel and of the Christian is to reveal God to the world, and for this to be accomplished there must be manifestations of full liberation. That is, liberation cannot simply be spiritual. It must have concrete implications (as Ellul wrote *Presence in the Modern World* to explain). On the other hand, the expression of this liberation must not conform to the pattern of this world—i.e., to the "progressive" development of the rest of society. There must simultaneously be a revelation of God and a submission to God's total sovereignty for any material liberation to be real, as Ellul explains in *False Presence of The Kingdom*. The Christian life

---

36. Ellul, *Ethics of Freedom*, 122.
37. See Ellul, *Reason for Being*, 298.
38. Ellul, *Ethics of Freedom*, 347–49.
39. Ellul, *Ethics of Freedom*, 97.
40. Ellul, *Ethics of Freedom*, 147.
41. Ellul, *Ethics of Freedom*, 96.

of exodus is therefore a constant interplay between discerning the forces of alienation, calling all to submit to God in Christ with his love, and acting in concrete ways to demonstrate this freedom.

Exodus as the Location of Christian Life

In *Living Faith* (whose original French title, *La foi au prix du doute*, translates as "Faith at the Price of Doubt"), Ellul concludes his reflections on faith, hope, and doubt with a long chapter on Jonah as the model for the Christian life. Jonah had to experience his own exodus, not when he ran from God and found himself in a big fish, but when he had to go to Nineveh. God's call was for him to leave his world behind and enter the world of his enemies—not to pursue his own task but to bring the revelation of God to a people under judgment.[42]

Christian faith is a movement for Ellul.[43] It is not a static state of being but a constant movement out of the world and to the world. Exodus is not about condemning of the world as evil, as with the flood of Noah.[44] Rather, it is liberation from the world, so that, free in Christ, one can bring the revelation of God's kingdom to a world bent on suicide.[45] Moving out of the world is obedience to the call to become a people of God, a holy people. But this people exists for the purpose of being sent into the world with the message of reconciliation. Within this movement comes formation, maturity, freedom. If this movement is schematized or turned into a static Christ and Culture model, like those of Niebuhr, confusion of holiness and mission results.

Thus, the Christian location is exodus, wilderness, or exile. The kingdom is not yet present enough that the Christian can live within it in a largely material way. But the kingdom is the call of the Spirit and the imagination. Thus, the actual location of the Christian tends to be in exile, unable to be part of the world, envisioning another, and working as exiles within the world for its reconciliation. The mere acceptance of Christ is to place oneself in exile. Exile is not a choice of the Christian life; it is the necessary condition. That means that Christian faith is the rejection of our land, our home, our milieu, our professions.[46] This exodus is a "mortal combat with the world."[47] But exodus is not the conclusion of the movement of the

---

42. Ellul, *Living Faith*, 277.
43. See Wagenfuhr, "Revelation and the Sacred Reconsidered."
44. Ellul, *Living Faith*, 277.
45. Ellul, *Presence in the Modern World*, 15.
46. Ellul, *Living Faith*, 274.
47. Ellul, *Living Faith*, 274.

Christian life, it is the prerequisite to entry into the world. This reentry is the calling of Jonah and his message, "Yet forty days" (which forms the French subtitle of *La foi au prix du doute*). This message is the preaching of God's judgment in love upon human alienation. This call is a total refusal to allow the world to march toward its necessary self-destruction. But Christian faith is not built on rescuing the world but on faithfulness to God.

Exodus and Freedom as Not Happiness

The act of liberation, as with Jonah's rebellion, is utterly devastating to a life integrated into the world. The experience of exodus is not happiness. Indeed, Ellul thinks that, if the act of liberating the world from its sacral attitudes toward its contemporary idolatries is not accompanied by a reason for living that can adequately sustain a will-to-life, it would have the tendency to drive the great majority of people to insanity or suicide.[48] Ellul often points to the Israelite desire in the wilderness to return to the perceived good life of slavery in Egypt. Interestingly, as Old Testament scholar and agrarian Ellen Davis points out, this good eating in Egypt was likely an accurate memory. Ancient Egypt had a varied and nutritious diet. She says, "No people would eat so well again for a thousand years."[49] This lends further credence to the reality about which Ellul is writing. Christian freedom is a lifestyle in direct contradiction to the lifestyle of happiness. Like the Israelites, humans generally seem prefer the security of bondage, which is regarded as happiness, to the risks of freedom. Freedom is risk, it is the "non-satisfaction of needs that we see as natural or essential,"[50] like those of security.

The Exodus Temptation of Jesus and the Self-Limitation of Freedom

One final aspect to point out is Ellul's regular use in his theology of Jesus's temptations. For Ellul, God risked everything by sending Jesus into the exile/exodus of temptation in the wilderness. Jesus was entirely free to choose to submit to his desires or the temptation of the devil, and it is on this risk that God's plan of reconciliation hinges. The wilderness is a place of dislocation, where there are no grounds of support. Ellul merges exodus, the flood of Noah, and the temptation of Adam all into this one event. It is the success in

---

48. Ellul, *New Demons*, 208.
49. Davis, *Scripture, Culture, and Agriculture*, 70.
50. Ellul, *Ethics of Freedom*, 262–63. See also Ellul, *Subversion of Christianity*, 167.

Christ of overcoming the temptations of materialism, power, and spiritual proof, temptations that led Israel into bondage throughout its history. Jesus resists temptation by accepting his relation to God. True freedom is, again, submission to the sovereign God alone. This alone is the force that can free people from determinations and necessities. Jesus demonstrates freedom by self-limitation. Rather than by an expression of his power, Jesus chooses limits for himself within which he is free.[51]

This concept of self-limitation and refusal of power finds expression throughout Ellul's works, including many of his sociological works in which he criticizes the uncritical implementation of what is possible.

Evaluation of the Exodus Theme in Ellul

I believe that Ellul has identified the heart of living the Christian faith by focusing so intently throughout his writings on the biblical themes of exodus and liberation. His understanding of an intolerable dialectical existence between slavery and freedom, and the careful elaboration of what that freedom truly means, is accurate. This aspect of Ellul's work has received great support from New Testament scholarship in recent decades, with the rise of the "New Perspective on Paul" and study of the genre of apocalyptic. An apocalyptic understanding of the radical inbreaking of the kingdom and its total otherness from the kingdoms of this world strongly resonates with Ellul's appraisal of New Testament theology. Furthermore, Ellul rightly understands that exodus is central to both the Old and New Testaments and is indeed one of their chief unifying elements. I find Ellul's understanding of the role of *torah* in the Bible, and its transition from Old to New Testaments commendable: it permits viewing *torah* as both the grounds of freedom and the source of slavery without creating a sort of Jewish-Christian opposition which sees Jews as legalists and Christians as concerned with freedom. This corresponds very well to the more recent reappraisal of the Pharisees in Second Temple Judaism,[52] though Ellul would not have known this.

But this leads to one area in which Ellul's thought about exodus is limited. The exodus under Moses was about the formation of a people of God. Ellul recognized this, but he did not develop much of an ecclesiology of freedom or exodus. The work of Christ in liberating people was not simply

---

51. Ellul, *Ethics of Freedom*, 51–62. See also Ellul, "Si tu es le fils de Dieu."

52. See Wright, *New Testament and the People of God*, 181–203. The Pharisees were not a people focused on legalism as a means of entry into heaven, but a complex and elusive group passionate about the national sovereignty and identity of Israel expressed through public and later exclusively personal purity.

for individual, personal relationships with God but for the formation of a community in which the Kingdom of God is plausible and tangible. This is a key ecclesial concept I elaborate in detail elsewhere.[53] Most basically it means that the Kingdom is not intended to be aspirational for individual experience, but a shared communal experience that normalizes the values of the Kingdom, and thus may be perceived as reasonable. Ellul does not develop much in the way of a communal life of liberty. There are a variety of likely reasons for this. His own ecclesial experiences did not fill him with hope in the institution of the church. Such disappointment has become an increasingly common experience among Christians in the North Atlantic as evidenced by copious data from major church research institutions on reasons for church decline, as well as in the necessary shift in the social function of church institutions under a post-Durkheimian late secularism.[54] This is a situation in which Moses figures are desperately needed. There must be the development of bold leaders who can take the risks of freedom in modeling and fostering exodus communities, for the Christian life of liberty to be plausible and tangible. These communities can then form the basis of a prophetic "Yet forty days!" that Ellul recognizes is necessary.

Along with his stunted ecclesiology, Ellul significantly under-develops a portrait of the life of the Kingdom. Perhaps ironically, Ellul focuses so much of his effort on explaining the reality of the Kingdom, the dialectic of its presence/absence, and the Christian's place within it, that he does not spend much time explaining his perspective of what characterizes the Kingdom. Put another way, Ellul does not say much about what freedom or liberation is for or to. What is that vision of the city of God of Hebrews? Certainly Ellul develops his view of *anakephalaiosis* or recapitulation,[55] in which God takes up the history of humanity and reconciles it with himself. But Ellul's eschatology lacks crucial dimensions that would otherwise round out his ethical call to "freedom to." Put another way, Ellul does not adequately spell out the mission of God's people. Rescue, salvation, liberation is not the goal but the beginning of God's purposes in the world. Certainly this is a theological weakness that Ellul shares with generations of theologians who have fixated on salvation as the core theme of Christianity.

And although Ellul (along with his friend Bernard Charbonneau) is himself a major forerunner of the ecological movement, he misses bringing the whole of creation into the exodus theme. Although Ellul believes in the salvation of all creation, he does not detail what the reconciliation of all

---

53. Wagenfuhr, *Plundering Eden*.
54. See Taylor, *Secular Age*, and Wagenfuhr, "Religion comme jeu."
55. See Ellul, *What I Believe*, ch. 16, and Ellul, *Meaning of the City*, ch. 6.

creation means or how that fits into his theory of Christ as the one who gives meaning to history. We might say that he runs the risk of seeing God as liberator of humanity without seeing God as the Creator who is rescuing all creation *from* humanity as well.[56] Exodus and the wilderness is replete with symbolic content to aid ecological thinking of exodus. Furthermore, Ellul makes a significant interpretative error in *The Meaning of the City* that perhaps prevents him from drawing more ecological conclusions. Does the history of creation not have meaning until humanity arrives on the scene? Certainly not. This anthropocentric danger is endemic in Ellul's Barthian Christocentrism that focuses on the centrality of humanity's salvation to the neglect of the restoration of creation. This does not mean that Ellul's ethic is anti-ecological, of course, only that it has a conceptual weakness which hinders it from becoming a major source for contemporary ecotheology.

Another element which is lacking is any real connection of liberation with jubilee or the practices of the sabbath year. Certainly, Ellul mentions the sabbath as a sign of liberty in the Old Testament and as a mark of Christian freedom.[57] But as he does so, he consistently fails to speak about the sabbath year and the year of jubilee. These legal frameworks would significantly bolster his theology of liberation in that they would add some content to a positive ecclesiology or view of kingdom life as intentionally liberating. They would also go a long way towards addressing the ecological deficit of his work on liberation. And it would further his theological ethic of self-restraint and exercise of non-power.

Certainly, Ellul's understanding of freedom and exodus is deeply rooted in his existentialism. This is both positive and negative. It is positive in the reminder that the life of Christian faith is not reducible to a formula, a static worldview, or applicable principles. It forces the Christian to meet with his or her own individual alienations in an encounter with Christ. But his existentialism is also one of his chief weaknesses. As we have seen, it prevents a more mature exploration of the people of God in a robust ecclesiology and eschatology. In the twenty-first century post-Durkheimian secular world, the formation of communities of faith will be increasingly a conscious and difficult effort, and sources of inspiration are needed for this task. It is therefore lamentable that Ellul does not provide much help for a time of building new communities and expressions of Christian discipleship.

All that said, Ellul's thinking about exodus is both an excellent microcosm of his theology in general, and a rather accurate and singular explanation of biblical theology.

---

56. Wagenfuhr, *Plundering Eden*.
57. Ellul, *Ethics of Freedom*, 129–30, 496; *Violence*, 128; *What I Believe*, ch. 12.

Liberation Theology?

We cannot conclude this essay without mention of Thomas Hanks's article "The Original 'Liberation Theologian'?" Hanks compares Ellul's thinking on liberation (as of 1985) with the development of liberation theology in Latin America. He finds, rightly, that Ellul was a precursor to the theologies of liberation that developed later in the twentieth century, though Ellul came from a different background and thus had different emphases. Hanks notes how Ellul shares with liberation theology the idea that salvation is liberation. He also quotes Geoffrey Bromiley, the major translator of both Karl Barth and Jacques Ellul, a quotation worth copying here:

> This freedom (unleashed at the cross) is received exclusively in Christ, making the gospel essentially one of liberation. Here again is a theme that recurs constantly in Barth's *Church Dogmatics*, and Ellul takes it up with vigor. Liberation, he thinks, provides the present age with a better figure of salvation than redemption does.[58]

Exodus helps inform Ellul's claim that in our time the concept of redemption is better understood as liberation and de-alienation.[59] This is partly due to the archaic nature of the concept of redemption but also due to the deeper alienations of modern life.

Ellul is not a liberation theologian in the Latin American sense of the term. He remained deeply critical of baptizing political movements and imagining that they represented the Kingdom of God. Thus, Hanks sees Ellul transcending liberation theology. Ellul perceived the centrality of exodus through Scripture, rather than seeing Scripture as a tool for revolution. In this way, Ellul retains a non-instrumental value for theology unlike other theologies of liberation.

Conclusion

This chapter examined the exodus theme in much of the corpus of Jacques Ellul. It was not comprehensive, and only touched on his much wider theme of liberation and freedom. This chapter has demonstrated that Ellul saw exodus as the central theme of the Bible and God's chief characteristic as liberator. It also showed that exodus provides a window into his theology as

---

58. Geoffrey Bromiley, "Barth's Influence on Jacques Ellul"; cited in Hanks, "Original 'Liberation Theologian'?," 21.

59. Ellul, *Ethics of Freedom*, 67.

a whole in its major outlines. In some ways, Ellul was a prescient precursor of more recent trends in New Testament scholarship regarding the centrality of exodus, even if he missed some key texts and themes that would have supported his view (i.e., Luke). His analysis is neither perfectly accurate nor comprehensive. It has weaknesses, but on balance I believe that Ellul's contribution to modern theology is vital to retain the dialectical movement of the life of exodus/exile/wilderness in which freedom is difficult and bondage is attractive. His work on liberation and exodus is not timeless, but it has aged well. It should not stand as the only word on the subject, but it still provides a needed voice of critique and encouragement in theology today.

Works Cited

Davis, Ellen F. *Scripture, Culture, and Agriculture: An Agrarian Reading of the Bible*. New York: Cambridge University Press, 2009.

Dawn, Marva. "The Concept of 'the Principalites and Powers' in the Works of Jacques Ellul." PhD diss., University of Notre Dame, 1992.

Ellul, Jacques. *Anarchy and Christianity*. Translated by Geoffrey W. Bromiley. Grand Rapids: Eerdmans, 1991.

———. *Apocalypse: The Book of Revelation*. Translated by George W. Schreiner. New York: Seabury, 1977.

———. *The Ethics of Freedom*. Translated by Geoffrey W. Bromiley. Grand Rapids: Eerdmans, 1976.

———. *False Presence of the Kingdom*. Translated by C. Edward Hopkin. New York: Seabury, 1972.

———. *The Humiliation of the Word*. Translated by Joyce Main Hanks. Grand Rapids: Eerdmans, 1985.

———. *Living Faith: Belief and Doubt in a Perilous World*. Translated by Peter Heinegg. San Francisco: Harper & Row, 1983.

———. *The Meaning of the City*. Translated by Dennis Pardee. Grand Rapids: Eerdmans, 1970.

———. *The New Demons*. Translated by C. Edward Hopkin. New York: Seabury, 1975.

———. *Presence in the Modern World: A New Translation*. Translated by Lisa Richmond. Eugene, OR: Cascade, 2016.

———. *The Reason for Being: A Meditation on Ecclesiastes*. Translated by Joyce Main Hanks. Grand Rapids: Eerdmans, 1990.

———. "Si tu es le fils de Dieu." In *Le Défi Et Le Nouveau: Oeuvres Théologiques 1948-1991*, 937–1016. Paris: La Table Ronde, 2007.

———. *The Subversion of Christianity*. Translated by Geoffrey W. Bromiley. Grand Rapids: Eerdmans, 1986.

———. *Violence: Reflections From a Christian Perspective*. Translated by Cecilia Gaul. London: SCM, 1970.

———. *What I Believe*. Translated by Geoffrey W. Bromiley. Grand Rapids: Eerdmans, 1989.

Ellul, Jacques, and Patrick Chastenet. *Jacques Ellul on Religion, Technology, and Politics*. Translated by Joan Mendès France. Eugene, OR: Wipf & Stock, 2005.

Ellul, Jacques, and William H. Vanderburg. *Perspectives on Our Age: Jacques Ellul Speaks on His Life and Work*. Translated by Joachim Neugroschel. Toronto: House of Anansi, 2004.

Hanks, Thomas. "The Original 'Liberation Theologian'?" *Cross Currents* 35 (1985) 17–32.

Taylor, Charles. *A Secular Age*. Cambridge, MA: Belknap, 2007.

Wagenfuhr, G. P. *Plundering Eden: A Subversive Theology of Creation and Ecology*. Eugene, OR: Cascade, 2020.

———. "Religion comme jeu: la situation au XXième siècle." In *Comment Peut-on (Encore) Être Ellulien Au XXième Siècle*, edited by Patrick Troude-Chastenet, 209–10. Paris: La Table Ronde, 2014.

———. "Revelation and the Sacred Reconsidered: The Revelation of God in Jesus Christ as Desacralising Reorientation to 'Milieu' in and Beyond Jacques Ellul." PhD diss., University of Bristol, 2013.

Wright, N. T. *Jesus and the Victory of God: Christian Origins and the Question of God*. Vol. 2. Minneapolis: Fortress, 1999.

———. *The New Testament and the People of God: Christian Origins and the Question of God*. Vol. 1. Minneapolis: Augsburg Fortress, 1996.

———. *Paul and the Faithfulness of God: Christian Origins and the Question of God*. Vol. 4. Minneapolis: Fortress, 2013.

CHAPTER 9

Ellul on Job
The Freedom of Waiting

AMY J. ERICKSON

THE CLAIM THAT OF all the biblical books, Job showcases the danger of theological technique *par excellence*, verges on the indisputable. As a direct result, we might expect to see Ellul's theologically subversive insights to emerge in full force in his reading of this tome. We would not be disappointed.

Ellul's comments on Job come to us through a transcript of a seminar series he led in 1974, made available in English by Willem Vanderburg.[1] In his reading of Job, Ellul expresses a distinctively figural mode of biblical interpretation that sets the stage for his dialectically driven insights. Figural reading, credited with deep roots in the Christian tradition, has gained renewed attention with the growing theological interpretation movement. John David Dawson's *Christian Figural Reading and the Fashioning of Identity*,[2] relying heavily on Erich Auerbach's seminal work *Mimesis,* is a vocal contemporary champion of the figural hermeneutic. Figuralism, as Dawson explains through Auerbach, identifies the spiritual connection between two entities: a figure, and its fulfillment. These may be separated by time and space, but they are ultimately united in God's authorship. In fact, figural interpretation presumes God's sovereign orchestration of both scripture and history, and it is displayed within the biblical text itself. Paul, for example, engages a figural interpretation when he claims in 1 Corinthians 5:7 that "Christ our Passover

---

1. Ellul, *On Freedom, Love, and Power*. Ellul's comments on Job are recorded in part two, "The Love That Seeks Us Out." The preceding and succeeding parts records Ellul's comments on Genesis 1–3 and Matthew, respectively.

2. Dawson, *Christian Figural Reading and the Fashioning of Identity*.

lamb has been sacrificed." The person of Christ in history fulfills the figure of the Passover lamb of ancient Hebrew ritual.

More art than science, figuralism maintains both discernible relations with and clear distinctions from allegory. Unlike allegory, which strains to release itself from historical particularity to achieve a lofty, higher meaning, figuralism finds significance by preserving the inherent, horizontal connection between concrete "figures" (e.g. the Passover lamb) and another concrete figure in which it finds its fulfillment (e.g. Christ's crucifixion). This "fulfilling" quality may draw lines with multiple figures across time and space, figures who ultimately credit God as their author. Christ is the ultimate figure of fulfillment, as the one who grounds meaning as such. Indeed, for the figuralist, Christ *is* the meaning of history. In this way, figural reading sensitizes its practitioners to see the gospel resound in kaleidoscopic form throughout the pages of scripture and the annals of history. Ellul applies this style of interpretation from the beginning of his reading of Job (or at least, as this reading has come to us.)

Ellul's comments on Job reach us fortuitously. Because the seminar recording on Job 1–37 has been lost, our entry point to Ellul's interpretation appears *in medias res*. We begin with Ellul's understanding of an oft-overlooked Joban figure: Elihu. Elihu's neglect is not without reason. Enigmatically reminiscent of Melchizedek (cf. Gen 14:17–20 and Heb 7:1–28), Elihu is distinguished from Job's three friends who have shouldered the grunt work of dialoguing with Job until now. He arrives unannounced and leaves without further mention; he is not included in the punishment of Job's friends at the book's close. Many interpreters insist that Elihu does little more than repeat the comments of Job's friends; Ellul insists they are mistaken.

Ellul overturns these prevalent misinterpretations of Elihu with a figural reading, albeit one which shifts in the course of the recorded lecture. Ellul begins by reading Elihu as a figure of Christ himself, but concludes by casting Elihu in the role of a John the Baptist-like prophet who prepares the way of the Lord. An etymological analysis tees him up: Ellul suggests that Elihu's in-text pedigree yields the meaning "YHWH is my God, son of Elohim's blessing, bearing the title of the despised servant, and coming from the heavens."[3] In this light, Elihu's discourse in chapters 32–37 unveils the nature of the wisdom and Word of God. This discourse achieves two ends: it reveals the humble nature of God's speech, which submits itself to human (mis)interpretation. (There is obvious and even explicit reference here to Ellul's *The Humiliation of the Word*.) But above all, Elihu illustrates that "God's actions are always announced first" in

3. Ellul, *On Freedom, Love, and Power*, 104.

order to maximize the opportunity for human response.[4] This allowance, Ellul adds, "leaves us a certain freedom."[5]

In the evident slippage of his figural interpretation of Elihu, by which Elihu shifts within the space of a few pages from a figure of Christ to a messenger of Christ, Ellul showcases the fluid and dynamic nature of figural reading. This refractive nature of figuralism and the reality it apprehends is echoed in poet Gerard Manley Hopkin's beloved line: "Christ plays in ten thousand places."[6] That is, a single scriptural "figure" might point us into a number of historical or biblical directions. Elihu may point us in the direction of John the Baptist or Jesus, just as the person of John the Baptist may remind us of Elijah or any number of contemporary prophets, or the person of Peter may draw our attention to either our ability to confess Jesus as Messiah or our capacity to deny of him. With these varied interpretations in mind, Ellul also broaches a deficit of figural reading (and of Hopkin's own poem): how does it account for those forms which proliferate in both scripture and world which are sinful distortions of—or aberrations from—Christ's form? Can figuralism give us a hermeneutic of sin? Again, Ellul's text is fortuitous. It addresses this concern in the series of Joban figures soon to come: Behemoth and Leviathan.

But first, when we arrive at chapters 38–39 we find that Elihu has accomplished his role as a messenger. After Elihu's announcement, God speaks. Ellul admits his initial disappointment at this juncture: "It makes God appear in the way non-believers often see him: a God who is only power, who crushes people, who reduces people to silence without replying."[7] Yet Ellul insists that there is here, as elsewhere in scripture, a hidden depth which is only accessible to those whose approach is one of faith. God's reply to Job's existential questions condenses to the assertion, "I am here." God, instead of dismissing Job's cries, takes them seriously. [8] Yet this affirmation does not present itself in declarative form. Instead, God responds to Job's questioning with more questions. These questions extend an invitation to reply which reveals "a much deeper sense to God asking us questions—it implies that we are free."[9] God's engagement with Job validates the freedom which he grants all humanity by virtue of his willingness to dialogue with us. Indeed, God's Word both creates humanity and sets us free. And humans are not the only ones revealed to be

---

4. Ellul, *On Freedom, Love, and Power*, 116.
5. Ellul, *On Freedom, Love, and Power*, 117.
6. Hopkins, "As Kingfishers Catch Fire."
7. Ellul, *On Freedom, Love, and Power*, 118.
8. Ellul, *On Freedom, Love, and Power*, 119.
9. Ellul, *On Freedom, Love, and Power*, 120.

free by God's discourse: creation, too, is liberated in God's speaking. From God's speech Job learns that creation was not made for humanity but exists on its own, even with "its own playfulness."[10]

Yet Ellul's reading of Job 40–41 puts an unconventional spin even on his understanding of creation as just set forth. These two chapters describe the mythic-like beasts Behemoth and Leviathan, often translated as a hippopotamus and crocodile. For many interpreters, these creatures of the Nile indicate the book's debt to Egyptian poetry. Yet in Ellul's estimation, this "positivistic" and literalist interpretation fails to account for how these two animals add any meaningful substance to the previous claims about creation and the creatures who inhabit it. Ellul suggests an alternative, and rather unconventional, understanding. Ellul attests that Behemoth "represents the power of living matter as a kind of blind force."[11] This explains why Behemoth was created first.[12] Descriptions of vain attempts to domesticate Behemoth in the fortieth chapter indicate humanity's own futile attempts to discover and control natural forces. Correlatively, if Behemoth signifies natural powers, Ellul concludes that Leviathan designates spiritual ones—specifically, the power of evil.[13] Accounts of human attempts to domesticate this beast parallel the vain attempts of Job's friends to explain sin and evil.

Together, these beasts form a figural response to Job's protest which has threaded throughout the book. In reply to Job's question—"why are you treating me this way?"—God has replied, "It is Behemoth and Leviathan who did all this."[14] Ellul insists that citing these beasts as responsible does not diminish the horror of evil, but rather heightens it. These horrors are so horrible that they must be spoken of sideways, so to speak, in the form of figures. They represent evil symbolically and allegorically, because evil cannot be logically or philosophically described, as Job's friends had foolishly tried to do. Furthermore, Ellul insists that although they are a part of creation, these beasts are not themselves created by God. Rather, they reveal how "when everything is reduced to matter . . . evil makes its appearance."[15] These creatures reveal how positivism itself gives rise to the evil spirit which then, in turn, animates and dominates all matter. (Luke 11:24–26 takes a new layer of meaning in this light.) Is Ellul committing

---

10. Ellul, *On Freedom, Love, and Power*, 121.
11. Ellul, *On Freedom, Love, and Power*, 129.
12. Job 40:19.
13. Ellul, *On Freedom, Love, and Power*, 130.
14. Ellul, *On Freedom, Love, and Power*, 131.
15. Ellul, *On Freedom, Love, and Power*, 132.

eisegesis here with his favorite bête noire, *la technique*? Perhaps; though it behooves us to consider his evidence.

Ellul summons inter-canonical support to confirm his interpretation of Behemoth and Leviathan. Although he concedes that Psalm 22 does not directly mention Behemoth and Leviathan, it does describe encircling bulls. These beasts are indirectly invoked when Jesus quotes Psalm 22 from the cross, where "Jesus is attacked by monsters and it is God who limits their powers."[16] If this connection seems tenuous, his second is stronger. Ellul notes that Behemoth and Leviathan bring to mind the dragon and beast in Revelation (cf. chapters 12, 13, and 19). There is further evidence that justify this evocation: the Septuagint text of Job uses the same Greek word to translate Behemoth and Leviathan that the Koine Greek of the New Testament also employs to describe the beast and dragon of Revelation. Moreover, Revelation describes *two* beasts: one emerging from the sea (13:1), the other from the earth (13:11). Together they validate Ellul's suggestion that Behemoth serves as a figure for material reality, encompassed by both land and sea.

We still might resist this interpretation. Does God not seem admiring, even proud of these creatures? Yet further consideration of the closing verses of this section buttress Ellul's reading. Job 41:33 describes Leviathan as a beast "without fear". The Hebrew word "fear" also appears in Genesis 9:2 to attest how all post-diluvian beasts would fear humans. This verbal allusion, however brief, confirms Ellul's suspicion that Leviathan signals something other than those creatures created by God; Leviathan is not that which fears humans, but that which humans fear. Indeed, all of Job has served as an extended catalogue of this fear. This is the evil Job has battled throughout the book, and nevertheless remains an entity which falls within the domain of God's sovereignty.

Not only does he showcase figural reading, which itself climbs into the dialectical mystery of the difference between what a text "meant" and what it "means," Ellul also opens and explores two key dialectics: that between reality and truth, and between divine and human freedom. In Ellul's conception, reality designates that which we *see*, truth that which we may only *hear* through God's Word. Because of the deformations of sin and evil, these domains are not interchangeable. Yet they coincide in the person of Jesus Christ, in whom we see God's Word. This metaphysic (if we can call it that) itself points to the gospel: in Christ God reunites his Spirit with human matter and in so doing conquers those same monsters which arose from their separation. In this, Ellul both exercises and dialectically amends figural reading. Even those

---

16. Ellul, *On Freedom, Love, and Power*, 132.

entities which fail to reflect God's creative intent unwittingly declare how God conquers monsters through the divine human Jesus Christ.

This dialectic between reality and truth interlocks with another: divine and human freedom. God exercises his divine freedom by curtailing the works of Behemoth and Leviathan, but not entirely. This divine restraint permits reality as humans experience it. This reality, in turn, opens the door for human freedom. Humans are not only free to respond to the reality which God has permitted, and which may lead to their rejection of God's Word. They are also free to temporarily forsake the truth, in a fashion, in order to exercise love. God's closing judgment on Job's friends, coupled with his direct dialogue with Job, displays the biblical truth that "no person is ever right."[17] To insist on one's rightness against another is not only impossible, it betrays a failure to love. (This is the point Paul makes forcefully in Romans 14.) Almost by definition, the Christian must resolve to "love the other more than truth."[18] We might extend Ellul's insight to claim that Christ, by visualizing truth, releases us from being its defendant and permits us to exercise our freedom out of compassionate love for that reality which does not always coincide with Christ's revelation. Such love is the product of the truest freedom, grounded as it is in God's own.

The scandal of God's freedom is intensified by Ellul's culminating reading of the entire book: "God is right because of Job."[19] In fact, not only does God permit Job to pardon him for permitting Behemoth and Leviathan to remain undomesticated by humans, God also *waits* for such pardon. In this scandalous reading of Job Ellul has seemingly subverted the gospel itself, turning it inside out from God's declaration of human righteousness to humanity's declaration of God's righteousness. In this subversion Ellul gestures towards Paul's references in Colossians 1:24 of 'filling up in his flesh what is lacking in Christ's affliction.' In this reading, the distortion suffered by material reality is borne through time in the form of suffering or, in other words, *passion*.

This crowning interpretation of Job, germinated in the soil of figural reading and irrigated by a series of dialectical explorations, yields promising fruit for the present day. As throughout her history, the church today should take her mold from a steeled resolve to wait upon Christ's return. But Ellul's interpretation transposes this waiting into a higher key. By way of Job, Ellul reveals that our waiting is not just *on* God, but *with* God. Even Paul's comments in Romans 8 are leavened by Ellul's reading. We are taken up above

---

17. Ellul, *On Freedom, Love, and Power*, 141.
18. Ellul, *On Freedom, Love, and Power*, 141.
19. Ellul, *On Freedom, Love, and Power*, 143.

creation's eager expectation for God's children to be revealed and pressed into the waiting of the Creator himself as he awaits our free response. What might this conviction do to our sojourn through time in an era in which—indeed, *to* which—material reality has been enslaved by a divisive and angst-ridden zeitgeist of technique, which bends its knee to the twin beasts of efficiency and profitability? How would our church gatherings, our rhythms and forms of discipleship, our daily lives change if we relinquished our grip on attraction, production, and busy-ness? Or sacrificed our illusions that our ivory-tower theologies or cutting-edge ministry practices are what the world needs most? What if we instead wasted our time reveling in the miraculous fact that our God is one who—at this very moment—*waits*? Then we would be free indeed.

Works Cited

Dawson, David. *Christian Figural Reading and the Fashioning of Identity.* Berkeley: University of California Press, 2001.

Ellul, Jacques. *On Freedom, Love, and Power.* Compiled, edited and translated by Willem H. Vanderburg. Toronto: University of Toronto Press, 2010.

Hopkins, Gerard Manley. "As Kingfishers Catch Fire." https://www.poetryfoundation.org/poems/44389/as-kingfishers-catch-fire.

CHAPTER 10

Ellul as a Reader of Ecclesiastes

Anthony J. Petrotta

When I started my studies at Fuller Seminary nearly thirty years ago, I took an elective class on "The Ethics of Jacques Ellul" taught by David Gill, then finishing his PhD studies on Ellul across town at USC.[1] At that time, I was taking classes mostly in Semitic Languages and wanted to go on in Old Testament studies. Ethics and theology were "recreational" reading for me. I had some interest in Ellul since a friend was urging me to read his books, and the class fit my schedule. I managed to talk Professor Gill into allowing me to write a paper on Ellul's hermeneutics, and he enthusiastically—as David often does!—accepted my proposal.

I found Ellul to be not only a sociologist, ethicist, and theologian, but somebody who had a deep interest in the biblical text and was conversant with the field. I found that a number of his concerns about interpretation were also being voiced by prominent biblical theologians (in particular, Brevard Childs).

Now, a generation later and with all that has gone on in the field of biblical studies, how does Ellul stand as an exegete, as a reader of Scripture?

I want to center my thoughts on Ellul as a reader of Scripture by looking at *Reason for Being*, his "meditation" on Ecclesiastes.[2] Ellul says that Ecclesiastes is the book of the Bible that he has explored more than any other book. It is a book he read, meditated upon, and taught for more than fifty years. I also want to compare what Ellul has said against two more recent (and more

---

1. An earlier version of this chapter was printed in *The Ellul Forum* 36 (Fall 2005), 3–5, reprinted in issue 61 (Spring 2018). The version presented here is lightly edited and revisited.

2. Ellul, *Reason for Being*.

traditional) commentaries on Ecclesiastes: Ellen Davis, *Proverbs, Ecclesiastes, and the Song of Songs*, and Michael Fox, *Ecclesiastes*.[3]

Ellul begins by reflecting on his reason and method for writing *Reason for Being* in his "Preliminary, Polemical, Nondefinitive Postscript," which, of course, appears as Chapter One, an instance of paradox that fits with Ecclesiastes' program of throwing contradictions together for the effect and truth they create. This chapter is very instructive; he reveals a lot about how he reads, and by implication, reveals some of what he considers the shortcomings of commenting upon Scripture in the modern sense of the term (Ellul is polemical).

Ellul is keenly aware that he is not going about his task as an academician might. He has not compiled an extensive bibliography and he has not interacted with the literature on Ecclesiastes current during his writing of *Reason for Being*. That is not to say, though, that he has not done the requisite work for writing an informed book on Ecclesiastes. Over the years he has read important studies on Ecclesiastes, which he notes. More importantly, he "slogged" through the Hebrew text and nine other translations as he was writing. After writing *Reason for Being* he went back and read through the literature again on Ecclesiastes. Though he saw no reason to change what he had written, he did check his thoughts against others who also have studied and written on the book. His reactions to these "historians and exegetes" he put in footnotes after the manuscript was completed.

Ellul says: "This approach seemed to me to be consistent with Ecclesiastes: once you have acquired a certain knowledge and experience, you must walk alone, without repeating what others have said."[4]

I am not sure that Ellul has "walked alone," at least in this sense: he has read the studies by those who have spent a lifetime reading Ecclesiastes (Pedersen, von Rad, among others). But I think his point is well taken. Ellul has absorbed the thoughts of others into his thoughts, arranged them, and set them down through his own extensive—and slow! ("slogged," he writes)—reading of the text itself. Ellul is not simply writing what he "feels" but what he has experienced as a reader; his experience of the text itself involves listening to those who have read the text and written through their knowledge and experience. Ellul is in a company of readers, but writes with his own voice. The distinction is important because he thus steers clear of merely reflecting the studies or opinions of others or lapsing into a pietism.

3. Davis, *Proverbs, Ecclesiastes, and the Song of Songs*; Fox, *Ecclesiastes*. These commentaries are not randomly chosen. They are commentaries in a more traditional sense than Ellul's study, but both authors are writing for lay people, pastors, and rabbis, and I know both to be very good readers of Scripture.

4 Ellul, *Reason for Being*, 3.

In an important footnote, Ellul spells this approach out a bit more by invoking the Jewish tradition of four kinds of interpretation: literal, allegorical, homiletical, and the "seed of life, from which new mysteries of meaning continually spring up." He believes that Qoheleth (the Hebrew term for the "preacher," and the name of Ecclesiastes often used in Jewish writings regarding this book) has given us a text where "new mysteries of meaning spring up, with or without new scientific methods."[5] Here Ellul quite clearly points to what he considers the limits of modern commentary, hinting at why he writes without those aids ready at hand. Ellul recognizes that however important philological and historical research is (and he clearly values these researches), a text is brought to life as readers open themselves to the forms and thought of the book, then thoughtfully respond.

The point that reading a text is more than simply understanding the words on the page is worth belaboring. Nicholas Lash talks of "performing" Scripture, of taking the marks on the page and making them alive in our life, much as a musician takes the notes of a sonata and realizes them in a recital. "The performance of scripture is the life of the church."[6] Ellul does not use this language, but it is implicit in his reading. In his discussion of this point, Lash similarly adheres to the importance of the historical-critical method, but also its limitation. Ellul and Lash (and others) see the reader doing more than making critical notes on a biblical text; as readers of Scripture, we move beyond simple comment to truths that must be lived out in our lives.

It is worth noting that both Davis and Fox make similar assertions about the role of interpretation. Fox, interacting with the tradition of Jewish midrash, recognizes that one role of an interpreter is to draw out "the fullness of meaning potential" in a passage.[7] Davis speaks of the medieval practice of "chewing" on the words of scripture. She wisely writes, "We are now a society that 'processes' words rather than one that ponders them."[8] As we shall see, both Fox and Davis are more restrained in their comments than Ellul; but I suspect this is more of an editorial constraint than an authorial one.

An example might help show how the subtle differences between Davis, Fox, and Ellul play themselves out. Eccl 12:12–14, the "epilogue" to the book, poses problems. First, Qoheleth is spoken of in the third person and no longer in the reflective first person that we find throughout most of the book (e.g., Eccl 1:13–14). There are also interpretive problems involving

---

5. Ellul, *Reason for Being*, 7.

6. Lash, *Theology on the Way to Emmaus*, 43.

7. Fox, *Ecclesiastes*, xxii. *Midrash* refers to both ancient Jewish writings on Scripture and to a method of interpretation.

8. Davis, *Proverbs, Ecclesiastes, and the Song of Songs*, 3.

what certain words mean in this context, and what they refer to beyond simple translation of a term.

Davis, Fox, and Ellul all agree that these verses are not a "pious" conclusion that is tacked on to an otherwise radical book, as has often been a line of interpretation linked with the rise of historical criticism.[9] Rather, these words are in keeping with the scope of the book; fearing God and God's judgment are not alien to the book. To support this view, Fox cites Eccl 3:17 and 11:9 on the judgment of God, and 5:5 and 7:18 on the fear of God. In adopting this approach, all three are trying to come to terms with the complexity of the book as a literary document, but also with the complexity of the thought of Qoheleth.

To what, however, do the words "they were given by one shepherd" refer? The translation is transparent; there is nothing ambiguous about the words. But to whom do they refer? We find different ways of explaining the "one shepherd" in Davis, Fox, and Ellul. Davis appeals to the shepherd as a moral authority, one who "goads" the sheep to new pastures where they will thrive and not overgraze the very ground that feeds them. She goes on to ask who might fulfill this role in our society. She answers, "Few teachers or clergy, or even fewer politicians."[10] She reflects on the role advertising has had on our attention to words and how slogans, euphemisms, and so forth have curtailed our ability to grapple with the complexity of truth, and to change our way of thinking and acting. These reflections, I think, would delight Ellul, though it is not the line of interpretation that he takes with this passage.

Fox gives a rather lengthy discussion of "shepherd." In the traditional interpretations of the rabbis, the term almost always referred to God. According to Fox, the rabbis say that even the words of someone as unconventional as Qoheleth derive from God. The rabbis often have this "extraordinary openness" to different interpretations of Torah. Fox questions this interpretation, however. Rather, the metaphor of shepherd usually refers to protecting and providing, not the giving of words. The words of the wise are not, in Fox's view, like that of law or prophecy. Fox settles on "sages" (not God) prodding people; hence the warning that follows: be careful, sages can overwhelm you with all their ideas (v. 12). This interpretation is similar to Davis in saying that the "shepherd" refers to the sages, not God, but differs in that Davis is lamenting the lack of sage advice in our society, whereas Fox focuses on the warning of endlessly listening to other people's

---

9. See Barton, *Ecclesiastes*. Barton calls the whole section a "late editor's praise of Qoheleth," and the final verses a "Chasid's [a pious person's] last gloss" (197).

10. Davis, *Proverbs, Ecclesiastes, and the Song of Songs*, 226.

advice. Ellul, I think, would find this last part sage advice from Fox; but this is not the approach that he takes.

Ellul goes in another direction. He focuses on the words "all has been heard," interpreting this line in two ways and at considerable length. First, God has heard all and "collects" these words, for which you will be judged (citing Matt 12:37). Second, all has been heard, we cannot go beyond the words of Qoheleth; we have reached "Land's End." From this interpretation, the injunction to fear God and keep his commandments is all that need be said, and Ellul reflects on what "fear–respect" and "listening–obedience" mean for the Christian. It is from these two poles that "the truth and being of a person burst forth."[11]

However, in a footnote (presumably written after Ellul's initial meditation on the text), Ellul draws upon a doctoral dissertation by Jacques Chopineau who ties the phrase "one shepherd" to Ps 80:1, "O Shepherd of Israel, hear . . . " and interprets the reference to God (as in the traditional interpretation). Ellul admits that he "spontaneously wanted" to interpret these words as a reference to God (and, hence, God's revelation), but felt "uncertain" and therefore did not mention that in the reflection proper.[12]

Ellul then goes on in the footnote to reflect on this interpretation.[13] If God is the true shepherd ("one"; Hebrew 'echad), then this ties and contrasts with Abel/Hevel ("vanity"), Abel being a shepherd also. God, the true shepherd, is the opposite of hevel/vanity. The book is thematically structured around the various vanities, but God is opposite by giving us his commandments, which constitute the "whole person" when we live by them. Chopineau thus gives Ellul further support for his interpretation of the Epilogue as a whole, that fear–obedience, the encounter with God, and our listening–obedience liberates our whole being. God as the One Shepherd gives us the commandments. In this respect Ellul goes beyond both Davis and Fox, though Davis might be more sympathetic to the revelatory nature of the shepherd/sage and the connection with the commandments.

Davis, Fox, and Ellul agree that fear of God and keeping commandments are the sum of the teaching of Ecclesiastes. Davis concludes her comments by invoking the Book of Common Prayer: "Therefore, orienting our lives toward the commandments enables us, 'while we are placed among things that are passing away, to hold fast to those who endure.'"[14] Ellul would quite agree. Fox

11. Ellul, *Reason for Being*, 299.

12. See Ellul, *Reason for Being*, 291–92, n56.

13. It is not clear to me if this reflection is part of Chopineau's interpretation or Ellul carrying it forward in his own inimitable way. I suspect the latter.

14. Davis, *Proverbs, Ecclesiastes, and the Song of Songs*, 228; the citation comes from the *Book of Common Prayer*, 234.

says, "The book allows readers to probe the ways of God and man, wherever this may lead, so long as we make the fear of God and obedience to the Commandments the final standard of behavior."[15]

To answer my question at the beginning of this chapter as to how Ellul's reading stands the test of time, I think that it does so rather well. Granted, in picking Davis and Fox, I am perhaps not being entirely fair, since they are both interested in writing for the laity and clergy of the Church and Synagogue; but that is Ellul's audience as well. Ellul lingers more in his reflections than either Davis or Fox. His is, after all, a "meditation" and not a commentary in the narrow sense. Ellul, though, stays close to the text, the Hebrew text in this case. Even in his "gut-level" interpretation of "shepherd" as God, he relegates his comments to a footnote; he is fully aware that this interpretation is not universally accepted, but still in consonant with critical possibilities (a point that Fox makes more sharply than Davis).

I do find it curious that Davis and Fox do not entertain the shepherd–God connection more than they do. That the shepherd is described as "one" seems suggestive in a book that uses words carefully and even playfully, in the sense that Qoheleth wants to tease the reader to consider that the obvious and the less-than-obvious can occupy the same space. Certainly, God as the shepherd is not obvious or necessary; but the fact that commentators have long split on this issue keeps it as a live option to consider. Curiously, Barton notes the options and says that since "shepherd" is usually an epithet of God, it is "probably so here."[16]

A final note on my reading of Ellul this time: in my journey as a reader of Scripture, I have found that good readers of Scripture are often those who have honed their skills as readers generally, not just those who are trained to do exegesis in the narrow sense that is taught in books on exegesis for seminary students. What I mean is that a good reader is one who is not just a technician, but one who has, as Proverbs teaches, learned to "acquire skill, to understand a proverb and a figure, the words of the wise and their riddles" (Prov 1:5b–6). Ellul weaves into his meditations, thoughts, and interactions with biblical scholars (both Christian and Jewish), as we should expect, but also philosophers, anthropologists, novelists, poets, and so forth. Ellul's experience as a reader is wide, which is why he can bring his experiences to the task of writing on Scripture and write with the depth and thoughtfulness that he does.

Ellul's skill as a reader comes out again in his "Preliminary, Polemical, and Nondefinitive Postscript." Ellul objects to commentators that must find

---

15. Fox, *Ecclesiastes*, 85.
16. Barton, *Ecclesiastes*, 198.

a "formal, logical coherence" in Ecclesiastes. This text is not like any other; scholars treat works on Roman law with more "congeniality" than many biblical scholars treat Ecclesiastes. The scholars would have a "purer, more authentic text" than the one we have received in Scripture (I think Ellul has his tongue firmly in cheek at this point!).[17]

Ellul does not say it this way, but the issue at stake is receiving this text as a Hebraic text, I think, and not as a Western text. However much Qoheleth may be interacting with Greek philosophical thought, he is still very much a Hebrew and employs Hebrew forms and Hebrew "logic." The ability to receive a text as it is written is a skill that most of us need to develop as readers of the Bible—especially since our current translations often go out of the way to obscure the differences between the world of biblical texts and our world.[18] We need to learn the language, structure, forms, conventions, and so forth before we can become competent readers of Scripture.[19]

The end of the matter is this: Ellul is a model reader for all of us, though he would be disappointed if we merely repeated what he has taught us and did not build upon his work.

* * *

Addendum

A few reflective thoughts reading this essay after the intervening years of its publication:

I wonder what Ellul would do if he were writing this commentary on Ecclesiastes today. Would issues of gender, global warming, migration, and so forth show their face in his comments? I would dearly love to hear what he has to say about our technological advances and social media. A hearty yet gracious, "I told you so . . . "? I suspect it would be more of a gentle, perhaps tired sigh, much as the "Preacher" of Ecclesiastes says, "Of making many books there is no end, and much study is a *weariness of the flesh*" (Eccl 12:12, italics added).

I think Ellul's meditation on Ecclesiastes has held up well over time, in the same manner as the works of Gregory of Nyssa, Luther, and Ellen Davis.

---

17. See Ellul, *Reason for Being*, 6–16 for a fuller treatment of Ellul's objections to some of the critical stances by biblical scholars.

18. Fox, *Five Books of Moses* is a wonderful counter example to the trend to be "contemporary."

19. I am thinking here not so much of form-criticism as Hebraic rhetorical forms of narrative and poetry. Form criticism often becomes reductionist rather than illuminating the poetic elements in a psalm, for example.

Like these individuals, Ellul's study shows him to be a generous, gracious reader (though he can certainly be polemical at times!). George MacDonald ends his story *The Wise Woman* with a word to his readers, "If you think [the story] is not finished—I never knew a story that was. I could tell you a great deal more concerning them all, but I have told more than is good for those who read *but with their foreheads* . . . " (italics added).

"Forehead" is a lovely, telling image about reading—or even an approach to life. I think the "Preacher" (Ecclesiastes) would smile knowingly at that image.

Ellul had said of his own work in the "Preliminary, Polemical, Non-definitive Postscript" (chapter 1): "This approach [not going to the commentaries first as he wrote, but letting his years of study and meditation on Ecclesiastes guide him] seemed to me to be consistent with Ecclesiastes: once you have acquired a certain knowledge and experience, you must walk alone, without repeating what others have said."[20]

This is perhaps the wisest approach to all our thoughts and writings. The "Preacher" (Ecclesiastes) told us so over two millennia ago: "Fear God. Do what he tells you. And that's it. Eventually God will bring everything that we do out into the open and judge it according to its hidden intent, whether it's good or evil" (Eccl 12:13–14, *The Message*).

Rev. Anthony Petrotta, PhD; Christmastide, 2019.

Works Cited

Barton, G. A. *Ecclesiastes*. Edinburgh: T. & T. Clark, 1908.

The Book of Common Prayer. According to the use of the Episcopal Church. New York: The Church Hymnal Corporation, 1979.

Davis, Ellen F. *Proverbs, Ecclesiastes, and the Song of Songs*. Louisville: Westminster John Knox, 2000.

Ellul, Jacques. *Reason for Being: A Meditation on Ecclesiastes*. Translated by Joyce Main Hanks. Grand Rapids: Eerdmans, 1985.

Fox, Everett. *The Five Books of Moses*. New York: Schocken, 1995.

Fox, Michael V. *Ecclesiastes*. Philadelphia: Jewish Publication Society, 2004.

Lash, Nicholas. *Theology on the Way to Emmaus*. Eugene, OR: Wipf & Stock, 2005.

---

20. Ellul, *Reason for Being*, 3.

CHAPTER 11

The Figure of Jonah in Ellul's Life and Work

JEAN-SÉBASTIEN INGRAND

TRANSLATED BY
JACOB MARQUES ROLLISON

Introduction

THE BIBLICAL BOOK OF Jonah is the "matrix" narrative par excellence:[1] it is as if the original brevity of the text had naturally provoked an infinite plurality of interpretations, appropriations, and metamorphoses, such that every age and generation has reread and appropriated the figure of Jonah. Ellul holds a place in the long lineage of authors who distinguish themselves in the labor of rewriting. In this respect, it is appropriate to examine his commentary on Jonah, which generally goes unnoticed in the long list of his writings.[2] It is true that the French text, which was simultaneously published as an article[3] and a small booklet,[4] was rather unknown for a long time.[5] However, this little book looms large in Ellul's oeuvre.

It is no coincidence that Ellul chose to comment on this portion of the Bible in 1952. Ellul was forty years old and found himself in a particularly

---

1. Bochet, *Jonas palimpseste*, 17, 164.
2. Rare exceptions to this rule include Darrell Fasching and Frédéric Rognon. Cf. Fasching, *Thought of Jacques Ellul*, 137–46; Rognon, *Jacques Ellul*, 83–84, 159–60.
3. Cf. Ellul, "Le livre de Jonas," 81–184.
4. Cf. Ellul, *Le livre de Jonas*.
5. Fortunately, the French text has been republished in Ellul, *Le défi et le nouveau*, 117–98.

prolific and transitional moment as a writer. At this precise moment[6] he wrote two of his most emblematic texts—*The Technological Society*[7] and *The Meaning of the City*[8]—i.e., two books which in many aspects represent his major sociological and foundational theological works. In the former, he describes a world heading inevitably to its doom; in the second, despite everything, he finds reasons to hope in the unfathomable mercies of God. The publication of these two texts closely accompanies his reflections on Jonah.

Moreover, let us note that *The Judgement of Jonah* complements *Presence in the Modern World*, the book which Ellul considered to be the general introduction to his whole oeuvre, which appeared four years earlier.[9] Both books were born amidst Ellul's active engagement in various groups: the *Associations professionelles protestantes* in France, the *Centre protestant d'études* in Geneva, and international ecumenical circles. Alongside prestigious theologians, he discussed themes such as "the Christian in modern society" and "Man's Disorder and God's Design" at length.[10] In this setting, Ellul's will to urge all Christians to an authentic presence in the world, a revolutionary presence turned towards a specific new style of life, comes out. This will is as notable in *Presence in the Modern World* as in *The Judgement of Jonah*.[11] The latter book allowed him to develop and refine a point which he only evoked in the former book: what is the particular role of the prophetic dimension among Christians?

This commentary on Jonah is interesting for reasons linked to two complementary phenomena: first, the influence of a decisive personal

---

6. *Judgement of Jonah* seems to have been written between 1950 and 1952: cf. Ellul, *L'Apocalypse*, 14n2.

7. Cf. Ellul, *La technique ou l'enjeu du siècle*.

8. *Meaning of the City* seems to have been written between 1947 and 1951: cf. Ellul, *Sans feu ni lieu*, 297; Goddard, *Living the Word, Resisting the World*, 76n58. Most of the fifth chapter (231–61) was already published in 1950: cf. Ellul, "La Bible et la ville"; Ellul, "Urbanisme et théologie biblique."

9. Cf. Ellul, *Présence au monde moderne*. This book seems to have been written already in 1946: cf. Mobbs, *Les origines et les premières années de l'Institut oecuménique de Bossey*, 16; Ellul, *Presence of the Kingdom*, x–xi.

10. Editor's note: Ingrand is referring to writings prepared for the First Assembly of the World Council of Churches, which took place in Amsterdam, August 22–September 4, 1948. These writings are collected in five volumes; Ellul's essay, "The Situation in Europe," is found in vol. III, *The Church and the Disorder of Society* (London: SCM, 1948), 50–60. The opening essay in the volume, "God's Design and the Present Disorder of Civilization," is written by Reinhold Niebuhr. Some other notable contributors to these volumes include Karl Barth, Emil Brunner, Richard Niebuhr, Lesslie Newbigin, Paul Tillich, and John Foster Dulles.

11. Cf. Ellul, *Présence au monde moderne*, 191–98; Ellul, *Le défi et le nouveau*, 110–13.

context. When he began to formulate his life's work, Ellul felt the prophetic calling. My first point, therefore, is that this commentary contains autobiographical elements. Second, Ellul conceives of the universality of the figure of Jonah in connection with the prophetic vocation of all Christians, in the service of all humanity. In the second portion of this paper, I will thus seek to highlight his universalist reading of the book of Jonah.

1. An Autobiographical Reading

Ellul's self-identification with the life of the prophet Jonah is an essential element for understanding the presuppositions underlying his reading of the biblical book.

a. A Revelation followed by a Conversion

In at least two texts, Ellul admits that he identifies with Jonah.[12] For Ellul, this process of identification is possible because the prophetic reality is not limited to era of the Hebrew Bible. Furthermore, the prophetic vocation and the call of Jesus Christ necessarily go together. For Ellul, the Christian is thus called by definition to fulfill the function of the prophet.[13] According to Matthew (12:39–41, 16:4) and Luke (11:29–32), Jesus says that the only sign given will be that of the prophet Jonah. For Judaism, however, prophecy ended with the biblical prophets. André Neher forcefully describes this approach: " . . . Jewish biblical prophecy . . . precedes any contemporaneity with a Christ. Prophetic time excludes the Parousia; the expectation of the Savior can only be that of an advent, never that of a return. In the Hebrew sense, biblical prophecy stops very precisely where Christianity begins."[14] It must be remembered that historically, Protestantism has at times harbored contested affiliations with the prophetic figures of the Hebrew Bible. As Ellul had been fascinated with the biblical prophets' sociopolitical proclamations since his childhood, assimilating his life and work to theirs was even easier for him.[15] In 1936, it seems he published his first article (which is currently lost) on the prophecies of Hosea.[16]

12. Cf. Ellul, *La foi au prix du doute*, 243; Ellul, "La charrue et l'étoile," 13; Ellul, *Penser globalement agir localement*, 272.

13. Cf. Ellul, *Présence au monde moderne*, 64; Ellul, *Le défi et le nouveau*, 47–48.

14. Neher, *L'essence du prophétisme*, 56.

15. Cf. Ellul, *Perspectives on our Age*, 13; Ellul, *Ellul par lui-même*, 31.

16. I am hopeful that it may be found one day—perhaps in one of the many journals published by French Protestant scouting associations.

But from the beginning, we can discern in Ellul's identification with biblical prophecy a pronounced ambivalence which never fades. On the one hand, he feels the prophetic calling; on the other hand, he violently rejects this cumbersome label. This is part of his constant and lifelong refusal to allow himself to be put into any kind of box.[17] In a 1939 text, he expresses himself quite eloquently on this point: " . . . I do not like to play this constant role of protester, of a small prophet in my corner. What [I] write has no value except for a profound conviction, and a maturing in prayer, by the grace of God."[18] Indeed, Ellul will go on to be understood as a prophet by a number of his readers, and will increasingly insist on refuting this identity.[19]

In his commentary, Ellul highlights that God apparently chose Jonah for no reason, and that it seems that it even seems to be a choice against all reason. The biblical story of Jonah begins when the Word of God is addressed to the prophet and says nothing of what may have happened beforehand. Likewise, in Ellul's thinking, his own work is largely the fruit of the Word of God which imposed itself on him and requisitioned him to be the bearer of this Word. Coming from Ellul's pen, the whole commentary on Jonah's election with regard to his mission strikes as particularly autobiographical.[20] For example, he aims to show that Jonah did not hear words coming from God, but rather that he had experienced a power which manifested itself—despite the textual evidence from the first verse ("The word of YHWH to Jonah"), which immediately recalls its status as a prophetic text, (even if we only know that Jonah is a prophet thanks to 2 Kings 14:25)! For Ellul, this Word of God is power, and it always accomplishes its purpose. He considers that he has personally experienced an election which concerns a mission, in which the presence of God imposed itself on him. We find this in one of two accounts of this experience which he gives: "It was the summer. I was staying at a friend's place in a large, closed dining room. I was translating Goethe's *Faust*. Suddenly it felt like a block of granite had sat down next to me, a completely unmovable presence. I remember writing at that moment: *"If God does not exist, neither do I."*[21]

In my estimation, this triple movement of revelation, conversion (he takes this term very seriously!) to the Christian faith, and prophetic call

---

17. And yet, he is put into this prophetic box quite regularly: e.g., Goure, "Conversation avec Jacques Ellul. Un prophète dans le siècle," 48–53; Drouin, "Un prophète libre," viii.

18. Ellul, "La politique et nous," 181.

19. Cf. Ellul and Chastenet, *Entretiens avec Jacques Ellul*, 166–67.

20. Cf. Ellul, *Le livre de Jonas*, 1520; *Le défi et le nouveau*, 128–32.

21. Ellul, "La charrue et l'étoile"; Ellul, *Penser globalement agir localement*. The other account can be found in Ellul and Chastenet, *Entretiens*, 86–87.

dates from summer 1930.²² While numerous French intellectuals were converting to Catholicism at this time, Ellul was set apart by the prophetic inflections of his protestant choice.²³ We should not stop at Ellul's desire to avoid appearing as a contemporary prophet, and thus as an intellectual of questionable seriousness—a desire which is easily understandable for a university professor. Beyond this refusal and beyond the distinctive label *prophet*, I would like to point out strong resemblances between two accounts of Jonah's and Ellul's vocation.

We must also note that if Ellul chose this particular biblical prophet, he did so because this book is profoundly different from all other prophetic literature—even if it is grouped with the prophetic books in the Hebrew Bible. The difference is that the prophet (and not the Word of God) is at the center of the story told by this book—even though the book says almost nothing about the life of the prophet.²⁴

b. Characteristics of Prophetic Election

For Ellul, there are five principle aspects of Jonah's election which we can also find present in his own life.

First, the Word of God is always singular. The man of God " . . . knows that the meaning and possibility of everything else will come from his personal struggle."²⁵ In other words, election is a personal affair. For example, it makes a person out of Jonah, who

> . . . only matters from the moment that the Word of God is upon him. He is personalized at this moment; before he was undoubtedly as important as anyone else, he was an individual, he could have great importance; but he had a destiny; he was submitted to destiny; now he is given a mission, singularized; he rules over destiny, and is called to change history for himself and for others.²⁶

---

22. On conversion, cf. Ellul, "De l'inconséquence," 177–99. On the dating of these moments, cf. Ellul, "From Jacques Ellul . . . ", 5; Ellul, *A temps et contretemps*, 17; Ellul, *Perspectives on Our Age*, 14; Ellul, "Pour plus de vitalité," 26; Elle and Chastenet, *Entretiens*, 86–88; Ellul, *Ellul par lui-même*, 33–34.

23. Cf. Gugelot, *La conversion des intellectuels au catholicisme en France (1885–1935)*.

24. Cf. Ellul, *Le livre de Jonas*, 6; Ellul, *Le défi et le nouveau*, 121. His friend Alphonse Maillot's thinking on this question was the exact opposite of Ellul's: cf. Maillot, *Jonas ou le sourire de Dieu*, 22.

25. Ellul, *L'espérance oubliée*, 247–48.

26. Ellul, *Le livre de Jonas*, 16–17; Ellul, *Le défi et le nouveau*, 129.

And, following Jonah, Ellul considers that the essence of his election is to try to change the world. In the dynamics of this starting point, we must understand the dialectical structure of his work, which constantly moves between sociology and biblical theology. In order to act on the world's development as a Christian prophet, Ellul must understand its essential *sociological* mechanisms. And in order for his message of protest to have an echo, he must grasp the *theological* consequences of the spirit of contradiction which Christian faith bears in relation to the world.[27]

Secondly, individual action does not come with any individualism. The elected human being is certainly singularized, but she remains the representative of a whole. For example, Jonah belongs to the elect people, and even if he is alone, in his solitude he nevertheless belongs to the larger group of witnesses of God. He represents the rest of Israel.

> In reality, Jonah represents the *whole* people of God, and if he is all alone, if he is the sole Remnant, well, he alone still represents the whole people: Israel and the Church. And this is also why God cannot be satisfied with an individual and arbitrary decision from Jonah. When he turns his back and runs, it is not simply Jonah who is at stake, but the whole Church and the world. And God cannot just let him do whatever he wants; this man is no longer independent of God because of the world to which he is sent.[28]

Likewise, Ellul remarks that in his own life, he often felt the weight of his responsibilities, yet this never caused him to turn away from service to the Church. For him, the prophet is more specifically the one charged by God to actively await the coming of his Kingdom when humanity does not know what they are doing (cf. John 4:11)[29] and Christians have stopped expecting this Kingdom. He has no qualms about saying so in his particular style:

> The kingdom comes, Christ returns by way of the one who awaits with this unrelenting firmness, with this unfailing rigor, with this exalted fervor, this obstinance which refuses to let anything divert it. The kingdom comes, Christ returns in this one alone, but not *for* this one alone. It is for everyone, just as the sentinel watches for everyone; as the prophet keeps watch for everyone.[30]

---

27. Cf. Ellul, *A temps et à contretemps*, 187; Goddard, *Living the Word, Resisting the World*, 154–64.

28. Ellul, *Le livre de Jonas*, 17; Ellul, *Le défi et le nouveau*, 129.

29. Cf. Ellul, *La raison d'être*, 266–67.

30. Ellul, *L'espérance oubliée*, 248.

A third aspect is that this election is always linked to a specific action, and God always perseveres in his choice. The Word spoken by God does not simply announce; it commits the man who receives it to a precise action. The singularization of a field of work is proper to election. "And when God has chosen a man who must fulfill a function, he never looks back ... He has chosen him for a precise action, and as long as this action is not accomplished, God pursues man. This is the case for all men in the Bible, even Judas."[31] Relying on biblical narratives and on his own experience, Ellul remarks that the singular man chosen by God enters into a relation in which he does not choose between *yes* and *no*, but in which he is led by God to say *yes*. The prophet is both the freest and the least free among men and women. He is freer because this Word obliges him to break with the world, and less free because he is committed to a mission which he did not desire. "And this adventure, in which man is obliged to go all in on a freedom which is given to him (but given only for this adventure), appears to be extraordinarily important for God. In a way, God commits himself to the work in which he engages man."[32] In the story of Jonah, the surest sign that this election is a serious matter is found in the outburst of natural forces in which human lives are at stake. All available means are employed to make the inflexible and stubborn man of God yield.

The fourth aspect is that election is always followed by a double phenomenon of the prophet's flight and acceptance. In the Bible, God's election of a person almost always goes together with this person's flight, until they end up accepting their mission. The formulation given in Jonah 1:3 insists on this flight, and on the terrible collective responsibility borne by the prophet. "The formula 'from God's presence' seems to indicate that the flight is a refusal of the prophetic ministry: one of the tasks of the prophet is indeed to remain *in God's presence* (cf. 1 Kgs 18:15, 22:21; Jer 15:19, 18:20)."[33] André Neher called this this classic phenomenon a state of *heaviness*.[34] Jonah is emblematic of the biblical prophet who refuses the action of God's hand upon him. Ellul understood this very well: " ... if one of my first books was *The Judgement of Jonah*, it is because from a spiritual point of view, my brutal conversion was followed by a frantic flight which lasted for years."[35]

Finally, the fifth aspect of election is that it implies a very demanding vocation: God clearly demands the impossible, always. From a purely

---

31. Ellul, *Le livre de Jonas*, 18; Ellul, *Le défi et le nouveau*, 130.
32. Ellul, *Le livre de Jonas*, 19; Ellul, *Le défi et le nouveau*, 131.
33. Lichtert, *Traversée du récit de Jonas*, 16.
34. Cf. Neher, *L'essence du prophétisme*, 320–33.
35. Ellul, *A temps et à contretemps*, 190.

human level, Jonah is absolutely right to head directly away from Nineveh, simply for fear of death. In Ellul's perspective, Nineveh is obviously a metaphor for the contemporary world.

> But above all, we must put the word 'Nineveh' back in its biblical perspective: Nineveh, the great city, like Babylon, is the place of man's omnipotence, man's counter-creation opposed to the creation of God, the place of human pride which allies itself with demons but rejects God, the world closed to God. In the spiritual sense, what Nineveh represents still exists . . . The drama is thus . . . profound. God commands Jonah to go precisely where he cannot go—like light into darkness. Nineveh is definitively "the world" in the theological sense of the term.[36]

Nineveh is the archetype of the cruel and bloodthirsty city which divinizes war, opposing both the people of God and God himself.[37] Like Babylon, she is the antitype of the new Jerusalem in the book of Revelation. In his work, Ellul frequently revisited this archetypal question of the city.[38]

2. A Universalist Reading

If Ellul strongly accentuates the prophetic vocation of Christians, he equally performs a universalist reading of the book of Jonah. Incidentally, this passage from the unique to the universal corresponds to the movement at the very heart of the biblical text.

a. A Universal Figure

Ellul highlights that the vocation of the prophet Jonah is surprisingly open to the outside world. He recalls that this biblical book is set apart by the fact that the word of God is not tied to Israel. "Here, the word is spoken to Nineveh and for Nineveh. There is no question of Israel, and this seems singularly striking, since all of the prophets are directly linked to the people of Israel. They are there for Israel, to bring her back to God; the prophet is inconceivable without the chosen people."[39] Ellul is attracted by the fact

---

36. Ellul, *Le livre de Jonas*, 21–22; Ellul, *Le défi et le nouveau*, 133.

37. Cf. Ellul, *Sans feu ni lieu*, 110–17; Ellul, *L'Apocalypse*, 235–36; Ellul, *Conférence sur l'Apocalypse de Jean*, 89–90; Maillot, *Jonas ou le sourire de Dieu*, 53–55; Bochet, *Jonas palimpseste*, 90–98.

38. Cf. Ingrand, "Bernard Charbonneau et Jacques Ellul," 108–16.

39. Ellul, *Le livre de Jonas*, 6; Ellul, *Le défi et le nouveau*, 121.

that the figure of Jonah breaks open the limits of the commonly accepted definition of prophecy. This openness to the outside world indirectly allows for a justifiable existence of a prophecy for today.

On these bases, Ellul seeks to show that the figure of Jonah is a universal figure who concerns the whole of humanity in an intemporal way. There is a subtle link between the personalization of the word by the prophet and his universal vocation. "If Jonah can be a sign *'for this generation'*—the generation of the Son of man, ours, others yet to come—it is because the word which is heard, which is *addressed* to him, belongs to this same universal and personal movement."[40] In other words, for Ellul, every reader of the book of Jonah—whether they are Christian or not—should be able to identify with the life of Jonah, who ultimately lives the story of every human being.[41]

> This agony of Jonah is in truth the agony of every man. Jonah is not the subject of some exceptional adventure. Jonah in the sea and Jonah in the fish is the situation of every one of us, in the crisis of our lives, and not only in the final struggle with death. For there is no great difference between a man who is spiritually dead because he wants to be separated from God, and a man physically engulfed in the raging sea."[42]

b. A Necessary Solidarity

Ellul uses the story of Jonah to affirm that there is a necessary solidarity between Christians and non-Christians. Without knowing it, the sailors are implicated in Jonah's flight. For Ellul, we could say today that non-Christians have set sail with a Christian. They are on the same boat, in the same storm, and their salvation depends on their respective actions. Ellul's insistence on the prophetic calling of Christians shows that this dimension alone can call humanity to change.

> The paradox between the last act of the people's faith and the beginning of the narrative is striking. In verse two, the Ninevites' evil has come up before YHWH. But these men must confront another problem, seeking its origin (YHWH) and cause (Jonah). The account of the action of these men—their marked

---

40. Manigne, *Génération Jonas*, 109.

41. Cf. Ellul, *Le livre de Jonas*, 23, 70; Ellul, *La foi au prix du doute*, 326–27; Bauer, *Le jeu de Dieu et de Jonas*, 28–29; Ellul, *Le défi et le nouveau*, 134, 171.

42. Ellul, *Le livre de Jonas*, 46–47; Ellul, *Le défi et le nouveau*, 153.

respect for the person of Jonah, their fear of YHWH, their conversion—advantageously replaces the initial intrigue aborted by Jonah's flight.[43]

For Ellul, the problem is not always where Christians (quite spontaneously) think it is. In the biblical text, if the sailors clearly play a role of a foil, they are nevertheless the ones who demonstrate religiosity, humanity and solidarity. At the heart of the storm, they do everything humanly possible. Then, they turn to imploring various gods and spiritual powers. Finally, the sailors speak to Jonah—but he does not feel concerned by their shared story. For Ellul, this is because Christians do not fulfill their mission: "Jonah, like Christians, is asleep."[44] And if Jonah decides to sleep in the eye of the storm, this means that he does not want to recognize God's presence therein. Echoing Ellul, Wilhelm Vischer affirms in turn in his provocative *Evangile selon saint Jonas*, [*The Gospel According to Saint Jonah*] that " . . . we cannot form a sleeping [C]hurch at the bottom of the boat of humanity in grave danger. We are the witnesses of Jesus on this boat."[45]

And if non-Christians end up talking to Christians, they do so with the feeling that these latter will be of no use. This is at the bottom of Ellul's incessant remarks on the abuses of institutional churches and the absence of a particular style of life among numerous Christians.

> Non-Christians do not perhaps expect very much from Christians; but on the off-chance, they awaken them anyway, requiring their participation in the drama. They awaken them—i.e., they oblige Christians to become aware of what is happening in reality. Even the very active Christian is distinguished by the fact that he nearly always ignores reality. He is lost in the sleep of his activities, his good works, his chorales, his theology, his evangelization, his communities, and every time he passes right by reality; as for the storm, he sees it as an outsider, not as one involved—even if (contrary to Jonah) he harbors no ill will. And the non-Christians end up obliging him to come out of his sleep and actively take part in their common fate.[46]

For Ellul, this is a recurring event in the history of the Churches (e.g., with Nazism or Communism). On these occasions, God uses non-Christians to awaken Christians.

---

43. Lichtert, *Traversée du récit de Jonas*, 21.
44. Ellul, *Le livre de Jonas*, 25; Ellul, *Le défi et le nouveau*, 136.
45. Vischer, "L'Evangile selon st Jonas [V]," 11.
46. Ellul, *Le livre de Jonas*, 26; Ellul, *Le défi et le nouveau*, 136.

It is thus after his reading of Jonah that Ellul is led to awareness of Christians' responsibility concerning affairs of the world in which they live. These Christians can very well continue to say no to God and sink with the rest of humanity.

> That really is our situation. If Christians divest themselves of their function in the common danger which weighs on the world, if the Christians who have received grace of inestimable value refuse to carry it to the world, well, the others—pagans, non-Christians, those who populate the initiatives in which we find ourselves—will perish. Christians must know that they hold the fate of their traveling companions in their hands. And I am weighing each of these words as I write them.[47]

This necessary solidarity between Christians and non-Christians is one of the essential motifs of the dual structure of Ellul's oeuvre. The two forms of discourse which he proposes (one part sociology and one part biblical theology) are offered to all. Everyone is free to take only one of these parts. For him, it is clear that Christians live in the same world and the same society as non-Christians. But Christians must have a specific message which inserts a gap into this world. Contrary to some of his detractors, Ellul's Christian faith does not lead to any scorn for non-Christians. For Ellul, the prophet Jonah is the paradigm of the universalism of the "in the world but not of it" (cf. Rom 12:2) so dear to him. This story is the archetype of the necessary solidarity between Christians and the rest of humanity.

c. A Performing Word Based on the Benevolence of God

Finally, for Ellul, the story of Jonah shows that God very rarely acts without a human intermediary.[48] He obviously could do without, but this would not be love. "God is not the one who scorns man, but the one who raises him to the dignified status of collaborator in his work. He is the one who patiently awaits man's consent to his work before carrying it out."[49] In this understanding of the story of Jonah *for* Nineveh, each human being is situated in the complete work of God.

Ellul forcefully incites Christians to see the true meaning of and take their inspiration from Jonah's calling for the world. God sends Jonah so that Nineveh would become aware of its situation before God.

---

47. Ellul, *Le livre de Jonas*, 31; Ellul, *Le défi et le nouveau*, 140.
48. Cf. Bauer, *Le jeu de Dieu et de Jonas*, 47.
49. Ellul, *Le livre de Jonas*, 87; Ellul, *Le défi et le nouveau*, 185.

Jonah's preaching is dramatically simple: he explosively announces the judgement and death of Nineveh; and in a mysterious and hidden way (even for himself), he announces its forgiveness. But Nineveh can only grasp this forgiveness if she accepts her condemnation. This is no preaching of a morality . . . It is the preaching of a decision of God. He places Nineveh before the will of God.

Obviously, the powerful Nineveh has every reason to treat Jonah with the greatest scorn, unless she considers him a bearer of a revelation which is unbelievable, but which should be taken into account. "And here we are in the presence of a mystery and a miracle: Nineveh does not react at all in the way that we might humanly expect. Confronted with the authentic preaching of the Word, there is an absolutely unpredictable side to man's reactions."[50] And for Ellul, the specifically Christian calling finds its reason for being in this unpredictability of human beings. Ellul is persuaded that Christians no longer believe in the possible performance of their word. For this to change, they must make their word specific and nonconformist. If at times Ellul wrote and spoke in a rather frenetic way, it is because he was persuaded that his word could have an impact. At a time when the figure of the Christian intellectual was crumbling, he steadfastly insisted that Christians have a message to communicate, and that this message can change the world.

Incidentally, Ellul carefully highlights that this prophetic work of transmitting a message must always begin anew. In chapter four, Jonah adopts the position of a spectator. Like all Christians who impatiently await God's judgement on the wicket, and who set themselves up as judges of other humans, Jonah wants to see, but no longer to do. This attitude is directly contrary to that of Abraham before God's judgement pronounced on Sodom (cf. Gen 18:16–33). Abraham feels a deep solidarity with a city which is not even his own, while Jonah impatiently awaits the destruction of Nineveh.[51] Instead of acting against Nineveh, God does something to benefit Jonah, offering him shade: he replaces the protection which Jonah had made for himself with his own protection. "The story of Jonah is thus doubly prophetic: it announces both a time of universal mercy from God, and the dismay of the man in charge of announcing it and paradoxically bearing its weight."[52]

Thus, for every person inclined to follow in Jonah's footsteps, the " . . . trial is threefold: first, the Word tells me what I have no desire to hear:

---

50. Cf. Abel, "La figure effondrée de l'intellectuel chrétien," 80–90.

51. This perspective is shared by Maillot, but not by Bauer: cf. Maillot, *Jonas ou le sourire de Dieu*, 90–99; Bauer, *Le jeu de Dieu et de Jonas*, 64–65.

52. Manigne, *Génération Jonas*, 13.

'Rise and go to Nineveh'; then, it tells me to say what I do not want to say: 'Yet forty days and Nineveh will be destroyed'; and finally, and most beautifully, it surpasses the expectations of the messenger."[53] In the end, and despite himself, Jonah reveals a God who is disconcerting, and profoundly merciful. If the hopelessness of Nineveh's inhabitants is the source of God's concern, then the horizon of this whole story—and of Ellul's entire thought—is the unexpected goodness of God. Humanity ultimately awaits this proclamation, yet only rarely do Christians dare to formulate it. It is precisely in the parallel work of writing "his" Jonah and his biblical theology of the city that Ellul is progressively led to think the universal salvation of all creation in the new Jerusalem.[54]

Conclusion

A detour through *The Judgement of Jonah*, a frequently forgotten work of Ellulian exegesis, is full of surprises. I purposely avoided an examination of his very Christological exegesis, which is strongly influenced by Wilhelm Vischer's *The Witness of the Old Testament to Christ*, and which poses incontestable hermeneutical questions.[55] I have tried to show that his reading of the book of Jonah is profoundly original. It is also symptomatic his manner of reading a biblical text, which manifests a nearly interactive labor of a preacher and his audience. On the one hand, he has a very personal way of implicating the reader in the work of commenting on the text. He has also written all his other commentaries in the first and third person, provoking the reader to take up a position.[56] Indeed, the reader is almost invited to become part of the biblical story itself. On the other hand, his way of approaching the Bible is very subjective and personal. It is never a sort of dead text which could be dissected disinterestedly. For Ellul, the Bible possesses a remarkable power to pose questions for today.

In certain aspects, the reading of Jonah performed by Ellul is dated. Nevertheless, we must not take this work lightly on the pretext that some sixty or seventy years have gone by since its publication. Ellul's fascination for Jonah was not restricted to this commentary; he never abandoned it,

---

53. Manigne, *Génération Jonas*, 120.

54. Cf. Ellul, *Sans feu ni lieu*, 249–61; Ellul, *L'Apocalypse*, 232–43; Ellul, *Conférence sur l'Apocalypse de Jean*, 81–93; Goddard, *Living the Word, Resisting the World*, 87–91; Rognon, *Jacques Ellul*, 85–87 and 98–100.

55. Cf. Vischer, *Witness of the Old Testament to Christ*. On these questions, cf. Maly, "Jacques Ellul, Meaning of the City," 255; Maillot, *Jonas ou le sourire de Dieu*, 8.

56. Cf. Pigeaud, "Regard sur Ellul bibliste," 10–11.

though it remained hidden for some time. Among his theological works, traces of this fascination are quite common.[57] It is visible in the subtitle of his book *La foi au prix du doute* (translated as *Living Faith*) nearly thirty years later: "Encore quarante jours . . . " ["Yet forty days . . . "] (cf. Jonah 3:4). He asserts his dependence on the figure of the prophet Jonah yet again: " . . . I . . . desire infinitely that Nineveh would not be destroyed, just as Jonah's prophecy was not executed. But I had to cry out, just as one must cry out today."[58] And with some disillusionment, he adds: "I tried everything. I seized every opportunity which seemed suitable. I thought so much. I have only been able to understand what happened . . . I saw correctly. I spoke. I warned. It was useless."[59]

To a large extent, it is possible to understand Ellul's oeuvre as an extension of the prophetic call which he said he had received. Certain critics employ this to affirm that his socio-political studies are *nothing but* the fruit of his Christian faith, and thus to be rejected as a whole.[60] All this happens in the name of the " . . . narrow-minded positivism of our culture, which (as Kant had already observed) never ceases to swing from excessive gullibility to excessive disbelief, in a monotheistic conception of the truth and reality which no monotheism ever dared to imagine."[61] The recurring accusations derived from scientism brought to bear on Ellul's oeuvre are an insult to his intellectual honesty. Even if, on occasion, he permitted himself inexact affirmations and pointless polemics, his Christian faith did not prevent him from showing a true scientific rigor, in both his sociology and his theology. This honesty even gives him the courage to call himself a prophet before the world of intellectuals, all while knowing that no prophet is welcome in his hometown (cf. Matt 13:57; Mark 6:4; Luke 4:24). In the light of his current notoriety in North America, we can confirm this statement.

Works Cited

Abel, Olivier. "La figure effondrée de l'intellectuel chrétien." *ContreTemps* 15 (2006) 80–90.

Bauer, Olivier. *Le jeu de Dieu et de Jonas. Grille de lecture pour un livre déroutant*. Poliez-le-Grand: Le Moulin, 1996.

---

57. Cf. Ellul, *La foi au prix du doute*, 241–327; Rognon, *Jacques Ellul*, 159–65.

58. Ellul, *La foi au prix du doute*, 244.

59. Ellul, *La foi au prix du doute*, 254.

60. Cf. Jacob, *Le retour de "L'Ordre nouveau,"* 185, 188; "Le paysan et le philosophe: José Bové et Jacques Ellul," 198–99.

61. Abel, "La figure effondrée de l'intellectuel chrétien," 90.

Bochet, Marc. *Jonas palimpseste. Réécritures littéraires d'une figure biblique*. Le livre et le rouleau. Brussels: Lessius, 2006.

Drouin, P. "Un prophète libre. Sur la pensée foisonnante de Jacques Ellul." *Le monde* 18134 (May 16, 2003) viii.

Ellul, Jacques. *Conférence sur l'Apocalypse de Jean*. Nantes: Editions de l'AREFPPI, 1985.

———. "De l'inconséquence." In *Denis de Rougemont. L'écrivain. L'Européen. Etudes et témoignages publiés pour le soixante-dixième anniversaire de Denis de Rougemont*, edited by André Reszler and Henri Schwamm, 177–90. Langages. Neuchâtel: La Baconnière, 1976.

———. *Ellul par lui-même. Entretiens avec Willem H. Vanderburg*. Edited with notes by Michel Hourcade, Jean-Pierre Jézéquel, and Gérard Paul. La petite vermillon 311. Paris: La Table Ronde, 2008.

———. "From Jacques Ellul . . . " In *Introducing Jacques Ellul*, edited by James Holloway, 5–7. Grand Rapids: Eerdmans, 1970.

———. "La Bible et la ville." *Foi et Vie* 48 (1950) 4–19.

———. "La charrue et l'étoile." Interview with Jean-Claude Raspiengeas. *Télérama* 1956 (1987) 12–15.

———. *La foi au prix du doute. "Encore quarante jours . . . "* Paris: Hachette, 1980.

———. "La politique et nous." *Le Semeur* 42 (1938–1939) 177–81.

———. *L'Apocalypse. Architecture en mouvement. L'athéisme interrogee*. Paris: Desclée, 1975.

———. *La raison d'être. Méditation sur l'Ecclésiaste*. Paris: Le Seuil (coll. *Empreintes*), 1987.

———. *La technique ou l'enjeu du siècle*. Paris: Armand Colin (coll. *Sciences politiques*), 1954.

———. *Le défi et le nouveau. OEuvres théologiques 1948–1991*. Paris: La Table Ronde, 2006.

———. "Le livre de Jonas." *Foi et Vie* 50 (1952) 81–184.

———. *Le livre de Jonas*. Cahiers bibliques de Foi et Vie. Paris: Foi et Vie, 1952.

———. *L'espérance oubliée*. Voies ouvertes. Paris: Gallimard, 1972.

———. *Penser globalement agir localement. Chroniques journalistiques*. Monein: PyréMonde, 2007.

———. *Perspectives on our Age. Jacques Ellul Speaks on His Life and Work*. Edited by Willem H. Vanderburg. Translated by Joachim Neugroschel. Toronto: Canadian Broadcasting Corporation, 1981.

———. *Présence au monde moderne. Problèmes de la civilisation post-chrétienne*. Geneva: Roulet (*Centre protestant d'études*), 1948.

———. *Presence of the Kingdom*. Colorado Springs: Helmers & Howard, 1982.

———. *Sans feu ni lieu. Signification biblique de la Grande Ville*. Paris: Gallimard (coll. *Voies ouvertes*), 1975.

———. "The Situation in Europe." In *The Church and the Disorder of Society*, 50–60. London: SCM, 1948.

———. *A temps et contretemps. Entretiens avec Madeleine Garrigou-Lagrange*. Paris: Le Centurion, 1981.

———. "Urbanisme et théologie biblique." *Dieu vivant* 16 (1950) 107–23.

Ellul, Jacques, and Patrick Chastenet. *Entretiens avec Jacques Ellul*. Paris: La Table Ronde, 1994.

Fasching, Darrell. *The Thought of Jacques Ellul: A Systematic Exposition*. Toronto Studies in Theology 7. New York: Edwin Mellen, 1981.

Goddard, Andrew. *Living the Word, Resisting the World. The Life and Thought of Jacques Ellul*. Paternoster Biblical and Theological Monographs. Carlisle: Paternoster, 2002.

Goure, C., ed. "Conversation avec Jacques Ellul. Un prophète dans le siècle." *Panorama. Le mensuel chrétien* 215 (1987) 48–53.

Gugelot, Frédéric. *La conversion des intellectuels au catholicisme en France (1885–1935)*. Paris: CNRS, 1998.

Ingrand, Jean-Sébastien. "Bernard Charbonneau et Jacques Ellul: des critiques similaires de la grande ville, au nom de la liberté." In *Bernard Charbonneau: habiter la terre. Actes du colloque du 2-4 mai 2011. Université de Pau et des pays de l'Adour*, 108–16. Pau: Université de Pau et des pays de l'Adour, 2012.

Jacob, Jean. "Le paysan et le philosophe: José Bové et Jacques Ellul." *Hérodote. Revue de géographie et de géopolitique* 113 (2004) 174–204.

———. *Le retour de "L'Ordre nouveau." Les métamorphoses d'un fédéralisme européen*. Travaux de sciences sociales 188. Geneva: Droz, 2002.

Lichtert, Claude. *Traversée du récit de Jonas*. Connaître la Bible 33. Bruxelles: Lumen Vitae, 2003.

Maillot, Alphonse. *Jonas ou le sourire de Dieu*. Paris: Lethielleux, 1997.

Maly, Eugene H. "Jacques Ellul, *The Meaning of the City* (Grand Rapids: Eerdmans, 1970)." *The Catholic Biblical Quarterly* 33 (1971) 255.

Manigne, Jean-Pierre. *Génération Jonas. Un prophète pour notre temps*. Chrétiens en liberté. Paris: Karthala, 2004.

Mobbs, Arnold. *Les origines et les premières années de l'Institut oecuménique de Bossey. Recueil de "souvenirs personnels."* Céligny: Institut oecuménique de Bossey, 1983.

Neher, André. *L'essence du prophétisme*. Epiméthée. Essais philosophiques. Paris: PUF, 1955.

Pigeaud, Olivier. "Regard sur Ellul bibliste." *The Ellul Forum for the Critique of Technological Civilization* 33 (2004) 9–11.

Rognon, Frédéric. *Jacques Ellul: Une pensée en dialogue*. Le champ éthique 48. Geneva: Labor et Fides, 2007.

Vischer, Wilhelm. "L'Evangile selon st Jonas [V]." *Réforme* 1233 (1968) 11.

———. *The Witness of the Old Testament to Christ*. London: Lutterwort, 1949.

CHAPTER 12

Reading 2 Kings with Jacques Ellul

CHRIS FRIESEN

2 Kings Revisited

STUDYING JACQUES ELLUL CAN make you want to read your Bible again.[1] I have experienced this effect both times in my life that I pored over *The Politics of God and the Politics of Man*, Ellul's penetrating study of the biblical book of 2 Kings. If the so-called "hermeneutics of suspicion" have undermined the possibility of a vital personal encounter with the Word of God in Scripture for many in our era, what we might call the "hermeneutics of avoidance" may be equally to blame. Many of us who claim to believe what we read in the Bible still skirt widely around certain landscapes of the Good Book for fear of what might blow up underneath us if we dare step there: whether scientific or cultural embarrassments, words that damage hope, or stories and images that seem impossible to reconcile with the love of God— both God's love for us, and our love for God. When was the last time you read 2 Kings devotionally? When was the last time you heard or preached a sermon on it? But Jacques Ellul has taken a biblical minefield and turned it into a treasure trove, modeling a creative and faithful hermeneutic as inspiring as the conclusions it draws.

Second Kings narrates the troubled political history of neighbouring Judea and Israel (products of the ten-versus-two tribal split that took place after David) from the death of Ahab to the fall of Jerusalem, emphasizing the interventions of God and his prophetic representative Elisha throughout that period. Viewing 2 Kings as "probably the most political of all the

---

1. This chapter presents an expanded version of an essay published in *The Ellul Forum* 6 (Fall 2005) 14–16.

books of the Bible,"[2] Ellul drew out two themes which he considered the book's preeminent witness. The first is the tangled risk, futility, and necessity of human action in the political realm, with "politics" understood narrowly as "the discharge of a directive function in a party or state organism" and broadly as "the sphere of the greatest affirmation of man's autonomy, of his revolt, of his pretentious attempt to play the role of God."[3] The second theme is the interaction of human freedom with divine sovereignty and foreknowledge, a grappling with the enigma of how "these deliberate acts which men do for their own reasons and according to their own calculations are the very ones which accomplish just what God had decided and was expecting";[4] how, from Eden to Calvary and beyond, "God finally accomplishes his purpose at the heart of our disobedience."[5] In relation to both themes—that is, politics and freedom—a set of questions runs through *The Politics of God and the Politics of Man*: Does human action mean anything? Does it accomplish anything? How does God relate to it? To what degree does he compel, negate, permit, or invite it? The book's brief concluding "Meditation on Inutility" brings a degree of resolution to the inquiry, proposing (even as it flirts with the pessimism of which Ellul is often accused) that "to do a gratuitous, ineffective, and useless act is the first sign of our freedom and perhaps the last."[6]

An Existential Reading

Those fascinated by the problems of political action and historical determinism, human efficacy and divine miracle, will find much grist for the mill in *Politics of God*. The present essay, however, is most interested in how Ellul's signature hermeneutics are on display in this book, as seen in the unapologetically Christocentric opening sentence—"All the stories we shall read are set in the perspective of Jesus Christ"[7]—and in the preliminary footnote differentiating Ellul's approach from the methods and interests of historical-critical study: "We are not pretending to be doing scientific work . . . We

---

2. Ellul, *Politics of God and the Politics of Man*, 13.
3. Ellul, *Politics of God and the Politics of Man*, 14.
4. Ellul, *Politics of God and the Politics of Man*, 16.
5. Ellul, *Politics of God and the Politics of Man*, 19.
6. Ellul, *Politics of God and the Politics of Man*, 198.
7. Ellul, *Politics of God and the Politics of Man*, 9. The prophet Elisha—whose miracles prefigure those of Jesus much as his relationship to Elijah prefigures Jesus's relationship to John the Baptist—represents for Ellul the type and image of Christ throughout the narrative, as he deftly outlines in the book's introduction.

shall adopt the simple attitude of the believer with his Bible who through the text that he reads is ultimately trying to discover what is the Word of God, and what is the final meaning of his life in the presence of this text."[8] One can characterize Ellul's hermeneutic approach as existential as opposed to legal, doctrinal, antiquarian, or even literary. Though not disregarding the data and hypotheses generated by the history-of-religions school, his interpretative work is not contingent on the form or development of the received text. Instead, it focuses on the dynamics of the human-divine drama playing out in the text, a drama in which we too are ongoing participants. Ellul prefers to look "along the beam" rather than "at it,"[9] believing that the best opportunity to encounter divine revelation arises by giving the narrative the simple benefit of the doubt. In the politically charged stories of 2 Kings, he maintains, "we are in the presence of life itself at its most profound and most significant. We must not let it slip away from us."[10]

What gives these stories any more significance than, say, Greek tragedy? It is that the Bible is not just a text among texts but the unique channel and locus of the Word of God—understood not only as God's message to individuals and situations but also as the action of God, the event of God, and above all, the incarnate presence of God in Christ, who is himself the Word par excellence. Hence, the Bible is the word of the Word in a singular manner. Ellul is absolutely firm on this point, occasionally throwing down the gauntlet: "Either Israel is the chosen people and receives a revelation from God, so that what it holds, transcribes, and transmits is a Word of God and not its own ideas, or Israel is not the chosen people and its ideas and myths and writings are of no more interest than those of the Aztecs or the Japanese."[11]

As Ellul applies his existential hermeneutic to 2 Kings, he engages the profound drama of that book through a series of character studies. He does not aim to draw moralizing "life lessons" or gather tips for good behavior, but rather to reveal each character's essential relation to the Word of God set before them. The characters believe or do not believe. They play their roles or abdicate them. According to their interests and natures, they may ignore the Word or try to commandeer it. We meet several commendable models: Naaman, the leprous general of Aram who ultimately accepts the modest and contestable invitations God presents to him; Hezekiah, the imperiled

8. Ellul, *Politics of God and the Politics of Man*, 12.

9. The two postures are contrasted in C. S. Lewis's "Meditation in a Toolshed" as an analogy for intellectual objectification versus sympathetic participation in a text or belief system.

10. Ellul, *Politics of God and the Politics of Man*, 16.

11. Ellul, *Politics of God and the Politics of Man*, 27.

king of Judah who recognizes the limits of politics and bring the alarming taunts of his enemy directly to the Lord; and of course, Elisha, prophet of the Eternal in solidarity with his people, who presents the Word and withdraws to let matters and individuals take their course. We also meet several cautionary models: Joram, the despairing king of besieged Samaria who would assassinate a prophet to get even with God; Joram's officer, who like his master is skeptical of the miracle of liberation and provision about to break upon them, and thereby forfeits it; Hazael, the usurping king of Aram, who enters eagerly through the gate a heartbroken Elisha opens before him to become the scourge of Israel; Jehu, the cunning and ferocious "religious cleanser" for whom the end justifies the means; Ahaz, an efficient political deal-maker who conforms the worship of Yahweh to the religion of his overlords; and finally, Rabshakeh, the Assyrian propagandist who heaps scorn, intimidation, and enticement on the people of Jerusalem just before his own nation's inexorable campaign unexpectedly collapses.

During this astute survey of characters, Ellul often turns his gaze abruptly to the contemporary landscape and shows us how we as church, state, world, and humankind are confronted with the same kinds of situations these ancient people faced. The same powers beckon accommodation and worship; the same faith is required in resistance. For example, when Naaman asks Elisha for forgiveness in advance since he will be continuing to bow before Rimmon in his role beside the king of Aram, Ellul turns on us: "Are we so sure, when we serve idols, that we can see they are idols? Are we so sure we have the same clarity of vision in relation to the nation, the state, the independence of peoples, socialism, progress, the army, cultures, money, etc . . . Are we so sure we have the honesty not to attempt to reconcile the two?"[12] He considers Naaman's dilemma to be the position of "every conscientious Christian who takes part in any way in the activity of society."[13] In a similar sudden turn to the present, Ellul brings into sharp relief the "frighteningly modern speech" made to Jerusalem by the Assyrian field commander, who becomes the archetype of both the modern world addressing the church ("Poor people . . . You are led astray by stories and fables. You are indoctrinated by theology, the catechism, and faith in general. We have now come to set you free"[14]) and the tempter addressing the child of God ("All these I will give you, if you will fall down and worship me"[15]). In this way, Ellul's readers become simultaneous targets and beneficiaries of his vigorous existential

---

12. Ellul, *Politics of God and the Politics of Man*, 37.
13. Ellul, *Politics of God and the Politics of Man*, 38.
14. Ellul, *Politics of God and the Politics of Man*, 155.
15. Ellul, *Politics of God and the Politics of Man*, 157; Matt 4:9.

hermeneutic, as well as of his penetrating intertextual imagination[16]—two important benchmarks of his biblical work that emphasize the unity and durability of the Word across time and space.

A Redemptive Reading

With this summary groundwork laid, we can examine Ellul's treatment of a particular character in 2 Kings—Jehu—to illustrate what may be the most integral and distinctive dimension of the Bible reading demonstrated in *Politics of God*: what we can term his "hermeneutic of hope." Underlying Jacques Ellul's trenchant theological and ethical applications of Scripture was a fixed belief in the ultimate redemption of history. While he may often seem to take sides with God and Word over against Man, Church, and World, his critical, dialectical stance operated within a larger trust that God's love would ultimately triumph for every single member of humankind—even those judged and condemned during their earthly sojourn. Discussing soon-to-be dethroned Joram and the skeptical officer trampled to death in 2 Kings 7:20, Ellul writes, "My own conviction is that in all this we simply have a rejection in time, a condemnation for the moment, not eternal damnation . . . *They are put outside God's work but not his love*."[17] For many of us, this conviction makes Ellul a trustworthy guide through some of Scripture's most fraught landscapes, knowing he will never simply leave us in shadow and say, "Sorry, folks, but since God is God, this is just the way things are." His hope-shaped hermeneutic is especially palpable during his analysis of the stimulus and outcome of Jehu's murderous career in 2 Kings 9–10.

In accordance with a word spoken years earlier to Elijah, Jehu is anointed king over Israel in place of the wounded Joram and proceeds to extirpate from the land (also according to prophecy) both Ahab's entire family and Baalism in general. On the face of it, his crusade is a righteous revolution in the name of Yahweh. Yet the manner of Jehu's bloody purge horrifies more and more as it unfolds. "He is a man of God, but he uses all the methods of the devil,"[18] our guide reckons. "[Jehu] wants to do what God has revealed, but he confuses what God has shown will come to pass with what God really loves."[19] Ellul grants without hesitation that God is jealous and terrible in his love and that God will not tolerate the ongoing loss of his creature's affection to idols or the ongoing destruction of his

16. Striking examples can be found on pages 37, 84, and 91 of *Politics*.
17. Ellul, *Politics of God and the Politics of Man*, 54, emphasis mine.
18. Ellul, *Politics of God and the Politics of Man*, 99.
19. Ellul, *Politics of God and the Politics of Man*, 115.

creature's life by sin. These evils are why "wrath happens." And yet, Ellul reminds us that the terrible God who unleashes Jehu is also the God whom Jesus has taught us to call Father. Because of God's self-revelation in Jesus, we must realize that "God as Father suffers from all that his creature, his Son, suffers." Consequently, "when he inflicts chastisement on man, God himself suffers it, for he does not withdraw from even the worst of men . . . He accompanies the one he condemns both to prison and to hell."[20] This leads Ellul to a startling outlook on the carnage of 2 Kings: "When Jehu fulfilled the prophecy, it was on God himself that his violence fell. It was God whom he massacred in the priests of Baal, none of whom was a stranger or unimportant to God, since the Father had numbered all the hairs of their heads too. All the violence of Jehu is assumed by Jesus Christ."[21]

Wrestling with Ellul's Reading

My heart leaps at Ellul's performance of a hermeneutic of hope. Theology like this can keep a person from turning away in misery from the Old Testament or the larger biblical corpus with its at times dismaying "many's" and "few's."[22] You or I might have been a distant relative of Ahab or a devotee of Baal; if we cannot honestly take that realization to heart, then we have a long way to go before we reach the true path of Jesus, who leaves the many to seek the few—and in another sense, who leaves the few to seek the many.

Nevertheless, after an initial reading of 2 Kings in this season, I was not exegetically convinced that God condemned Jehu's violence as fully as Ellul proposed, or that Jehu's entire career had been based on the unauthorized modification of Elisha's message by the junior prophetic intermediary. The tone and details of the various prophecies seemed severe, not to mention the activity of their initial bearer Elijah after the showdown on Mount Carmel.[23] The intermediary's addition, "You are to destroy the house of Ahab your master [etc.]" (2 Kgs 9:7–10), might simply have been an expanded word he had heard from the Lord; or perhaps the entire discourse had been implied

20. Ellul, *Politics of God and the Politics of Man*, 109.
21. Ellul, *Politics of God and the Politics of Man*, 110.
22. Cf. Matt 7:13–14; 22:14.
23. "Elijah said to them, 'Seize the prophets of Baal; do not let one of them escape.' Then they seized them; and Elijah brought them down to the Wadi Kishon, and killed them there" (1 Kgs 18:40). This scene raises its own hermeneutical dilemma, as Ellul acknowledges elsewhere, for rather than some innately violent Jehu as protagonist, "the prophet of life . . . has hands covered in blood." Ellul goes on: "We must know that this is how it is, but we should not accept it. That is the whole difficulty" (Ellul, *To Will & To Do*, 2: forthcoming from Cascade.)

within Elisha's terse message. Moreover, God's approval of Jehu after the fact—"you have done well in accomplishing what is right in my eyes and have done to the house of Ahab all I had in mind to do" (2 Kgs 10:30)—was patent in the text. I was not eager to think of Jehu differently than Ellul construed him; but what if our eminent interpreter had not so much discovered a disassociation of God from violence in the text as he had projected that disassociation onto it with his own strong vision?

After further study, my mind (not just my heart) was won over to Ellul's viewpoint for four reasons: 1) Elisha brackets his brief message with the instructions, "Then open the door and run; don't delay!" giving credence to the notion that the intermediary's expansion of the message, delivered while failing to run immediately as instructed, is unauthorized.[24] 2) Yahweh's approval of Jehu in 2 Kings 10:30 does convey the sense of reticence Ellul highlights,[25] in contrast to the tenor of the Lord's relationship with other of his servants in Scripture. 3) Historically, Jehu's next three descendants "did evil in the eyes of the Lord," continuing in the sin of Jeroboam ("using God to enhance the state," in Ellul's analysis),[26] as did Jehu himself—a fact the text relates straightaway after God's restrained commendation. 4) And finally, all this evidence is crowned by the astonishing judgment of Hosea 1:4—"I will punish the house of Jehu for the blood of Jezreel" (the NIV reads "for the massacre at Jezreel")—which indicts the violence that occurred at the very place Jehu destroyed the main portion of Ahab's house, including Jezebel. These textual indications led me to agree with Ellul's judgment of the distance between Jehu's heart and the heart of the God (cf. 2 Kgs 10:31), the God whose will he sought to prosecute as his own cause. "For [Jehu] is a type of the man who is unfaithful even in his faithfulness . . . To be sure, he is always loved by God in spite of his lies, assassinations, and treacheries. But he is also rejected by God because of his commandeering of the Word and the harshness of his loyalty."[27]

Thus were my exegetical misgivings resolved. But at the same time, my initial failure to track with Ellul's redemptive hermeneutics stirred up a question which has been on my mind since I first studied *The Politics of God and the Politics of Man* fourteen years ago. Might there be another approach to biblical "minefield moments" than simultaneously maximizing

---

24. Ellul does not miss the opportunity at that point of the discussion for a quick contemporary jab: "In the same way the Word spoken by God in Christ is undoubtedly modified by the church, and not for the better" (Ellul, *Politics of God and the Politics of Man*, 98).

25. Ellul, *Politics of God and the Politics of Man*, 107.

26. Ellul, *Politics of God and the Politics of Man*, 88.

27. Ellul, *Politics of God and the Politics of Man*, 118.

loyalty to the goodness of the Lord and loyalty to the goodness of the text? When suspending oneself with arms akimbo between these two commitments seems an unattainable feat by a weaker hermeneutical gymnast, might there be a legitimate, faithful way to shift some weight from the second commitment back to the first? For example, if a perceived contradiction happened to arise between the perfection of Scripture and the perfection of the love Scripture tells us that God is, could we ever choose to side with God over against a text whose presentation of his ways seemed to fall short of the glory revealed in Jesus? Or would such a move represent, at best, merely a new version of the hermeneutics of avoidance and, at worst, the collapse of the whole enterprise of biblical faith?

The Vulnerable but Effective Word

As I have understood him, Ellul did not feel the need to make an either-or choice of this kind. The interpretive lens of Jesus the Word of God was a comprehensive and sufficient theodicy for him. Perhaps the true weakness behind the dilemma of loyalties I have described, then, is Christological rather than hermeneutical. Perhaps what is needed is a stronger inclination and ability to perceive that "everything [in Scripture] leads to Jesus Christ, just as everything comes from him."[28] I accept that. I am willing to build new Christological interpretive muscles. And yet, I would still wish to pose the following to Jacques: if God truly deals with human beings in the flexible way you describe—and I believe God does—then did not the same non-coerciveness, the same tolerance of error, the same willingness to adapt to human choice and preference and to assume human attempt and aspiration, obtain in relation to those human beings who inscribed the words of revelation that became our Bible? If "God does not mechanize man," as you say, did God mechanize Scripture?[29] And if God did not do that, then did God ever allow Scripture to portray his character or actions in an inadequate way? If he ever did, how would we identify where? These questions may sound largely rhetorical, as though I already know the answer and just want to persuade others, but that is not the case; I really do wonder.

---

28. Ellul, *Politics of God and the Politics of Man*, 9.

29. Ellul, *Politics of God and the Politics of Man*, 16. In Ellul's article "Darwin and the Bible" (ch. 15 in the present volume) he unequivocally answers no: "If this God is above all the Liberator, how can we even conceive of a mechanical and literal inspiration of the Bible? How would this God transform his witnesses and prophets into typewriters? On the contrary, each of them transmitted Revelation using their own means, taking full responsibility, in their own conceptual framework."

This is not the moment to contrive an extended reply-in-character from the master or to develop from his oeuvre a full account of how fallible human words can reliably bear the faultless Word of the Wholly Other. But we can at least recall in the volume under consideration his depiction of God's finesse in accomplishing the full divine intention through freely executed human acts—including, one would assume, literary ones. Ellul believed that the inherent vulnerability of "translation into language with all the risks this involves" is precisely what God intends for the presentation of his Word,[30] so much does God respect human freedom. He also believed that despite the fragility of human linguistic and documentary means, the true Word of God is readily available everywhere in Scripture to those who approach it with a disciplined construal[31] along the lines of *fides quaerens intellectum* ("faith seeking understanding"). For this reason, I am curious about Ellul's modest selectivity of engagement with the text of 2 Kings, best illustrated by his silence on the opening narrative in which Elijah casually burns up multiple companies of men by calling down fire from heaven. Perhaps these are simply further examples of people "put outside God's work but not his love," but I suspect that if Ellul were pressed to comment on the story, he would interpret 2 Kings One through the lens of that New Testament moment when two disciples wanted to call down fire from heaven on others "as Elijah did," and Jesus rebuked them. In other words, I suspect that, like most of us, Ellul implicitly considered the Word of God to be more apparent in some biblical texts than others. Moreover, I expect that, even as he concurred with the highest traditional and Barthian view of Scripture's function, he entertained subtle but important qualifications of Scripture's divine origination and flawlessness, whether or not he felt the need to expound on them.

And why did he not do so more often? Presumably, in the shadow of the historical-critical scholarship peering over Ellul's shoulder as he penned his biblical reflections, it would have been banal rather than adventurous to innovate a nuanced retake of the church's doctrine of Scripture. What was needed far more was a live demonstration of how the Bible really could pose the transcendent, world-shattering, life-transforming Word of God. For it is above all when people *experience* Scripture speaking to them as

---

30. Ellul, *Politics of God and the Politics of Man*, 21.

31. Discussing the origin of a particular verse in 2 Kings, Ellul comments, "Whether we like it or not, the incident has now been inserted in the book which was accepted by God's people as God's Word" (Ellul, *Politics of God and the Politics of Man*, 27). Later, in reference to the model of the Jerusalem temple, he remarks, "the directions are given in Holy Scripture, and we have to take this seriously even if we do not take it absolutely literally" (130).

God's Word, personally and existentially, that they are prepared to embrace Scripture's divine origin, authority, and reliability. Jacques Ellul made that demonstration, and continues to furnish such an experience, encouraging this particular believer, for one, to seek again "the final meaning of his life in the presence of this text."

Works Cited

Ellul, Jacques. *The Politics of God and the Politics of Man*. Translated by Geoffrey W. Bromiley. Grand Rapids: Eerdmans, 1972.

———. *To Will & To Do: An Introduction to Christian Ethics*. 2 vols. Translated by Jacob Marques Rollison. Eugene, OR: Cascade, 2020.

CHAPTER 13

A Short, Complementary Note on Romans 13:1

JACQUES ELLUL

TRANSLATED BY
JACOB MARQUES ROLLISON

THOUSANDS OF PAGES HAVE been written on this verse![1] It has been used as a foundational argument both for the divine right of monarchy, and (later on, in the same manner) to support absolute obedience to the authorities, whatever their character might be. Others (though fewer in number) have seen in this verse a Pauline reaction to rebellious tendencies among Christians. And then there is the illuminating doctrine of the *exousiai* (e.g. in Cullmann, etc.). But it is difficult to find a truly satisfying response. I will not claim to do so here! I only wish to add a piece of information which I have rarely seen taken into account.

As is commonly done, I have taught that ever since Augustus, the *imperator* was qualified as "divus" for the duration of his lifetime and included among the gods after his death. After Domitian's brief and quickly rejected attempt to be called *deus* during his lifetime, the title was permanently attributed to all emperors after Aurelian (270). Incidentally, this is much less important than we might think, and has absolutely no bearing on Paul's epistles in any case. But I recently read a thesis which alerted me to something which could change the interpretation of this text in light of the context in which it was situated.

---

1. This is a lightly-edited translation of "Petite note complémentaire sur Romains 13:1," *Foi et Vie* 89 (1990) 81–83. Special thanks to *Foi et Vie* for permission to translate and print this text.

In all likelihood, the Epistle to the Romans was written in 57 AD. This would locate it during the reign of Nero, emperor from 54 to 68 AD. Now, this is interesting: when he took power, Nero declared "Among all mortals, it is thus I who have been designated and chosen to play the role of the Gods on earth" (Seneca, *De dementia*). In the same era, Lucan went even further: Nero is a God, and not just one God among others, but *the* divinity, superior to the other gods.[2] "All divinity will yield to you" (*Pharsalia*), Nero is "the center of the universe." Moreover, it is not just the assembly of the gods which confers divinity and primacy over themselves on Nero, but so does Nature itself![3] And "Nature will allow you the right to choose what kind of God you will be" (Lucan). Therefore, it is the very principle which founds the order of the world which allows Nero to claim divinity. And in several texts, Nero is *identified* with Jupiter and Apollo, who are themselves allegories of the Logos. "Jupiter-Logos" is the figure of the rational principle which governs everything. And Nero is thus integrated with this Jupiter.

Now, this construction, which is unthinkable for us, was not simply an idea of several flatterers and courtiers: it was philosophically grounded and propagated throughout the Empire (and above all in Rome) through the mediation of the Stoics. And it did not remain confined to intellectual circles; we know that this thought was diffused among the people after having been spread among the aristocracy. This is evidenced by the timidity and retreat of the Senate. Based on this conception of power, the delirium of omnipotence which seized Nero is understandable.

But in this case, we can also understand Paul's text much better: it is ultimately a text of contestation and refusal! This text enacts the same desacralization in relation to political power which Genesis effects regarding nature. Nero is in no way what the official doctrine proclaims. He is not god. He is not the center of the world. He is not the master of Nature: if he has any power, it is *attributed* to him by the God of Jesus Christ. Certainly, there must be a power in society. But the order is not that of Nature; it is the order willed by God. The authorities are first and foremost servants of the will of God, and none can claim to compare themselves to our God. On the contrary, they must obey this God; and we must obey them precisely to the extent that they obey God.

In light of the dominant ideology under Nero, a declaration such as Romans 13:1 was a veritable sacrilege! But the emphasis should not be placed on "You must obey," but rather on "the higher authorities come from the God of Abraham and Jesus" and they have no power on their

---

2. Pena, *Le stoïcisme et l'Empire Romain*; see also Brun, *Le Stoïcisme*.
3. And we know how important Nature was for the Stoics.

own. This is certainly included in the command that we must obey God rather than men.

Works Cited

Brun, Jean. *Le Stoïcisme*. Paris: PUF, 1980.
Pena, Marc. *Le stoïcisme et l'Empire Romain*. Aix-Marseille: Presses Universitaires d'Aix-Marseille, 1990.

―――― CHAPTER 14 ――――

Review of André Chouraqui's Translation of the Bible

Jacques Ellul

TRANSLATED BY
Lisa Richmond

WHAT WE HAVE HERE is a truly new translation of the Bible.[1] It is new not only in the sense that it has just been produced but new particularly in its aim. All translators who place themselves within the traditional scholarly mentality of our day view translation first and foremost as formal and grammatical fidelity to the text, semantic precision, accuracy in going from one language to the other according to the standard scholarly rules. But the translated text has to be correct in terms of grammar and vocabulary. Let us also note that whatever the claim to objectivity, every translation involves a large number of implicit assumptions that remain unstated. A translator works from within a particular theology, and the translation will vary accordingly and influence the reader's mind in the direction of that theology, if only by the choice of key words. Moreover, translations since the 18th century have been marked by a certain moralism and sense of propriety. The biblical text, which is often violent, raw, and harsh, was reduced to drawing-room language. In Chouraqui we have a translator who takes a clear stance. He restores the text to life. He gives readers the shock that might come from reading the original.

---

1. Editor's note: This chapter is a translation of a book review originally published in *Revue des Deux Mondes*, 4th trimester 1977, 507–12. Special thanks to *Revue des Deux Mondes* for permitting this translation. See https://www.revuedesdeuxmondes.fr/.

In other words, what we have here is the move that Vahanian[2] described so well between *scripta* and *scriptura*. When we describe the Bible as scripture (*scriptura*), we lose sight of the term's meaning entirely, and we read it as if it were *scripta* (writings).[3] But it is not *scripta*—in the past, finished, closed, already written. The biblical texts are *scriptura*—in the future, that which must always be written again. And this is also true of the dialectic writing/speech:[4] the Bible is speech, spoken on God's behalf by man to man and living through this relation. This speech was fixed in a scripture, it became an object, a thing (the Canon), unchanging, completed, and in this sense dead. But it is continually called to become speech again, to become address, message, call, proclamation. André Chouraqui's translation restores a text-speech to us, a text that is active. This is why some people now refer to "Chouraqui's Bible."[5] I do not agree with this. The Bible is not Chouraqui's. It is God's and the witnesses' who have been his spokespeople. It is not Chouraqui's in the sense that we may say that the Gospel of Jesus offered by Barbusse belongs to Barbusse.[6] André Chouraqui is a messenger who gives a new meaning to the words of the tribe.[7] But these are not his words!

The life-giving stance of André Chouraqui (comparable to that of Luther, who had a similar aim for his translation) produces, needless to say, a sense of disorientation for the reader accustomed to a certain style of "fine French," a certain religious droning, or a certain reticence on the

2. See Vahanian, "Scripta et scriptura." (This and the footnotes that follow are those of the translator unless otherwise stated.)

3. In Latin, *scripta* is the past-tense, passive-voice participle of the verb *scribere*, "to write." As such, it means "having been written," or, when used as a noun, "what has been written." *Scriptura* is the future-tense, active-voice participle and means "going to write," or, when used as a noun, "what is going to write." The two words as nouns can be distinguished further. The *Oxford Latin Dictionary* offers the following for *scripta*: "text," "writing," "written composition," and for *scriptura*: "text," "(the activity of) writing," "the expression (of ideas) in writing," "the art or process of writing."

4. The French word following the / is *parole* and is typically translated into English as "word" or "speech."

5. Here Ellul is reacting against citations like this one from André Neher, a Jewish philosopher and professor at the University of Strasbourg after the Second World War: "In André Chouraqui there is a range of original aspects which prevent us from speaking of his translation in relation to others, but, absolutely, of André Chouraqui's Bible." This citation is found (alongside an endorsement from Ellul himself) inside the front cover of Chouraqui's translations of several biblical books, including his translations of the four gospels (editor's note).

6. Henri Barbusse (1873–1935) published a trilogy of novels about the life of Jesus from a Marxist perspective in the 1920s.

7. A phrase from "Le Tombeau d'Edgar Poe" by the French poet Stéphane Mallarmé (1842–1898).

part of Old and New Testament professors due to how they conceive of translation. For some, there is not enough respect for grammar;[8] for others, the language they are reading is improper French (one has described it as "franbreu"[9]). But they are focused on the wrong question. Is it a question of Hebrew knowledge? André Chouraqui knows Hebrew extremely well as a classical and a living[10] language, but in a way *other* than that of a university specialist. Is the question one of applying a scholarly method of translation? Chouraqui's complex method, which I will return to, is extremely rigorous, but here again it is not so much *less* scholarly as it is scholarly in a different way. Or is it a question of using irreproachable French? But which French? The French of textbooks and grammarians, or that of the poets and creators of the language?

When we broach this newly translated text, we are thrown off by a different rhythm, a different vocabulary. The titles of the biblical books are different from the ones we are used to. Proverbs is now "Examples [to Imitate]," Exodus is "Names," Deuteronomy is "Speeches." Numbers is "In the Desert." And this transformation is quite characteristic. Chouraqui has restored the direct Hebrew meaning lying beyond the traditional names that have come from Greek or Latin translations and that, strictly speaking, no longer communicate. Which one speaks more to a new reader: "Numbers" (is this an arithmetical treatise?) or "In the Desert," which is the literal translation of the Hebrew title? But this is upsetting to our religious habits. The same goes for the change from the traditional chapter titles, which have been replaced by running heads at the top of the page, forming a sort of table of contents for each book as the narrative proceeds.

But above all, on first reading we are struck by this text's simultaneously rough and sophisticated character. It is rough in its rhythm, like barbarian poetry, in the violence of attack and call, in the linguistic bluntness that restores a whole aspect of the Old Testament to us—one that we had completely lost, used as we are to confuse polished and pious language with the word of the living God. It is sophisticated in the choice of careful and scholarly words, sometimes archaic (*dilection*, for example[11]),

---

8. Author's note: And because Chouraqui chooses to put most of the verbs in the present tense, although there is no present tense in Hebrew but only "completed" and "incompleted," university specialists of Hebrew do not agree with this rendering.

9. A combination of the words *français* and *hébreu*, which could be rendered as "Freebrew."

10. Ellul is able to draw on both senses of the French adjective *vivant*, a point that is difficult to make in English translation. *Vivant* means "alive," "living," but in the context of a language it also means "modern," i.e., currently spoken, not a dead language.

11. *Dilection* (a word archaic in French and obsolete in English) is spiritual love or

sometimes in the creation of completely new words, or in the way that these verses seem at times like modern or ultramodern poetry, poems that sometimes have no clear logical meaning.

As a result, we observe another difference from most current translations, which generally try to bring the text closer to the reader, making it accessible in vocabulary and expression, adapted to the current way of thinking (the traditional word *mercenaire* is replaced with *ouvrier* or *salarié*, for example[12]). They "modernize" it. Whereas with Chouraqui, it is not a matter of making the reading easier but of eliciting the shock of the unexpected. This is not incidental. The usual translation is situated at the level of what is reasonable for average understanding. André Chouraqui's is situated beyond intellection. After all, modern people are gripped by pop music, Rolling Stones lyrics, Miró's painting—even when they are not able to say "what it means." The point is not to offer a newspaper article; it is to set forth a proclamation. Not to hand out information, but to demand a response, to put the reader's back to the wall. This is also the reason for choosing the present tense: the text becomes active not by form but by the way in which the reader is made contemporaneous with the event being described. Today is the day that the story of David is unfolding. This is your story. You cannot not be involved in it. We see, then, that nothing is arbitrary here; every choice is intentional.

And this leads us to say a few words on the scholarly method of this translation. André Chouraqui himself specifically addresses this. It is important. One characteristic is obviously that Chouraqui lives in Jerusalem, and for him Hebrew is a living language. Of course, this is not to say that modern Hebrew is biblical Hebrew. But it is false to say, as some do, that the two are as far apart as are Cicero's Latin and modern French. We must not forget that modern Hebrew has been recreated, born anew a half-century ago, based on biblical Hebrew. All of the new words, modern adaptations, argot, etc., of this modern Hebrew language are rooted in an immediate way in biblical Hebrew, and there is a reciprocal current between the two. Whether one wants it or not, a French person has more affinity of understanding for the language of Racine than a Japanese person does, even one who knows French very well. As A. Neher[13] put it so well, it is the relationship between an *existence* and a *culture* that is being effected here, and this is what Chouraqui is conveying to us in this translation. This is why it is

---

affection, the love between God and humankind.

12. *Mercenaire*: hireling, mercenary, someone who works (only) for money. *Ouvrier*: laborer, manual worker. *Salarié*: waged worker, salaried employee.

13. André Neher (1914–1988), French-Jewish scholar. Ellul is possibly drawing on Neher's *L'existence juive*.

indispensable. In addition, he is providing us with an outstanding witness to the resurrection of Hebrew, a phenomenon that is worth meditating on. This development is the reverse of Latin's, which went from an everyday language to a religious language. Here the religious language has become a living one. But in his rigour, Chouraqui does not let himself be carried off by current-day Hebrew: he constantly plays on the triple register of the etymological meaning, the meaning specific to the text's historical period, and the modern meaning.

And this leads to a second aspect of this scholarly method. The books of the Old Testament were written in very different times and correspond to different "genres." While other translators have followed their own inclinations and their own style for the entirety of the Bible, Chouraqui has sought to express the style specific to each book. The Psalms are not "expressed" in the same way as Deuteronomy, and neither of them in the same way as Isaiah. He has made a detailed effort to reproduce the uniqueness of each one (a scholarly approach if there ever was one!). Moreover, he has imposed an extremely strict rule on himself: for one Hebrew word, one French word (the same one each time), and for each Hebrew word, a different French word. All other translations, by contrast, allow themselves the easy way out of rendering five or six different Hebrew words by the same one French word when their meaning is "more or less" the same (but if so, why are there several words?). And conversely, they translate the same word in the text by different French words, as the case may be. Admittedly, this rigour of Chouraqui's can seem somewhat mechanical; it sometimes seems to restrict the text. For example, [the Hebrew word] *ruach* has customarily been translated sometimes by *souffle*, sometimes by *esprit*.[14] Chouraqui opts radically throughout for *souffle* (in line certainly with the Bible's anti-spiritualizing "materiality"!), and this robs us of a certain mysterious feeling. But it also causes us to better reflect on the relationship of the Creator and the creature, which is neither abstract nor immaterial. Similarly, in his strict submission to the text, Chouraqui does not try to impose a clear meaning on obscure, incoherent, or mysterious passages. Translators have always attempted to make texts logical and comprehensible even when they are not so in the original. Chouraqui prefers to abruptly set us down in the heart of this incomprehensibility, and why not? We thus perceive a double reversal: On the one hand, Chouraqui seeks to convey the very "inspiration" of the Word, its deep meaning, even if this requires modifying a particular literal element (the present tense, for example). On the other hand, he radically submits to the letter of this text,

---

14. *Souffle*: breath, wind. *Esprit*: breath, spirit, mind.

inverting the customary position, i.e., grammatical fidelity plus attribution of a logical meaning (even where it is not present).

Finally, the last aspect of this method to be noted is that André Chouraqui has applied what has been called "the law of breath."[15] The biblical text possesses a breath, a breathing, a rhythm of its own; there is a movement to grasp hold of. Just as there is a specific breathing for the Ciceronian period or the Shakespearean soliloquy, so also the biblical text has its rhythm, which is not compatible with our traditional division into chapters and verses. The true translator must therefore find the punctuations, the divisions, the periods, the rhythm (and this is especially important for our day, when rhythm and movement are so prominent). This is precisely what Chouraqui has done, by bringing the text to life from the inside, and it is what admittedly gives a Baroque character to the French sometimes, because French does not necessarily have the same rhythm. The different breaks require "reading the text again" in a way different from our usual one. We thus observe that, in his translation, Chouraqui has in no way just followed his imagination, neither has he wanted his work to sound effusive, following instead a precise method and strict rules.

We must come now to a singularly important aspect. It appears that André Chouraqui is the first Jew to have translated the New Testament. This took courage. He could have been viewed by some of his brethren as a kind of renegade for taking these deceptive pages seriously. But from the outset, he presents this New Testament as *"pages of my people's history."*[16] And this sets the whole tone: he reminds us powerfully (which we certainly admit, but rather reluctantly!) that Jesus, his disciples, Paul, the first Church, are Jews. They think as Jews, they are permeated by the Bible, they express the innermost revelation given to the Jewish people. Paul in any case is utterly shaped by the Jewish method of interpretation. And as a result, there is a Hebraic infrastructure underlying the Greek text of the New Testament. André Chouraqui's chief effort is thus to retrieve this Hebraic character within the Greek, and even beyond the Aramaic. It is in no way a matter of adding to the Gospels or Paul; it is a matter of restoring them!

I can say, as a Christian, that I have been struck by the care and respect that Chouraqui shows, in regard to the Pauline message for example. Nothing is watered down or ambiguous. He is even willing to give Jesus the divine title of Adonai. The great novelty is the concrete rediscovery of the

---

15. A formula used by F. Rosenzweig and taken up by A. Neher in his solid article in the *Revue des études juives* [Review of Jewish Studies], 1975. Translator's note: This is a third French word for breath—*haleine*—and refers to the inhalation and exhalation of the lungs.

16. Ellul's italics in original.

Hebraic roots, the passing beyond Greek thought. This is fundamental. Because the New Testament is written in Greek, we have always been tempted to interpret it in the form and context of Greek thought (and often even more in Latin!). But this has been an error, one that led to almost all of the heresies. This Greek language transmits a Hebraic way of thinking, and this is what is to be brought out, in agreement with the Old Testament. How can we not see this, when this Greek text is constantly punctuated by the reference "according to the Scriptures"? This great effort of Chouraqui's, testifying to the movement toward Jewish-Christian reconciliation, calls Christians to make a similar effort to rethink their theology in relation to this one revelation in the two "Testaments."

Is this to say that I have no criticism to make about this great work, that I am an unconditional admirer? No, I have many reservations. [For one,] I do not see the value of retaining the original spelling for the names (one sometimes gets the impression that the translator is throwing the reader off balance "just for the fun of it"). This doesn't matter too much. [Second,] I would dispute many terms. I do not find the word *dilection* to be apt for expressing the love of God toward his people. Replacing the term *foi* with *adhésion*[17] has the advantage of giving a precise meaning and avoiding familiarization as well as inconsistency, but there is still a whole dimension that disappears. Adhesion (which of course for a contemporary will evoke adherence to a political party) expresses more an act of intellect or judgement; one adheres to a doctrine, an association, a movement. There is a whole aspect of feeling, imagination, confidence, fidelity, love, of relation of one being to another, that seems to me to disappear. Sometimes the chosen words weaken the text's impact: to often replace *orgueil* by *fierté*[18] removes the profound nature of sin, the rupture in relation to God.

But the central point concerns the very name of God. That Chouraqui might have refused to use the word *God*, so equivocal, so laden with misapprehensions, is quite understandable. One can try to avoid confusion. And certainly we can stress that the God who reveals himself in Scripture, the God of Abraham, Isaac, Jacob, and Jesus Christ, is not god, is not an avatar of Jupiter or Manitou; he is the opposite, he is the enemy of Zeus, Baal,

17. *Foi*: faith. *Adhésion*: adherence, cleaving, attachment, devotion.

18. *Orgueil*: pride considered as a disposition, as an acute sense of self-worth that can become excessive in comparison to others, in which sense it has an unfavourable meaning. It may also be used in a favourable sense however, as a synonym of *fierté*: pride considered as a usually more benign, even partly impersonal, feeling, often arising on behalf of others or of things more or less associated with oneself, as the pleasure that one takes in high accomplishment or in the recognition of certain favourable attributes. But *fierté* too may sometimes be used in an unfavourable individual sense, as in *faire le fier*, to put on airs.

etc. This is excellent. But in the New Testament, Chouraqui has constantly translated *Theos* by *Elohim*. And here I cannot agree. The God of Jesus is not Elohim but YHWH. He is not the "objective" god, so to speak, but the god who reveals himself, who not only gives his name but, much more, manifests his being in Jesus. He is the god of most personal, most intimate, relationship. The Father is not Elohim but YHWH. I understand completely why André Chouraqui could not possibly use this translation. But as a Christian, I have to note this great difference.

That said, and to conclude, I would like to recall that translation (which, in the well-worn expression, is compared to "betrayal" by the Italian wordplay[19]) is *transducere*, to lead across or beyond. This is precisely what André Chouraqui has accomplished. He leads us beyond the literality, he restores the text's own freedom, by means of the translator's freedom (but, as we have seen, how disciplined a freedom it is!). He has given us a text without baggage and without heaviness, without fatalism, without conformism, but not without tradition. He thus forces us to actually read this text, not to replace it with our mnemonic devices, our conventions and justifications. He restores a newness to the text that produces a shock, a breath that takes the place of our breathlessness. This poetic creation of the translator is, here, a creation of faith, and André Chouraqui has conceived this translation as a call. We must be willing to receive it in this way to understand at once its accuracy and its depth.

Works Cited

Neher, André. *L'existence juive: solitude et affrontements*. La condition humaine. Paris: Seuil, 1962, 1991.

Vahanian, Gabriel. "Scripta et scriptura." In *Le don et la dette*, edited by Marco M. Olivetti, 605–10. Biblioteca dell'Archivio di Filosofia 34. Padua: CEDAM, 2004.

---

19. That is, *traduttore, traditore*: to translate is to betray.

Part III

Ellul and the Bible Today: Contemporary Dialogue

CHAPTER 15

Darwin and the Bible

JACQUES ELLUL

TRANSLATED BY
MATTHEW T. PRIOR

THESE PAST FEW MONTHS we have been reminded of religious assertions based on a fundamentalist reading of the Bible, which made a reappearance on the occasion of the "year of Darwin,"[1] and which consider Darwin's theory to be of the devil.[2] This conflict is not as passé as we might suppose.

We know very well that there have been legal proceedings on this question in America, but even in France the debate is not over! I have received a number of letters arguing that according to the genealogies, the Bible tells us that the creation took place in 5542 BC, and therefore we should believe that today we are in the year 7500 (or thereabouts) and that all that prehistory, astronomy and geology tell us is mistaken . . .

I would like to recall at this point that I consider this literal interpretation to be wrong. I could sum up my view in a few simple words: *the kind of questions* which bother us were of absolutely no concern to the Jewish writers (at least before Greek influence) or to the early church fathers. It simply was not "their issue!" And they never claimed to give any answers to this question since they didn't even ask it!

---

1. Ellul is likely referring to centenary events in honor of Charles Darwin, as this article was published one hundred years after Darwin's death in 1882.

2. This article is a translation of Ellul, "Darwin et la Bible," which originally appeared in *Réforme* 1954 (October 2, 1982) 10. Special thanks to Nathalie Leenhardt at *Réforme* and to the Ellul family for granting permission to publish this article. See www.reforme.net.

Let's outline briefly, however, how "creationism" and "fixism"[3] are based on several assumptions. First there is inerrancy, according to which the biblical text can contain no errors of any kind. This, in turn, rests on two other assumptions: the omniscience of God (which I do not contest) and the idea that God reveals *everything* (and thus cannot have transmitted errors to human authors), and that he reveals it through a mechanical kind of inspiration (God dictates his Word to the human author, who writes it down word for word). There is one final assumption: the Bible answers every question and gives us the truth about everything, describing exactly what happened in everything, whether concerning biology, or history, etc. And because Genesis reveals that God spoke the words "everything is very good" over his creation, this means that nothing should change and no evolution is possible. The world today is just as it was created.

However, I argue that this seemingly self-evident construction rests upon several errors, both of exegesis and of theology. The Bible is not a science textbook, nor is it an Encyclopaedia. In God's revelation, we are not given a physics class. God's revelation gives us the truth about God himself and the relationship between humanity and God. There is absolutely no reference to the material origins of the world or the evolution of History.

The Bible is a message, a proclamation about Salvation, and nothing else, whether physics or metaphysics. And when reading a book, one must at least ask oneself why and for what purpose it has been written!

After this general reflection, let us examine a few points in short order. In the first few chapters of Genesis, we find some clues which tell against creationism. First of all, it is not a case of creation *ex nihilo* (this is a foreign idea) ... God "fashions" and "makes" the world, and there is an element prior to this act. This is referred to as *Tohu wa bohu*, which is untranslatable. The fact is that we are told *nothing* about point zero, or about a "big bang." The text doesn't even say "*In* the beginning" but "*Within* the beginning ... "

Next, God's action is not a "creation" but a *separation*. In the second chapter we find ourselves in a universe ("the heavens") in which is situated a garden for humanity, Eden. We might well understand this to refer to galaxies and *an* earth, our garden ... When we come to the plants and the animals, they are "created" *according to* their kinds, but this does not imply fixism, for the Hebrew preposition implies a sort of movement "with a view to" or "towards" their kind—a word which can be translated also as order or genus. Finally, we see clearly that everything has been put in place, organised in relation to humanity. Is this a naïve anthropocentrism? Not at all! It's just that the account aims to give humans a meaning for their lives, a response to their situation in the world.

---

3. Editor's note: "Fixism" is a theory which holds that current extant species correspond to ancient species, practically denying any sort of evolutionary adaptation.

This then leads to a second order of problems. It must be said that the Genesis account has very little place (it is very rarely cited) in the later texts of the Hebrew Bible. The founding text for the Jewish people is the Exodus. The founding act is the liberation of Israel: the first revelation of God is as liberator. The formation of the book of Genesis therefore aims to answer the question: *who is this God who has set us free*? And nothing else.

If we need further confirmation, we find it in the polemical nature of the first chapters of Genesis, which make a mockery of the existing cosmogonies of the surrounding religions. We are not being given a new cosmogony here!

Moreover, if this God is above all the Liberator, how can we even conceive of a mechanical and literal inspiration of the Bible? How would this God transform his witnesses and prophets into typewriters? On the contrary, each of them transmitted Revelation using their own means, taking full responsibility, in their own conceptual framework. A prophet had no greater geographical knowledge than anyone else, and it must be admitted that Jesus shared the knowledge and ways of thinking of the people of his time. He had no special insight on physics or chemistry.

Finally, the whole Bible is not a descriptive text but a mythic text, sometimes symbolic, which means neither "false," nor "wrong," nor "interpretable as the reader desires"! Myth and symbol evoke a deeper sense, the only one that counts. The reader's freedom is what is at stake as they read such a text *before God*.

Above all, we must not read it with *our* mentality of scientism, seeking *to know the exact facts and how things happened*. This text was to bear the revelation of meaning, designed for the discovery of meaning, bearing witness to God's presence from the beginning and guiding towards an ultimate goal, but without describing the process from one to the other. Our Science (Darwin) seeks an answer to the question "how" rather than the question "why" or the question "what does this mean?" To reduce the Bible to the explanatory framework of the "how" is to deny its true value.

What I have just recalled here (I have said nothing new!) goes to show that challenges such as those brought by Darwin invite us not to an outright rejection or a defensive stance but to read more attentively the Hebrew text itself, to return to Talmudic interpretations (for example) and the interpretations of the Early Church Fathers who were not caught up in other issues.

We can quickly perceive how fruitful this shift can be for today. There remains though the question: how could the meaning of the biblical text, which was quite clear and well understood by those theologians of earlier times, have been so lost? *How have we gotten so mixed up in these scientific debates*? But that should one day be the subject of another article . . .

CHAPTER 16

Giving under God's Gaze

*Figures of the Gift in the Bible and
in the Work of Jacques Ellul*

PATRICK CHASTENET

TRANSLATED BY
CHRISTIAN ROY

"God's sole behavior is the gift.[1]*"*
"Le don n'est pas la valeur centrale de l'Evangile."[2]

WHILE MARCEL MAUSS COULD see in the threefold obligation to give, to receive and to give back the matrix of any human society, the Christian understanding of the gift is essentially dynamic, strongly favoring the gift as much as it condemns the refusal of the counter-gift.[3] As an expression and a fruit of God's love, the gift is at the very heart of the Biblical message. God gives life: creation. God gives the Law (Torah): the Covenant. God gives what is dearest to him: his Son, his incarnate Word. Jesus gives his life to redeem all the world's sins. Charity, that is, love (*agapè*), thus logically gets to be termed the most important[4] of the three theological virtues (which have

---

1. Ellul, "L'argent," 65.

2. "The gift is not the central value of the Gospel" (Laupies, "La complexité évangélique du don," 388).

3. Unless otherwise indicated, biblical citations are English renderings of verses taken from the translation offered in the *Bible de Jérusalem*. I wish to thank Sylvain Dujancourt who, once more, has given me his time to complete my readings or throw light on them.

4. However, Vincent Laupies is right to underline that the Gospel's central value is

God as their object and relate to salvation), coming before faith and hope (1 Cor 13:13). Charity (*agapè*), "which binds them all together in perfect unity" (Col 3:14), links them and orders the other Christian virtues. "If I do not have love, I am nothing" (1 Cor 13:2). Or in the summarizing words of Saint Paul, placing charity (*agapè*) above all: "It bears all things, believes all things, hopes all things, endures all things" (1 Cor 13:7).

If the gift is a universal phenomenon, we shall attempt here to locate what it is about Scripture that could favor the privileging of this social act. From a sociological standpoint, the gift is defined by Alain Caillé as "a provision of goods or services performed without guarantee of return, in view of creating, sustaining or recreating a bond, socialness, between people.[5]" From a theological standpoint, the gift is viewed as man's response to God's love, the act of generosity that allows the believer to establish a spiritual bond between the one who gives and the one who receives. The Biblical survey that we are putting forward here is meant to distinguish the gift inspired by Christianity from the generosity of natural man. There exists a congruence between certain interpretations of Scripture favoring the gratuitousness of the gift and certain forms of public generosity. In other words, one may interpret a number of manifestations of solidarity toward the poor, the homeless or migrants, for instance, as gestures of secularized charity. We are proposing here to go back, if not to *the* source, then to one of the sources of public generosity, in the sense of generosity issuing from private persons toward the hungry, the destitute, those "without," the sick, the handicapped, etc. The body of values originating in Christianity lives on far beyond the circle of the faithful. Without referring to it explicitly, it inspires some of our more altruistic social behaviors, even willy-nilly. Max Weber and Ernst Troeltsch have, each in their own way, underlined the ambiguity of religions which, in order to have social efficacy, had to become embodied in practices that could lead to results far removed from original intentions.[6] Yet it is those intentions that interest us here, as we find them expressed in the Bible, even if the Churches have tended to maintain constant confusion between the Word of God and human morality—e.g., by turning the gift (a free and gratuitous act of love) into its exact opposite (i.e. a moral duty, an obligation supposed to secure a certificate of right Christianity; in short, the driver of that Christian good conscience that supremely annoyed Jacques Ellul).

---

not the gift, but the love of God and neighbor. "La complexité évangélique du don," 388.

5. Caillé, *Don, intérêt et désintéressement*, 236.

6. Weber, *Protestant Ethic and the Spirit of Capitalism*; *Sociology of Religion*; Troeltsch, *Protestantism and Progress*.

In agreement with Ellul, we aim to demonstrate that the question of the relation between "man and money"[7] is absolutely central in the Bible, since it is an expression of the creature's trust towards the Creator. If what people usually remember is that the believer cannot serve two masters at once, we tend to forget that the only Christian attitude is one of desacralization of money by means of the gift, as an individual and prophetic act. Because there is no power more contrary to God's action than Mammon, Ellul makes the gratuitous gift the culmination of all of his ethical reflection on money, but also the major act by which Christians place their full trust in God. The gift is a complete and joyful surrender to the hands of God, not the result of any legalism or suffering.

Ellul quoted Paul, who recalled the words of Jesus: "It is more blessed to give than to receive" (Acts 20:35). These words will guide us as we ask five fundamental questions: why give, to whom, what and how much, and above all, how?

I. Why Give?

What does the act of giving mean in a Christian perspective? If natural man can show generosity, e.g. to create social bonds, the believer who refers to the Bible has additional reasons to exercise his generosity. It is not that altruism is the monopoly of Christianity, but this religion favors charity to the point of making it the most important of the virtues. The believer is thus called upon to imitate his Lord Jesus.

1. Giving to Imitate Jesus: The Mimetic Gift

"In the Bible, the living God bestows his grace through the inestimable and gratuitous gift that he bestows upon the world in the person of his son Jesus Christ[8]". Gratuitousness is the hallmark of Christian grace and it is precisely due to Christianity's lasting impact that it "has persisted in many sectors of our culture as the hallmark of the gift, until Mauss at least."[9] The gift holds a fundamental place in Christian theology. The sacrifice of Jesus on the cross means that although he is the Son of God, he agreed to abase himself to the point of dying as a common criminal for the salvation of all. Rich as he was, he became poor in order to save us. Or, to put it as the apostle Paul did

---

7. That is, the original French title of Ellul's *Money and Power*, "*l'homme et l'argent.*"
8. Roux, *L'argent dans la communauté de l'Église*, 13.
9. Tarot, "Don et grâce, une famille à recomposer?," 477.

in his admonition to the Corinthians about generosity: "For you know the grace of our Lord Jesus Christ, that though he was rich, yet for your sake he became poor, so that you by his poverty might become rich." (2 Cor 8:9) By this gift, God enriches men and allows them to act without a calculating spirit. God's gift calls forth the gift of Christians who are invited to imitate Christ's example (2 Cor 1:7; 8:1 and 8:5). The Gospel shows that it is good to ask, to receive and to give. Jesus himself, weary after a long walk, asks the Samaritan woman for a drink (John 4:7) And when she shows surprise that a Jew would ask her to do him a favor, Jesus answers: "If you knew the gift of God, and who it is that is saying to you, 'Give me a drink,' you would have asked him, and he would have given you living water." (John 4:10) Finally, by dying on the cross, Jesus reminds us that "it is in the image of this God who is nothing but Love and Gift that mankind has been created."[10] We may therefore speak of sacrificial generosity with a God who is at once priest, the offerer, and the offering itself. When Paul talks to Timothy, we see again that the main model of Christian generosity (and its true motivation) is to be sought in the person of Christ: "They are to do good, to be rich in good works, to be generous and ready to share, thus storing up treasure for themselves as a good foundation for the future, so that they may take hold of that which is truly life" (1 Tim 6:18–19).

2. Giving to Be Spiritually Enriched: The Gift as "Investment"

In Catholic moral theology, good works enrich the Christian and open to him the doors of the eternal Kingdom. After what may be referred to as mimetic gift—one gives in order to follow the example of Jesus—we thus find again here a recurring theme of the Bible, from the Old Testament to the first epistle to Timothy: the gift enriches the one who gives. One could almost speak of calculative reason or of a gift out of self-interest. A spiritual gift to be sure, but interested nonetheless, since the Christian expects a reward from God. Even if the words "enrichment," "capital," and "acquisition" are not to be interpreted according to the categories of economic rationality, nor even within the framework of a pure material logic, they mean that it is in the interest of the believer—and thus of each one of us—to display generosity. The Book of Proverbs is particularly interesting in this regard, as its apparent simplicity, not to say its prosaic aspect, makes it an accessible text that is widely circulated in the form of moral maxims.

---

10. Debergé, *L'argent dans la Bible*, 97.

One gives freely, yet grows all the richer; another withholds what he should give, and only suffers want. (Prov 11:24)

Whoever is generous to the poor lends to the Lord, and he will repay him for his deed.[11] (Prov 19:17)

Whoever gives to the poor will not want.[12] (Prov 28:27)

True wealth cannot be capitalized; it grows through perpetual self-consumption.[13] It is not to be sought in possession, but in sharing. "For whoever gives you a cup of water to drink in My name, because you belong to Christ, assuredly, I say to you, he will by no means lose his reward" (Mark 9:41). Generosity alone enables one to gather up in one's soul a treasure for eternity: God himself. And yet, in Mark we find the promise made by Jesus to his disciples that they would receive one-hundredfold—here and now—at home, in their family, or in the fields, according to whatever they gave up to follow him (Mark 10:30). The promised wealth generally applies to the beyond. This theme comes back through Scripture like a leitmotiv: "He who gives enriches himself." In Catholic theology, however, this means spiritual wealth, the true treasure consisting in the Kingdom of God. We also find this norm of reciprocity in Ben Sirach's counsels, but it must be noted that the gift is limited here to coreligionists, whereas in Christian ethics it is universal: "If you do good, know to whom you do it, and you will be thanked for your good deeds. Do good to the devout, and you will be repaid—if not by them, certainly by the Most High." (Sir 12:1-2); "Lay up your treasure according to the commandments of the Most High, and it will profit you more than gold. Store up almsgiving in your treasury, and it will rescue you from every disaster." (Sir 29:11-12) The idea of gift and counter-gift also finds expression in Luke: "Give, and it will be given to you: good measure, pressed down, shaken together, and running over will be put into your bosom. For with the same measure that you use, it will be measured back to you." (Luke 6:38) This idea of retribution is usually underscored when the prophet Isaiah draws a parallel between fasting and the gift: "Is this not the fast that I have chosen: To loose the bonds of wickedness, [. . .] to share your bread with the hungry, And that you bring to your house the poor who are cast out; [. . .] if you extend your soul to the hungry and satisfy the afflicted soul, then your light shall dawn in the darkness, and your darkness shall be as the noonday.

---

11. According to the translation used by Jean Kressmann. Compare with the *Bible de Jérusalem*: "Qui fait la charité aux pauvres prête à Yahvé qui paiera le bienfait de retour."

12. *La Bible de Jérusalem* reads: "Pour qui donne aux pauvres, pas de disette."

13. Kressmann, *Le piège du Dieu vivant*, 394.

The Lord will guide you continually; [. . .] you shall be like [. . .] a spring of water, whose waters do not fail." (Isa 58:6–11) Better than the practice of fasting, the gift, which is also both a sacrifice and a privation, enables one to glorify God and to announce deliverance. In Catholic theology, generosity toward the neighbor in this world can be likened to an investment that is going to pay off later in the beyond. This is why the "gift for gain" can be one with the gift that sanctifies and purifies.

3. Giving to Save One's Soul: The Purifying Gift

As Tobit tells his son: "So you will be laying up a good treasure for yourself against the day of necessity. For almsgiving delivers from death and keeps you from going into the Darkness" (Tob 4:9–10). Charity can thus earn one the treasure of eternal life and keep away the flames of hell. In the Catholic tradition, giving purifies, sanctifies. One gives in order to save one's soul, to attempt to redeem one's sins. In the Old Testament, this is what Tobit tells his son Tobias: "For almsgiving saves from death and purges away every sin. Those who give alms will enjoy a full life . . . " (Tob 12:9) A message confirmed by Ben Sirach in his collection of sayings: "As water extinguishes a blazing fire, so almsgiving atones for sin. Those who repay favors give thought to the future; when they fall they will find support" (Sir 3:30–31). The purifying and sanctifying dimension is perfectly explicit in these verses of Ecclesiastes devoted to charity toward the poor. About those rich people who bequeathed considerable amounts to religious institutions or gave back their belongings to former debtors, Max Weber uses the beautiful term "conscience money."[14] Even today, it is not infrequent to find sceptics and people indifferent to religion who, before the fatal moment, try either to hedge their bets in the face of the uncertainty of the Judgment, or at least to reconcile with God through gifts. And yet, Peter's answer to Simon Magus ought to disabuse all those who think they can buy spiritual goods with money (Acts 8:18–21): "Your money perish with you, because you thought that the gift of God could be purchased with money! You have neither part nor portion in this matter, for your heart is not right in the sight of God." What behavior could be more interested—for a believer—than one that is supposed to "secure" him eternal life? Without overlooking what can be inaccurate about this presentation due to its oversimplifying character, we must here contrast two traditions: the Catholic understanding of reciprocity and the Protestant understanding of gratuitousness.

---

14. Weber, *L'Éthique protestante et l'esprit du capitalisme*, 76.

Based mostly on the mediation of the clergy, the former preaches salvation by (good) works, to the point of having experienced all its excesses through its history (e.g., with the sale of indulgences). The gift allows the sinner to redeem his sins. However, it must be pointed out that only God (and not the Church) can grant the remission of sins. The latter view is opposed to any idea of a meritorious work on the part of the creature (man), and views the gift as a gesture of gratitude toward the Creator (God)—and certainly not as a means to obtain forgiveness. "And what do you have that you did not receive? Now if you did indeed receive it, why do you boast as if you had not received it?" (1 Cor 4:7) One does not make offerings in order to be saved, but because one has been chosen, by grace; one expresses love for God by giving freely and with joy. On one side, one gives, if not to placate God, then to try to catch his attention; on the other side, one gives in order to thank God and to glorify him. Some Reformed believers still often reproach their Church (and the Roman Church) for turning the Word of God into a human morality and mixing divine law and natural law. As it happens, Catholics sometimes tend to confuse the gratuitousness of the gesture of charity with a moral obligation. Furthermore, the gift can also degenerate into its opposite: i.e., alms, here in the sense of a practice that promotes the giver as much as it humiliates its beneficiary.[15]

4. Giving Out of Duty

Since they came out of Egypt, as Pierre Debergé writes, the people of God has taken upon itself "a fundamental duty: almsgiving."[16] In the more recent texts of the Old Testament, almsgiving is indeed viewed as a duty: "Do not add to the troubles of the desperate, or delay giving to the needy" (Sir 4:3), and as one of the wellsprings of happiness: "No good comes to one who persists in evil or to one who does not give alms" (Sir 12:3). Alms are thus identified with the gift and come to be termed in turn "a fundamental duty,"[17] "a duty of concrete solidarity with the poor,"[18] and a "duty"[19] for all Christians. We have already noted that the practice of almsgiving was strongly urged throughout the Book of Tobias: "Give some of your food to the hungry, and

---

15. An idea that we also find in this African proverb: "The hand that gives is always above the one that receives." Which is, of course, the opposite of almsgiving as advocated in the Gospel.

16. Debergé, L'argent dans la Bible, 118.

17. Debergé, L'argent dans la Bible, 118, 137, 142.

18. Debergé, L'argent dans la Bible, 120.

19. Debergé, L'argent dans la Bible, 132.

some of your clothing to the naked. Give all your surplus as alms, and do not let your eye begrudge your giving of alms." (Tob 4:16) "Prayer with fasting is good, but better than both is almsgiving with righteousness. A little with righteousness is better than wealth with wrongdoing." (Tob 12:8) This counsel is all the more important, insists Debergé, highly representative in this of Catholic moral theology, as almsgiving (*tsedaka*) and justice are referred to by the same word in Hebrew. After having quoted Ecclesiastes: "Do not grow weary when you pray; do not neglect to give alms" (Sir 7:10), he reminds us that "any prayer that is not made concrete in care for the poor is useless." Christian solidarity must be active if faith is to have any substance. And he quotes one of the pillars of the Catholic confession, the famous "no faith without works!" of Saint James. "What does it profit, my brethren, if someone says he has faith but does not have works? Can faith save him? If a brother or sister is naked and destitute of daily food, and one of you says to them, 'Depart in peace, be warmed and filled,' but you do not give them the things which are needed for the body, what does it profit? Thus also faith by itself, if it does not have works, is dead" (Jas 2:14–17).

Generosity to the needy is a moral imperative for all Christians. The commentary of the School of Jerusalem's (Catholic) Biblicists is also unambiguous: "Following Christ, man's answer to the gift of faith is works; through them, man gives witness to Truth."[20] The letter to the Hebrews also reminds us that charity is the best worship that may be given to God (Heb 13:16). The service of God is necessarily accompanied by "service of brethren in the faith." With the radical tone that characterizes him, Luke had already opened the way: "Sell what you have and give alms; [. . .] For where your treasure is, there your heart will be also" (Luke 12:33–34). According to him, the first Christian community in Jerusalem did not include any needy person, and Luke constantly emphasizes the duty of solidarity of the rich toward the poor. As the Pharisees were told: "But rather give alms of such things as you have; then indeed all things are clean to you" (Luke 11:41). The Christian is called upon to free himself from the power of money through the gift.

5. Giving to Desacralize Money

The theme of money is so important that it deserves a special discussion. Let us confine ourselves here to the essentials of the Biblical message: the invitation to enter into the Revelation of God, which is precisely that of

---

20. *La Bible de Jérusalem*, 2461.

gratuitousness.[21] The gift allows us to stand the test of money and to resist its ever-tempting autonomous power. Offering up liberates us because it turns us toward the Wholly Other. It is not a duty, but "the health of religious life," as Antoinette Butte nicely put it.[22] While we live in a world where everything is bought and sold, the God of the Gospel offers us a spiritual reversal: entering a world in which nothing is bought and everything is given. While money belongs to the "sacred" of modern man, the gift is a sign of gratuitousness and freedom that enables us to break free of its hold. Giving without counting is to express one's generosity, but it also means desacralizing money, a particularly salutary work in a society driven by the religion of profit. The Christian, for his part, is invited not to conform to this world and to follow Jesus in entering the world of dispossession: "though He was rich, yet for your sakes He became poor, that you through His poverty might become rich" (2 Cor 8:9). God gives grace, for it would be impossible for us to pay its true price if we had to buy it. "God's sole behavior is the gift," as Ellul sums it up.[23] Even if we spoke above of giving as an "investment" in the spiritual sense, we have to underscore from the outset that the Gospel's general tone is distinctly anti-utilitarian, as evidenced in the story of the perfume offered by Mary. For Jesus accepted that 300 pieces of silver should be spent on him, which is the equivalent of over 300 workdays of an agricultural laborer. In John's narrative, the action takes place in Bethany six days before Easter, while Jesus is dining at Martha's with her brother Lazarus—having been raised from the dead—and her sister Mary:[24]

> Then Mary took a pound of very costly oil of spikenard, anointed the feet of Jesus, and wiped His feet with her hair. And the house was filled with the fragrance of the oil. But one of His disciples, Judas Iscariot, Simon's son, who would betray Him, said, "Why was this fragrant oil not sold for three hundred denarii and given to the poor?" This he said, not that he cared for the poor, but because he was a thief, and had the money box; and he used to take what was put in it. But Jesus said, "Let her alone; she has kept this for the day of My burial. For the poor you have with you always, but Me you do not have always." (John 12:1–8)

21. As a counterpoint to Pierre Debergé's book cited above, see Ellul, *L'homme et l'argent*; available in English as Ellul, *Money and Power*.

22. Butte, *L'Offrande*, 12

23. Ellul, "L'argent," 168.

24. These two sisters seem to have the same character traits as those described in Luke 10:38–42. Mark 14:1–9 and Matt 26:6–13 do not specify the identity of the woman with the alabaster jar. In their narrative, it is all of the disciples who cry waste about what Jesus calls a "good work."

From the moral standpoint, the lavish character of this gift seems unjustified. From a utilitarian standpoint, this act of devotion looks like a disproportionate and senseless expense. But what does "the reasonable" have to do in the whole story of Christ? As Paul puts it so well: "Let no one deceive himself. If anyone among you seems to be wise in this age, let him become a fool that he may become wise. For the wisdom of this world is foolishness with God. For it is written, 'He catches the wise in their craftiness'" (1 Cor 3:18–19). The teaching of Jesus turns upside down economic rationality and human morality that would convert the price of this offering, deemed frivolous, into a useful gift for the needy. How better to desacralize money than by wasting this perfume or by stating, against the full force of evidence, that "it is more blessed to give than to receive" (Acts 20:35)?

Jesus stigmatizes the worship of Mammon and not money in-itself, (that is, money as mere material instrument). Nor does he condemn property, and he even counted several rich men among his friends. The lesson on the two treasures has sometimes been understood as the opposition between the material and the spiritual, when it is a difference of attitudes toward riches. It is only because the disciples of Jesus accept to lose everything to follow him that property again becomes something possible in God's eyes, "but then it ceases to be a right and becomes a gift."[25] Faith is just what allows us to proclaim our detachment with respect to this tempting power that is Mammon, symbolized by the betrayal of Judas who sells Jesus out for thirty pieces of silver. When Jesus states that no servant can have two masters, he is acknowledging an impossibility and is not articulating a prohibition. Moralists have turned into a legal prohibition ('you must not') a parable aimed at revealing a radical impossibility ('you cannot'). The love of God is exclusive, as is the love of money. The two are antithetical. Smarmy bargaining between them is just not possible! "No one can serve two masters; for either he will hate the one and love the other, or else he will be loyal to the one and despise the other. You cannot serve God and Mammon." (Matt 6:24; Luke 16:13) Such is the true conclusion of the parable of the wise steward, better known under the name of the parable of the "false servant."[26] Luke's narrative is inviting us here to desacralize money, against the grain of human morality and far beyond its canons. A rich man learns that his steward is squandering his goods and asks him to account for his management. The steward is more incompetent than dishonest, since he has not accumulated a nest egg and finds himself genuinely anxious at the thought of losing his job. He takes advantage of the respite granted to him to

---

25. Roux, *L'argent dans la communauté de l'Église*, 19.
26. On this point, see the essential book by Kressmann, *Le piège du Dieu vivant*.

make friends where we would be tempted to see but mere accomplices. "So he called every one of his master's debtors to him, and said to the first, 'How much do you owe my master?' And he said, 'A hundred measures of oil.' So he said to him, 'Take your bill, and sit down quickly and write fifty.' Then he said to another, 'And how much do you owe?' So he said, 'A hundred measures of wheat.' And he said to him, 'Take your bill, and write eighty.' So the master commended the unjust steward[27] because he had dealt shrewdly. For the sons of this world are shrewder in their generation than the sons of light." (Luke 16:5–8) The steward is thanked for having fraudulently given goods that had first been virtuously saved. He shows himself generous with riches that do not belong to him. Human justice is not served! But by reducing the debt of his master's debtors, he breaks the circle of sales and corruption and makes his new friends enter the world of gratuitousness. "In that, this steward is unfaithful to money and faithful to grace," as Jacques Ellul puts it.[28] "And I say to you, make friends for yourselves by unrighteous Mammon,[29] that when you fail, they may receive you into an everlasting home" (Luke 16:9)—a very embarrassing admonition for all those who would shutter the words of Christ in a treatise of morals! Spiritual truth is here difficult to reconcile with a catechism of any kind. Even so, desacralizing money does not mean making a vow of poverty; Ellul insists on this point. Wanting to be poor is wanting to be sick, as the first Lutherans already said. It is even a crime with respect to poverty that is suffered. Not only does the Bible not praise voluntary poverty, but it invites Christians to fight destitution. One therefore also gives to fight poverty, but here the question of the why logically brings up another one: whom does one give to?

II. Giving to Whom?

According to Scripture, one gives to God, to the Church, and above all to men. "For all things come from You, and of Your own we have given You" (1 Chron 29:14). Or again, as Saint Augustine wrote: "God does not need sacrifices [. . .] Will he who drinks at a spring say that this spring benefits from it?"[30] Charity already had a central place in the Old Testament. "The merciful lend

---

27. "Unjust steward" is translated as "*intendant de l'Iniquité*" ("steward of Iniquity") in Jean Kressmann's book and by "*intendant avisé*" ("shrewd steward") in the *La Bible de Jérusalem*.

28. Ellul, "L'argent," 176.

29. We are partial to the French *Traduction œcuménique de la Bible* (TOB), which renders this phrase as "argent trompeur" ("deceitful money").

30. Saint Augustine, *De civitate dei contra paganos*, book X, ch. 5.

to their neighbors; by holding out a helping hand they keep the commandments" (Sir 29:1). Jesus confirmed the importance by making charity (*agapè*) the first of his commandments: "This is My commandment, that you love one another as I have loved you." (John 15:12) In the 1960s, liberation theologian Gustavo Gutierrez devised the expression "preferential option for the poor," later taken up by the bishops of North America and eventually adopted by the Vatican.[31] And yet, if the neighbor can obviously appear in the guise of the needy person, what are we to understand by the poor?

1. Giving to the Poor

> Give some of your food to the hungry, and some of your clothing to the naked. Give all your surplus as alms, and do not let your eye begrudge your giving of alms. (Tob 4:16a)

> He who despises his neighbor sins; but he who has mercy on the poor, happy is he! (Prov 14:21)

> He who oppresses the poor reproaches his Maker, but he who honors Him has mercy on the needy. (Prov 14:31)

> He who gives to the poor will not lack, but he who hides his eyes will have many curses. (Prov 28:27)

> My child, do not cheat the poor of their living [. . .] Do not grieve the hungry, or anger one in need. (Sir 4:1–2)

> Stretch out your hand to the poor, so that your blessing may be complete. (Sir 7:32)

> Nevertheless, be patient with someone in humble circumstances, and do not keep him waiting for your alms. Help the poor for the commandment's sake, and in their need do not send them away empty-handed. (Sir 29:8–9)

And yet, in the Old Testament, wealth was long viewed as a sign of divine blessing and poverty as the sanction of impiety.[32] It will take the Books of Job and Ecclesiastes (Qohelet), two texts particularly dear to Ellul, for a rupture to appear in this doctrine of earthly retributions. Material wealth no longer need go hand in hand with justice and happiness; destitution is no longer

---

31. Puebla Conference (1979) and Encyclical *Sollicitudo Rei Socialis*, no. 42, 30–12, 1987.

32. This understanding, of course, is that of the Protestant entrepreneurs described by Weber, *L'Éthique protestante et l'esprit du capitalisme*, 156ff.

described as the wages of sin. Nevertheless, poverty is never presented in the Bible as a desirable state. Saint Luke even makes its disappearance an essential feature of the first Christian community in Jerusalem. The question has been raised of whether limits ought to be set to this generosity. No, answers for instance Jacques Ellul, for whom "it is not for us to calculate whether the destitute is in need by his own fault or by chance, whether he deserves our gift or not: these calculations are still those of Mammon [. . .]."[33]

2. Giving to All the Poor?

The Protestant (and more particularly the Reformed) tradition holds that when it comes to gifts, "the Bible does not distinguish between those who are worthy of receiving it and those who are unworthy," but only looks for those who need it.[34] *A contrario*, Catholics could invoke Ben Sirach's doctrine as expounded in Ecclesiastes: "If you do good, know to whom you do it, and you will be thanked for your good deeds" (Sir 12:1). Along the same lines: "No good comes to one who persists in evil or to one who does not give alms. Give to the devout, but do not help the sinner" (Sir 12:3-4). This restriction shocked Saint Augustine, incidentally, and induced him to soften its rigor by commenting this verse roughly as follows: 'Do not give to the sinner as a sinner, give to him as a man,' with no thought of what he may or may not have done to end up in this position. Or again, in the parable of the ten maidens, the five foolish virgins are turned away for their lack of foresight by the five wise virgins: "'Give us some of your oil, for our lamps are going out.' But the wise answered, saying, 'No, lest there should not be enough for us and you; but go rather to those who sell, and buy for yourselves'" (Matt 25:8-9). Finally, even more explicitly: "Do good to the humble, but do not give to the ungodly; hold back their bread, and do not give it to them, for by means of it they might subdue you [. . .] Give to the one who is good, but do not help the sinner" (Sir 12:5-7). One has to admit that the Gospel brushes aside this type of restrictions when it comes to the Kingdom to be built.

3. Giving to All

Relating the words of Jesus in his Sermon on the Mount, Matthew writes: "Give to the one who asks" or "To the one who asks, give" (Matt 5:42), an

---

33. Ellul, "L'argent," 190.
34. Ellul, "L'argent," 190.

exhortation transcribed as follows by Luke: "Give every time to any supplicant" or "Give to everyone who asks of you" (Luke 6:30). The Gospel message is thus to give not to those who deserve but to everyone who asks, which incidentally assumes that all those who ask for help need it. Furthermore, including for Ben Sirach whose hardness toward the impious we have seen, one is advised to give to friends and to brothers, without exception nor any particular condition (Sir 29:10). Nowhere does it say that the gift is limited to an interaction between rich and poor. The Gospel speaks of the poor more often than of poverty. One needs to carefully distinguish within the Hebrew vocabulary all the meanings of the English word "poor"—indigent, needy, exploited, but also humble, small, modest, afflicted—in order to avoid confusing love for the poor and love for poverty.[35] The idea that poverty represents a privileged road to God is not without danger. Pushed to an extreme, it has even given rise in history to heresies like that of the Fraticelli.[36] When somebody writes: "some situations of poverty can preserve one from the snares of material wealth and of power, and thus lead to God, the only wealth," or "in the depths of destitution, the poor person experiences the nearness of God," or again, "only the one who accepts becoming poor and making himself vulnerable truly opens himself to the world of God," there is a serious risk of buying into a false alternative: either poor with God, or rich without or against God.[37] Now, for the Christian, the real ethical question is that of making his financial situation of whichever kind an instrument of the glory of God. Nor does the Bible say that charity can be reduced to a gift of money alone.

III. Giving What, and How?

The good Samaritan who stops to help an injured man he met on his path does not only give him money, but also his time, his compassion, his love (Luke 10:30–35). While those whose functions should have brought them to show

---

35. It is no small difference to translate (Zeph 3:12): "I will maintain a humble and modest people in your midst" (as in the French Jérusalem translation), or "humble and small" (as in the French Louis Segond translation), as "a remnant of humble and poor people" (as in the French TOB translation).

36. Coming from the so-called "spiritual" faction of the Franciscan order, the Fraticelli and other Dulcinians, or "Apostolics," were popularized by Umberto Eco's famous novel *The Name of the Rose*.

37. Debergé, *L'argent dans la Bible*, 81, 84, 86, 87. The theologian writes thus about the "twofold Biblical perception of poverty: on the one hand, an evil to be fought; on the other hand, the site where a human being can truly be born to his identity as Son of God and universal Brother."

more charity—the priest and the Levite—did not want to sully themselves with this impure blood, the Samaritan, for his part, takes the time to rescue this unknown person whom plunderers have severely beaten. He bandages his wounds, puts him on his mount, takes him to an inn and finally pays for his stay before announcing that he will come and visit on his way back. Mary, the sister of Lazarus, as we have seen, offers Jesus a jar of perfume. "Indeed, does not a word surpass a good gift?", as Sirach says (Sir 18:17). In reality, as we know, Christ's main commandment is that we love each other as he has loved us. The heart of the biblical message is thus love for the neighbor, but it is easier to send a check to UNICEF once a month than to love the neighbor who makes your life miserable with the barking of his dog or the noise of his TV. However, the gift of money is needed in certain circumstances and this is the one we are going to emphasize here. How much should we give? All that is superfluous, whatever is needed, a tenth?

The main thing according to Saint Luke is not to hoard, or even for Christ's disciples to give up all of their possessions (Luke 14:33). Provided however that sharing among the community is not a function of some moral law but of free choice. On this point, not without some variations, a Catholic and a Protestant can agree.[38] On the basis of the description given by Luke of the first Christian community: "Nor was there anyone among them who lacked" (Acts 4:34), some theologians have held that the main issue was not to know what one had to give or keep for oneself, but what one had to give in order to put an end to the scandal of poverty. This verse is thus often translated as: "None among them was poor," in a context where Luke expresses strongly egalitarian values. The temptation is great then to deduce from this an invitation to give everything to the poor and to confuse as a result equity and equality. For we do find this type of admonition in the Gospel: "Sell what you have and give alms." (Luke 12:33) "So likewise, whoever of you does not forsake all that he has cannot be my disciple." (Luke 14:33) Or again in the parable of the rich young ruler: "Sell all that you have and distribute it to the poor . . . " (Luke 18:22) And finally in the parable of the treasure and the pearl: "Again, the kingdom of heaven is like a merchant seeking beautiful pearls, who, when he had found one pearl of great price, went and sold all that he had and bought it" (Matt 13:45–46). If he wants to access the celestial riches, man must give up all that he possesses in this world. To soften the rigor of this commandment, either it is pointed out that it is exceptional in the Bible, or that it is addressed primarily to the small number who have received this calling, even if it potentially concerns all Christians.

---

38. At a quantitative level, let it suffice to mention here that countries of Protestant culture (the USA and the UK in particular) give a lot more than countries of Catholic culture (France and Italy especially).

We must recall here the words of Paul in the second epistle to the Corinthians, devoted precisely to the organization of collection and the motivations of generosity.[39] "I speak not by commandment, but I am testing the sincerity of your love [. . .] For I do not mean that others should be eased, and you burdened; but [that what is needed is] equality [. . .]" (2 Cor 8:8–13). Ben Sirach, too, had counseled: "So help your neighbor as much as you can, but protect yourself against the dangers involved" (Sir 29:20).

While the Christians of Macedonia had given "beyond their means," Paul asks Corinthians only for the superfluous, as there must not be any place for savings. The money earned must be used to satisfy our needs and the surplus must be fully redistributed. In accordance with the rule established for the manna given by God: "He who gathered much had nothing left over, and he who gathered little had no lack" (2 Cor 8:15). For during the march in the Sinai, God had caused manna to fall from heaven; "every man had gathered according to each one's need" and "he who *gathered* much had nothing left over, and he who *gathered* little had no lack" (Exod 16:18). Paul is confirming here a basic principle taught during the Exodus and that governs the whole of Jewish and Biblical ethics with respect to wealth. To sum up, one can see very well that it is more a matter of equity than of equality: "All who believed were together and had all things in common; they would sell their possessions and goods and distribute the proceeds to all, as any had need" (Acts 2:44–45). Luke repeats in chapter four that they shared everything and confirms: "They laid it at the apostles' feet, and it was distributed to each as any had need" (Acts 4:35). The rich publican Zacchaeus, for instance, only gives half of his possessions to the poor (Luke 19:8). And yet, when Jesus mentions the widow's offering before his disciples, he shows that to make a true gift, it is not enough to give the "superfluous;" one must also give up the necessary. By giving her two small coins, the poor woman took from her very indigence, she "has put in everything she had, all she had to live on" (Mark 12:44; Luke 21:4). There are those who have thought it possible to "objectify" the question of the "how" by invoking the practice of the tithe in force under the Old Covenant (Lev 27:30–32): giving the tenth part of what one earns, quite simply. The genuine answer however is not a matter of percentage. In reality, it is by starting again from the Second Epistle to the Corinthians that we find the main indication:

> The point is this: the one who sows sparingly will also reap sparingly, and the one who sows bountifully will also reap bountifully. Each of you must give as you have made up your mind, not

---

39. This text concerns a solidarity collection for the benefit of the church of Jerusalem. The gift is used here to ensure the unity of the early church.

reluctantly or under compulsion, for God loves a cheerful giver. And God is able to provide you with every blessing in abundance, so that by always having enough of everything, you may share abundantly in every good work. (2 Cor 9:6–8)

Everything is said here: the main thing is not the how much, but the how.

IV. How to Give?

As soon as charity becomes a chore, once giving becomes an obligation, when gratuitousness degenerates into a technique, as soon as love for the neighbor becomes a moral rule, the believer's conscience may perhaps be at rest, but he is no longer in tune with Biblical truth. "For I desire mercy, not sacrifice" (Hos 6:6). God prefers goodness to burnt offerings, as the prophet Micah confirms (Mic 6:8). Mark says nothing different: Jesus asks first that one love God and the neighbor as oneself. Which is worth "more than all whole burnt offerings and sacrifices" (Mark 12:30–33)

When it comes to the giving, the manner of giving is at least as important as the gift itself. More precisely, it is what grounds its true worth in the eyes of God. "My child, add no reproach to your charity, or spoil any gift by harsh words. Does not the dew give relief from the scorching heat? So a word can be better than a gift. Indeed does not a word count more than a good gift? But both are offered by a kind person" (Si 18:15–17). As Saint Paul says, even though I might know all mysteries and all science, I might have faith that moves mountains, I might give away all my possessions to the poor, if I "do not have love, I gain nothing" (1 Co 13:1–3). If I lack love, all my qualities are useless since I am nothing. Love opens hearts, but it also opens the eyes. Mammon closes them. If money is such a fearsome thing, it is because it makes us blind. Our generosity or our blindness are not hidden from God's sight. All through the Gospel, the theme of the gaze has pride of place when it comes to our relation to Money. The eye is thus termed by Matthew the "lamp of the body." If the eye is healthy, the whole body will be in light; if the eye is sick, the whole body will be plunged in darkness (Mt 6:22–23). If our inner light does not shine, our night will be darker that that of the blind. Is it a coincidence if these two verses are lodged between those on the true treasure and those on money? The "No one can serve two masters" of Matthew (Mt 6:24) happens to echo the Decalogue: "You shall have no other gods before me" (Exodus 20:3)—a first command which itself precedes the prohibition of ritual images and that of the worship of idols.

The *gaze* is therefore constantly at issue between man and God, rich and poor, the one who gives and the one who receives. "The poor man and the oppressor meet together; the Lord gives light to the eyes of both" (Pr 29:13).

"Whoever gives to the poor will not want, but he who hides his eyes will get many a curse." (Pr 28:27) One theme keeps coming back like a leitmotiv: sin consists less in not giving than in ignoring, to the point of not seeing those who need our generosity. "Turn not away thy eyes from the poor [. . .] and turn not away thy face from the needy," as Sirach sums up (Si 4:1–5). "Do not turn your face away from any poor man, and the face of God will not be turned away from you," as Tobias advises his son (Tb 4:7), further specifying that a genuine gift is done wholeheartedly: "[. . .] and do not let your eye begrudge the gift when you made it." (Tb 4:16)

In the parable of the wicked rich man and the poor man Lazarus (Lk 16:19–31), the rich man's sin is not that he has refused to give alms, but that he has not even noticed the poor man covered in sores and dying of hunger at his door. The wicked rich man, being possessed by money, fails to cast even a single glance on the poor man who is dying in front of his house. We are not meant to admire and honor the rich in this world and to turn our eyes away from the poor according to the world (James 2:1–6). If "charity is an excellent offering in the presence of the Most High" (Tb 4:11), it must also be done away from the eyes of men. God sees it; that is more than enough. "Thus, when you give alms, sound no trumpet before you, as the hypocrites do in the synagogues and in the streets, that they may be praised by men," Jesus says in the Sermon on the Mount. "But when you give alms, do not let your left hand know what your right hand is doing, so that your alms may be in secret; and your Father who sees in secret will reward you" (Mt 6:1–4). Generosity must therefore not be displayed on the public square, be trumpeted everywhere; it must not be practiced ostentatiously, but in secret. (Ellul insists on this fundamental point in *Money and Power*, extending his analysis in his 1952 article.[40])

The gaze is again involved in the widow's offering. Jesus sits in front of the Temple and looks at how each person slips an offering in the collection box. His intention is deliberate. Jesus did not sit on that spot by chance but to observe, less what people were giving than the way they were giving: "And he sat down opposite the treasury, and watched the multitude putting money into the treasury. Many rich people put in large sums. And a poor widow came, and put in two copper coins, which make a penny" (Mk 12:41–42). And Jesus calls his disciples to tell them essentially that the

---

40. See Ellul, *Money and Power*; "L'Argent."

greatest offering in the eyes of God comes from this poor woman who has given a ridiculous amount in the eyes of men, but who has "put in everything she had, her whole living." When it comes to money, Jesus observes not the amount being given but the way it is given. "However small the gift may be, if it is loaded with intention, it can establish a vast dialogue," as Antoinette Butte writes.[41] But the gift must never degenerate into alms, in the sense of some kind of superiority of the giver over the needy, implying all that might be humiliating about this for the latter.[42] The Christian gift must give the lie to the African proverb according to which "the hand that gives is always above the hand that receives." Almsgiving is a search for personal satisfaction, whereas the true gift is above all a gift of self. Alms are still a money-based relation, whereas the gift is above all a relation of love. The gift must not be a duty, but a personal act that allows us to break free of the power of money. "As long as we feel too great a sadness in giving, something wrenching, an annoyance, it is better not to give," counsels Jacques Ellul, who saw in the rich young man's sadness (Mt 19:22) the sign that he is far from the grace of God.

In conclusion, the question of how to give—especially when it is broached by intransigent Christians like Jacques Ellul—can only detach numerous daily acts of generosity from the biblical message. For his part, Vincent Laupies is right to highlight the evangelical complexity of the gift and the dangers of a selective reading of the Bible. The injunctions calling the hearer to give to all who ask are nuanced by others which are there to remind Christians that "the gift should not be a reflex."[43] Incidentally, it is still possible to call upon the letter to better besmirch the spirit. We have certainly forgotten how the emperor Haile Selassie—an Orthodox Christian—explained why his government did nothing to help the victims of the 1973 famines. "We have said that wealth must be earned through work; we have said: the one who does not work shall not eat." [44] Is this not a gross instrumentalization of Paul's second epistle to the Thessalonians? "If anyone is not willing to work, may he not eat either" (2 Th 3:10). Yet in context, Paul only intended to call to order several of his fellow disciples who had already forsaken all work in the expectation of the glorious arrival of the Messiah.

And yet, if it might seem presumptuous to affirm a direct lineage from the biblical Word to the multiple contemporary figures of the gift in our

---

41. Butte, *L'Offrande*, 14.

42. See Ellul, *Money and Power*, 190.

43. Laupies, "La complexité évangélique du don," 390.

44. Sentence quoted by L. Wiseberg, "An International Perspective on the African Famines," in Sen, *Repenser l'inégalité*.

secularized societies, we can at least speak of select affinities. Certainly, a very imperfect translation of certain doctrinal elements is often involved, many times in contradiction with the original message—as we have tried to render it here in any case—but also, sometimes, in complete harmony. Just as the Protestant Puritan and Weber's capitalist entrepreneur do not speak the same language yet understand one another, the charitable believer can entertain a fruitful dialogue on the topic of the gift with the generous natural man, and in a completely different register, with the sociologist. For in fact, the biblical message is perfectly soluble in the Maussian triple obligation: give, receive, give back. Even in the situation of pure cognitive dissonance in which we find ourselves by virtue of our market societies—which, on the one hand, make the rituals of individual performance, economic success, and universal competition into the religion of modern times, and on the other hand, unceasingly call upon compassion, selflessness, gratuitousness, and generosity towards the various categories of the excluded—it is helpful to highlight, with Durkheim, the intrinsic normativity of human societies.[45] As for the Christian, properly speaking, he or she has further reasons to express his or her charity. Ellul holds his or her relation to money to be a spiritual trial, for this money is unjust and deceitful; Ellul invites the Christian to desacralize it by means of the gratuitousness of the gift.

Works Cited

Butte, Antoinette. *L'Offrande. Office sacerdotal de l'Église*. Strasbourg: Librairie Oberlin, 1965.

Caillé, Alain. *Don, intérêt et désintéressement: Bourdieu, Mauss, Platon et quelques autres*. Lormont: Le Bord de l'eau, 2014.

———. "Du religieux. Esquisse d'une grammaire en clé de don." *Revue du MAUSS semestrielle* 49 (2017) 185–217. Paris: La Découverte.

Chanial, Philippe. *La société vue du don*. TAP/Bibliothèque du MAUSS. Paris: La Découverte, 2008.

Debergé, Pierre. *L'argent dans la Bible: ni pauvre ni riche*. Racines. Montrouge: Nouvelle Cité, 1983.

Eco, Umberto. *The Name of the Rose*. New York: Harcourt, 1983.

Ellul, Jacques. "L'argent." *Études théologiques et religieuses* 27 (1952) 29–66. Reprinted in *L'Économie*, edited by Patrick Troude-Chastenet. Cahiers Jacques-Ellul. N.d.: Le Bouscat / L'Esprit du temps, 2005.

———. *L'homme et l'argent (Nova et vetera)*. In *Le défi et le nouveau. Œuvres théologiques 1948–1991*, 199–345. Paris: La Table Ronde, 2007.

Kressmann, Jean. *Le piège du Dieu vivant. Essai sur la parabole de l'économe infidèle*. Paris: Je sers, 1948.

45. On this subject, see Debergé, *L'argent dans la Bible*, particularly 28–31; Caillé, *Don, intérêt et désintéressement*.

La Bible de Jérusalem. Paris: Editions du Cerf/Fleurus, 2001.

Laupies, Vincent. "La complexité évangélique du don." La Découverte, *Revue du MAUSS semestrielle* 47 (2016) 387–98.

Roux, Hébert. *L'argent dans la communauté de l'Église*. Cahiers de Théologie de l'Actualité Protestante 18. Neuchâtel/Paris: Delachaux et Niestlé, 1947.

Sen, Amartya. *Repenser l'inégalité*. L'Histoire immédiate. Paris: Seuil, 2000.

Tarot, Camille. "Don et grâce, une famille à recomposer?" *Revue du MAUSS semestrielle* 32 (2008) 469–94.

Troeltsch, Ernst. *Protestantism and Progress*. New Brunswick, NJ: Transaction, 2013.

Weber, Max. *L'Éthique protestante et l'esprit du capitalisme*. Paris: Plon/Agora, 1985.

———. *The Protestant Ethic and the Spirit of Capitalism*. Radford, VA: Wilder, 2009.

———. *Sociology of Religion*. Boston: Beacon, 1993.

CHAPTER 17

Nature and Scripture in Bernard Charbonneau's *The Green Light*

Christian Roy

HAVING RECENTLY TRANSLATED JACQUES Ellul's posthumous book on *Theology and Technique*[1] for Wipf & Stock, I was struck by the way that it makes explicit the intertwining of these two strands of his lifelong investigation.[2] His studies of Christian faith and the sociology of the modern world, carried out in the parallel series of books devoted to their respective ramifications, come together here at last. A crucial issue on which that convergence comes to bear is that of "Limits", to which Ellul devotes an important chapter. It deals, among other things, with the thesis, fashionable since Lynn White's famous 1966 article about "The Historical Roots of Our Ecologic Crisis"[3], that locates the latter in Biblical religion's "departure from the origin where there were limits to man's enterprise over nature," when, "surrounded by a sacred universe, man knew himself to be limited in his enterprises. He might have techniques, but he could not use them just anywhere nor anyhow." The Promethean hubris of the "unlimited remained a virtuality, but prohibitions remained more powerful." Summarizing a common view of how Christianity altered this situation, Ellul writes:

> And so it comes about that Christianity intervenes in this equilibrium, by desacralizing the world, deritualizing religion and

---

1. Ellul, *Theology and Technique*, translated by Christian Roy (forthcoming from Wipf & Stock). As this translation is not yet published, citations will include page numbers for the French edition.

2. This chapter originally appeared in *The Ellul Forum* 64 (Fall 2019) 5–16. The version presented here has been lightly edited.

3. White, "Historical Roots of Our Ecologic Crisis."

negating magic. It brings things down to being only things, it refuses the limits of a sacred that it manifests as imaginary, it kills the gods of the forest, the earth and the waters, and as a result puts all things at the disposal of man who can, from now on, use 'nature' as he sees fit, without limits imposed from the outside. Why should one respect what is now no more than matter?

And we must here pay heed to B. Charbonneau's call-out: by spiritualizing God too much, by making him radically heavenly and Transcendent, man was necessarily pushed away toward Matter, his action was materialized, man's material instinct was liberated . . . . Christianity has separated what the ancient world, and the traditional world, had carefully joined, balanced. From that moment on, man may seek the most efficient means and use everything without limits and without shame. The unlimited is inherent to Christianity itself, perhaps not the Christianity of theologians, but Christianity as experienced by the masses of the faithful, and producing effects that were not so much spiritual (having to do with holiness), but concretely historical ones.[4]

Ellul's acknowledgement here of the influence of his lifelong friend Bernard Charbonneau invites us to carefully examine how the two thinkers negotiate the interrelation of Christianity, limits and nature.

Carl Amery's Ecological Challenge to Christianity: Contrasting Responses of Ellul and Charbonneau

In this passage, Ellul seems to be referring to what may have been an early draft of the chapter on "Nature and Christianity" in Bernard Charbonneau's 1980 book *Le Feu vert. Autocritique du movement écologique*[5], as well as to Bavarian writer and environmentalist Carl Amery's 1972 book *Das Ende der Vorsehung. Die gnadenlosen Folgen des Christentums* (which translates as *The End of Providence. The Merciless Consequences of Christianity*). Both Ellul and Charbonneau engage at length with the latter's 1976 French translation as *La Fin de la Providence*, albeit with different emphases. Charbonneau is much more positive about Amery's critique, whereas Ellul remains rather defensive and apologetic. This is what enables Ellul's mention of Charbonneau's challenge to Christians cited above to seamlessly segue into an implicit account of what sounds more like Amery's own positions about Christianity's

---

4. Ellul, *Théologie et Technique*, 181–82.
5. See my English translation of this work: Charbonneau, *Green Light*.

ambiguous "success" in a disenchanted world of its own making than like the position actually developed in Charbonneau's writings.

Ellul feels the challenge of Amery's book so keenly that he devotes to it a whole "Annex to the Fifth Chapter" on "Ethical Mediation." On the one hand, he locates it as part of the trend that traces "all the evil of modern Western society" to Christianity as such. "Christianity set out on a quest for the final Kingdom and only ends up in a general conquest of the world", in the guise "of technical expansion, of 'planetary revolution.'"[6] That hardly seems controversial to the world historian that I sometimes purport to be; that is, at least if we are talking about a specifically Western Christianity in which (under Charlemagne for the first time) the "mechanical arts" came to be theologically valued as instrumental in the gradual restoration of the full power over Creation that Adam had enjoyed before the Fall, a power that made him the image of God on earth. This conflation of the divine image with human power over the world as a totality fuelled the technological revolutions that spread from monasteries to fields, and thence from cities to the State, driven by a Church mandate to gather the ends of the earth and make it one, as a proper vessel for the end times of a historicized millennial Kingdom. Far from being the result of the intrusion of non-Christian impulses soon after the Reformation as Ellul insists, the Western drive to cosmic mastery was always intimately linked to this eschatological pattern. It is manifest in myriad forms, ranging from the Scientific Revolution effected by millenarian evangelical Christians who sought the mind of God in the laws of nature, to the Positivists who took them as scripture of a new religion of industry, and beyond to the current transhumanist endeavour to remake reality as the new creation of omnipotent "spiritual machines" (Howard Rheingold).[7] Whether this really existing historical and cultural Christianity is true to the essence of the faith is of course a different matter. As a Christian whose loyalty is to the Gospel rather than to Christendom, Ellul is quite ready to take a stand against the latter's dubious holdovers, alongside non-Christian critics of technological society, such as Charbonneau and Amery. However, Ellul's other problem with the latter is that "what he puts forward as an ethic, to which I readily subscribe, has no chance of being born for lack of a *positive* motivation" for "post-Christian man who lives without hope, in anguish, in the shadow of death. What could be the use of driving him deeper, of telling him no one

---

6. Ellul, *Théologie et Technique*, 299.

7. See Noble, *Religion of Technology*. I am indebted to this book in my own account of "Space, Time and the Christian Matrix of Faustian Man."

will come to his help?"[8] He views *The End of Providence* as "actually just an iteration of Death of God Theology."

> Man must be persuaded that nobody is going to come to his help, that the God on whom he was relying is absent, and that he must manage on his own with the problems he has raised.[9]

> Now, I say that without hope and without the certainty of a Transcendence, the situation in which we are can only lead to suicide. Amery, with his book, seems to me to hasten the temptation of collective suicide.[10]

Charbonneau has a very different, even sympathetic assessment of this very stance of Amery's that troubles Ellul so much. In keeping with their common early calls for "an ascetic City so that man may live . . . "[11], Charbonneau holds that "faith alone will be able to impose the asceticism" required to recognize the material limits of embodied life in all areas. "We may say with Carl Amery that, since the sacrifices needed to save the earth and man 'can hardly find justifications in our immediate interests, the call to a religious renewal seems well-founded.'"[12] And Charbonneau proceeds to quote at length as the ground of this call the same passage that seemed so dispiriting to Ellul—as though his friend could not brook the hypothetical bracketing of reliance on a divine breakthrough awaiting ahead in time to save us. But Ellul appears to misunderstand this as an a priori exclusion of that possibility, when it may be a precondition for it in Charbonneau's reading of Amery—who, invoking Job's "lived experience of human and earthly finitude", writes that "we have to treat the future itself 'as though' it could and should be defined in purely human ways," in order to be responsible for our actions.

> And we must not allow any agency, be it divine or human, to leave half-open the least way out, to count on any miraculous intervention whatsoever, to spare us the sufferings we have laid in store and inflicted upon ourselves with our own hands. We must, to speak in theological language, tend towards this final kenosis, this ultimate self-emptying: the renunciation of any

---

8. Ellul, *Théologie et Technique*, 306.
9. Ellul, *Théologie et Technique*, 299.
10. Ellul, *Théologie et Technique*, 306.
11. This is the title of the last section of their 83 "Directives pour un manifeste personnaliste" (1935), in Charbonneau and Ellul, "Nous sommes des révolutionnaires malgré nous," 80.
12. Charbonneau, *Green Light*, 74.

guaranteed future. It is only by losing it that we will win it . . .
We have entered a new phase of divine unfathomability.[13]

This could well be read as an illustration of Ellul's crucial contrast of *espoir* and *espérance*: the former has to be lost or renounced for the latter to come into play as an opening to unforeseeable possibilities, with no certainty to fall back on, only *faith*.[14] And this is precisely the point that Charbonneau makes—arguably more Ellulian than Ellul himself here—in support of Amery's insistence on "lowering the growth rate to restore equilibrium," which he sees as a road without end that begins at our own feet, no matter one's situation or the timescale involved, regardless of the odds of success as we take one small step after the other.

> Despite a glaring emergency, it is only very gradually that it will be possible to perform such an about turn, after many conflicts and compromises with large interests and the public's habits (let us only think of the car), with mythologies, such as ideological and nationalist passions. To take on such an adversary with our eyes open, hope is but a feeble help; it will take faith in the meaning and necessity of that enterprise. But the choice is between the latter and nothingness.[15]

Charbonneau's words, written forty years ago, neatly capture the predicament we can no longer evade today and the kind of spiritual resolve required to face it. This is what he likes to call a post-Christian situation, assuming a Christian problematic of incarnation, yet independent of continued belief in the religious objects of faith. In line with Amery's kenotic approach to eschatology, not speaking as one himself, Charbonneau feels that "a Christian can answer such a challenge only by effecting a Copernican reversal at the level of religion itself; if it puts Christian faith in question, it does seem true to its general direction though."

> The current crisis finds us fundamentally involved in the earth which we had purported to escape. And it is no longer from the heavens or from nature or from History that rescue will come, but from the—paradoxically spiritual—experience of an Earth where man forever more makes a decision against entropy, death and necessity in a struggle that may be crazy, but that is the only meaningful one. Only the freedom that is its conscience will be able to save us: this time in the sense in which we say that

---

13. Charbonneau, *Green Light*, 75.
14. See Ellul, *Hope in Time of Abandonment*.
15. Charbonneau, *Green Light*, 185–86.

we save ourselves from drowning. But it is written somewhere that the spirit became incarnate in a body.[16]

Charbonneau's Ambivalent Reading of Christian Scripture

Shorn of its dogmatic content, this last sentence is at the core of Charbonneau's existential thought as it directly issues in ecological commitment. This is the foundational insight he takes from Christianity and remains ever faithful to, and in light of which he assesses the way it has translated in this religious tradition that has much to answer for in terms of its historical and environmental impact, but to which he is indebted for his moral compass. I will not attempt here to give a survey of Bernard Charbonneau's thinking on Nature and Christianity, a topic that exercised this reverent agnostic all his life, largely in uneasy but mutually fruitful dialogue with the staunch (if critical) Christian Jacques Ellul. An admirable paper along these lines has already been given by Frédéric Rognon at the Bernard Charbonneau conference in Pau in 2011.[17] But in keeping with this volume's theme, I will confine myself here to skimming Charbonneau's close reading of the Bible over the first half of the "Nature and Christianity" chapter of *The Green Light*, which marks his most sustained published engagement with Christian Scripture itself as a focus, rather than Christian civilization in general, in order to tease out the dynamics and paradoxes of the denial of limits which has largely driven the latter.

From the outset, Charbonneau draws from the Creation story a rebuttal of its simplistic anti-environmental interpretation by non-Christians (and even by some Christians, such as those supportive of the recent U.S. withdrawal from the Paris agreement), since "man received as his property the earth that Providence created for him. But nowhere does it say that he has the right to destroy God's handiwork. This sovereignty given to man has another, even more basic reason. If God gives it to him, it is because God created him in his image: sovereignty over nature belongs to the very being of the God of Jews and Christians," since, unlike "Greek or Oriental 'pagans'" who divinized nature, "the personal and transcendent God distinguishes himself from it."[18] Likewise, "the Old Testament reminds man that he was drawn from the silt of the earth," and to that extent stands over against it as a distinct and autonomous *human* being, i.e. one that comes

16. Amery as quoted in Charbonneau, *Green Light*, 75–76.
17. Rognon, "Bernard Charbonneau et la critique des racines chrétiennes de la Grande Mue."
18. Charbonneau, *Green Light*, 66.

from the ground (*humus*) but is not reducible to it, though he returns to it in his fallen historical state.

> The sovereignty he has been granted is not absolute like that of his creator, it is bounded by Adam's finitude, and due to sin, his work is never purely good. If, instead of being the vague sense of a general and abstract evil, the awareness of sin and evil was that of our own limits and of human weakness, it could be the wellspring of a more realistic view of nature, and warier of man and his works.[19]

But the exile from Eden into a nature now fallen along with man and turned into "a jungle ruled by the survival of the fittest"[20] instead launches its former lord on a path of precarious mastery, where he constantly feels the need to defend and consolidate the limits of his uneasy comfort zones. It is thus "the divine curse that condemns him to build the city"[21]—the foundational act of civilization as one of disobedience to God, for which Ellul blames man in his theology of the city based on the Biblical stories of Cain and Babel.[22] But Charbonneau seems to be suggesting that man's own creation of a social and technological microcosm, shielding him from the elements with artificial barriers to unmediated reliance on unpredictable, hostile nature, was not simply the declaration of independence from divine Providence that Ellul sees in it. For Charbonneau, it was really an inevitable and hence legitimate response to the new conditions into which God allows man to find a footing in his exile.

> Condemned to till the earth, he is less and less in magical communion with things, brought to mere utility by a will to power that reduces them to dust as soon as he lays hold of them. An ambivalent curse since it was imposed by God, work is both a duty and a blessing that happens to come along with the promise of deliverance from it.[23]

But according to Charbonneau, a perverse interpretation of this "curse-blessing" afflicts many one-sided readers of the Bible, such as the Puritans, who "had a religion of work that they transmitted to capitalist societies":

---

19. Charbonneau, *Green Light*, 70.
20. Charbonneau, *Green Light*, 67.
21. Charbonneau, *Green Light*, 70.
22. See Ellul, *Meaning of the City*.
23. Charbonneau, *Green Light*, 67.

> As long as we are going to bear suffering and inflict it upon ourselves, we might as well derive delight from it, either by enjoying other people's suffering out of sadism or our own suffering out of masochism: a specifically human and Christian vice, doubtless unknown in nature. But look at all these new pleasures![24]

The this-worldly asceticism of the Protestant work ethic was so successful in its unintended consequence of producing an embarrassment of riches[25] that, transfigured by Fordism's use of mass purchasing power to drive the industrial economy, the guilty pleasures that money can buy eventually became hallowed as an unmixed blessing and sign of election, in the new dispensation of a consumer society driven by an endless stream of new technological distractions—proof of the bounties of a secular providence that hardly needs explicit religious validation by a prosperity gospel. "For, always for good or ill, the old man lives on in the new: the pagan in the Christian,"[26] just as Christian patterns live on in the purportedly heathen hedonism of a post-Christian civilization.

"But it would be a mistake to reduce the Old and even the New Testament to a progressive ideology," Charbonneau insists, for "there is hardly a chapter without its own retort:"

> At the same time as the condemnation of nature, we find in the Bible its glorification. It is everywhere in the Old Testament, rooted (or mired), far more than the New, in its soil and its people: in the Promised Land that is not in Heaven but smack in the middle of a geographic and historical crossroads.[27]

Still, "the State, if not society as meticulously regulated by Deuteronomy, is what Yahweh and his prophets are wary of."[28]

> Money, and worse still, the royal census, are works of the devil: what does Yahweh think of a national accountancy that ends up surveying everything with its computers so as to completely master nature and man? [. . .] The Heavenly Jerusalem is not of this world, and things go awry every time man attempts to build it on earth. Babel, which wants to dominate the planet, is the work of an evil spirit, and it is annihilated for this reason. If the desert is the source of all virtues, Sodom and Babylon are

---

24. Charbonneau, *Green Light*, 67.
25. See Weber, *Protestant Ethic and the "Spirit" of Capitalism and Other Writings*.
26. Charbonneau, *Green Light*, 68.
27. Charbonneau, *Green Light*, 69.
28. Charbonneau, *Green Light*, 69–70.

> the mothers of all vices. And the *Psalms* and the *Prophets* constantly renew the condemnation of any human work that wants to equal that of God. [...]
>
> Although the New Testament continues the spiritualist and universalist tradition of the prophets, it remains nonetheless rooted in a Galilean countryside peopled by shepherds, agriculturalists and fishermen, where nature is omnipresent. The purest Gospel speech has the clarity of springs, the simple and sharp colours of spring meadows.[29]

In the guise of the birds and the lilies of the fields, "far from being cursed, nature is held up as an example to men, with their anxiety and greed for power and money."

> But the glorification of nature in the New Testament is not exactly that of the Old. It is no longer its power that is praised, but its humble beauty and its carefreeness. What is put into question by the Gospel and the prophets, more than nature, is the social power that does it violence, as it does to men. It is war, money, the Law.[30]

Oblivious to this serious business of human affairs, Christ thus lives "like an anarchist who ignores the economy and politics, without which men would have little power over nature. If Christians had strictly followed the Gospel's teaching, their power would hardly have gone beyond that of a tribe of gypsies or Indians," and there would have never been such thing as Christian civilization to upset the old ways of all human societies throughout the world, leading it at once to unity and to the brink of collapse. Just as Biblical transcendence tends to "bring upheaval to the earth in the attempt to realize an impossible ideal," "Gospel anarchism is condemned to subvert a society that can only realize the conditions of freedom by translating them into laws and sanctions," a process known as civilization. "But if the old law is abolished, it is in favour of another one that belongs to personal conscience and love," as a new way of approaching not only the neighbour as an irreplaceable person regardless of social function or context, but also a nature now stripped of the power once wielded by its divinized features, and likewise given over to human care and respect in its vulnerable if daunting otherness.

> If Christ finishes the process of disembodying the spirit, he re-embodies it on the other hand as no other religion has done,

---

29. Charbonneau, *Green Light*, 70.
30. Charbonneau, *Green Light*, 70.

in a God-man who, through his body, lives, experiences death throes and then expires on a cross in his time and place.[31]

Disentangling Christianity and Progress

The kind of behaviour that led Jesus to this divine consecration of human life is inseparable from his corporeal assumption of its mortal limits, so that incarnation refers not just to Christ's theological status or his sacramental incorporation of elements of the world, but to the consistent translation of ethical principles into action within these limits: "hearing these words and putting them into practice." This demand now has to go deeper than ritual observance and socially sanctioned propriety; since "no law determines how that is supposed to happen, it is up to freedom to do it. When that happens, nothing is negligible anymore: neither earth nor history; at every moment, a game is being played out in which the stakes are personal and universal salvation."[32] However, it will no longer do to view this salvation in mostly otherworldly terms, now that "a secularized, rogue Christianity is at work throughout the human species,"[33] exposing it along with most other species to the Sixth Great Extinction in the history of life on Earth. For this one coincides—not coincidentally!—with the Anthropocene, a geological era starting with fossil-fueled industrialization in which human activity overtakes all natural factors in reshaping the planetary environment, precipitating its entropy and collapse. Only recently recognized by science, the advent of the Anthropocene becomes unmistakable with the Great Acceleration, which is the very same process identified by Bernard Charbonneau a hundred years ago as the Great Molting (*la Grande Mue*),[34] whereby technological society becomes man's second nature—even more overwhelming than the original nature from which he first sought distance and a measure of freedom in the shelter of cultural forms and civilized enclaves.

There is no denying that Western Christianity has been instrumental in tipping the balance away from any natural moorings, towards the exponential growth and worldwide spread of increasingly artificial living

31. Charbonneau, *Green Light*, 71.
32. Charbonneau, *Green Light*, 71.
33. Charbonneau, *Green Light*, 72.

34. This "major transition" was one where "the characteristic habitat of the human species, which for several millennia had been the village, now was becoming the city." Steffen et al., "Anthropocene." Charbonneau came to the same realization from his own everyday experience at an early age in Bordeaux, where he was born in 1910—the date of the beginning of the incubation period of the Second Stage of the Great Acceleration, officially starting in 1945. Charbonneau described it in those terms that very year in a public lecture entitled "The Year 2000," putting Hiroshima in that wider context. See Charbonneau, "An Deux Mille."

conditions. Like it or not, "Progress, the continual development of science and technique, is inseparable from evangelical Christian faith; without it, it would have lacked an engine, nothing would have driven humans, until then steeped in the sacred, to break with the gods, except for the God-Man"[35] who brought a new heaven and a new earth within their reach. This alone could make it possible for the given earth and sky to eventually be seen as little more than springboards or fuel reserves for the historical journey to a better world as *telos* of all thought and activity, be it the New Frontier of outer space or a Brave New World at the end of history. To be sure, with Christianity also came the only antidote to the reckless excess it unleashed as the fall-out of misconstrued spiritual freedom and misplaced temporal embodiment, in a new bond "that belongs to personal conscience and love."[36]

> But if the old chains binding man to the earth and man to man held on their own, the new link can only be tied freely by every man, at the risk of losing himself.[37]

This is why Charbonneau welcomes Carl Amery's call for an end to Providence as the assumption of a divinely ordained happy end to the human adventure on this planet. He agrees that people now need to be disenchanted of this salvation history that remains under the guise of Progress, in the wake of the disenchantment of all other forms of the sacred it has enabled. It is a personal leap of faith in meaningful life without ultimate guarantee that Charbonneau demands of every human, no matter his or her beliefs or lack thereof, to defy the hopeless odds of steering mankind on the narrow path to collective survival. Where Ellul takes Amery to task for leaving out the transcendent hope that he deems indispensable to keep the future open, Charbonneau finds support in this thinker for both the spiritual and practical value of entertaining, like he always has, the uncomfortable question of the "only thing we can hold against pure Christianity" of the kind his friend is a reliable witness to:

> Is not the challenge it puts to the hominid mammal, that of a new Law embodied in an individual freedom, too far beyond its capacities?[38]

This question is not a rhetorical one to this agnostic. Yet even in the worst-case scenario of irredeemable environmental doom, Charbonneau maintains there is no way back to conditions prior to Biblical Revelation and its possibly fatal world-historical consequences: "the old order is crumbling

---

35. Charbonneau, *Green Light*, 71.
36. Charbonneau, *Green Light*, 72.
37. Charbonneau, *Green Light*, 72.
38. Charbonneau, *Green Light*, 72.

and we do not have any other way" beyond the dead end of Progress than that Way of personal freedom opened by the embodied Word as revealed in Christian Scripture —for better or for worse.

> If it happens that man is not up to the challenge of his own destiny, then that will have been the mistake of his Creator, whether God or nature.[39]

Works Cited

Charbonneau, Bernard. "An Deux Mille." In *"Nous sommes des révolutionnaires malgré nous." Textes pionniers de l'écologie politique*, by Bernard Charbonneau and Jacques Ellul, 193–215. Anthropocène. Paris: Seuil, 2014.

———. *The Green Light: A Self-Critique of the Ecological Movement*. Translated by Christian Roy. London: Bloomsbury, 2018.

Ellul, Jacques. *Hope in Time of Abandonment*. Translated by C. Edward Hopkin. New York: Seabury, 1977.

———. *The Meaning of the City*. Translated by Dennis Pardee. Jacques Ellul Legacy Series. Eugene, OR: Wipf & Stock, 2011.

———. *Théologie et Technique. Pour une éthique de la non-puissance*. Edited by Yves Ellul and Frédéric Rognon. Geneva: Labor et Fides, 2014.

Noble, David W. *The Religion of Technology: The Divinity of Man and the Spirit of Invention*. Harmondsworth, UK: Penguin, 1999.

Rognon, Frédéric. "Bernard Charbonneau et la critique des racines chrétiennes de la Grande Mue." In *Bernard Charbonneau: habiter la terre. Actes du Colloque du 2–4 mai 2011, Université de Pau et des Pays de l'Adour*, edited by Cazenave-Piarrot, 108–16. Université de Pau et des Pays de l'Adour, 2011. http://web.univ-pau.fr/RECHERCHE/SET/CHARBONNEAU/documents/Actes_colloque_Bernard_CHARBONNEAU_Habiter_la_terre_SET.pdf.

Roy, Christian. "Space, Time and the Christian Matrix of Faustian Man." Paper given at "100 Years after the Publication of *The Decline of the West*: Oswald Spengler in an Age of Globalisation," October 17–20, 2018, Blankenheimerdorf and Brussels. Video available at https://www.youtube.com/watch?v=H7O9JUcBRvQ; article available (pending publication of the proceedings) at https://www.academia.edu/39267384.

Steffen, Will, et al. "The Anthropocene: Are Humans Now Overwhelming the Great Forces of Nature?" *Ambio* 36 (2007). http://www.ambio.kva.se.

Weber, Max. *The Protestant Ethic and the "Spirit" of Capitalism and Other Writings*. Edited and translated by Peter Baehr and Gordon C. Wells. London: Penguin, 2002.

White, Lynn, Jr. "The Historical Roots of Our Ecologic Crisis." *Science* New Series 155 (March 10, 1967) 1203–7. http://www.brontaylor.com/courses/pdf/White—HistoricalRootsEcoCrisis(1967).pdf.

---

39. Charbonneau, *Green Light*, 72.

CHAPTER 18

Review of Ellul, *On Being Rich and Poor:*
Christianity in a Time of Economic Globalization

BRIAN BROCK

THIS IS THE SECOND volume of a fascinating, idiosyncratic and—I would argue—fruitful project undertaken by Willem Vanderburg.[1] The basis of the text is a series of intensive and structured Bible studies which Jacques Ellul led with small groups of graduate students and professionals in Bordeaux between 1973 and 1978. Vanderburg participated in most of these sessions and tape-recorded them. He is now releasing them in English translation. The idiosyncrasy of the project lies in the editing and translating procedure. Vanderburg admits that turning oral Bible studies into a prose text was a difficult undertaking, not least because the events often included questions from the other participants.

In order to fill out the text Vanderburg has weaved in material from studies of the same books that Ellul did with other groups during this period. The difficulty of this construction process led Vanderburg to forego producing a French version of the text. The complexity of this process, combined with Vanderburg's admitted lack of Hebrew or Greek, is bound to leave the academic reader wondering how close the published text is to Ellul's original words.

This volume follows a recently re-released and expanded version of the first volume, *On Freedom Love and Power*. That volume contained verse-by-verse theological readings of Genesis 1–3, Job 32–42, the parables of Jesus as recounted by Matthew, and the prologue of John. In terms of content, that volume pulled together Ellul's reflections on what he understood to be

1. This review of Ellul, *On Being Rich and Poor*, appeared in *The European Journal of Theology* 27 (2017) 2, 197–98.

fundamental themes: the nature of morality and religion, the dynamics of repentance and redemption, the main features of the kingdom of love established by Jesus, and the Christological inner logic of the life of the Trinitarian God. *On Being Rich and Poor* brings these themes down to earth in the life of the Christian in the modern world. It does so by way of an extended exegesis of the entire books of Amos and James.

The treatment of Amos opens with a fascinating account of Old Testament prophecy which makes it clear that Ellul himself modelled his own mode of cultural analysis on these prophets, and especially on Amos. Amos is presented as a new kind of prophet within the development of the prophetic traditions of Israel, who for the first time levelled criticisms not just at individual kings or ruling groups, but at the people of God as a whole and in all its parts. Ellul consciously tries to distance the biblical prophet from the contemporary crusaders for social justice who were presenting him in the persona of a secularized defender of social justice and economic redistributionism.

The second half of the book opens with Ellul presenting Kierkegaard as 'one of Protestantism's greatest theologians' whose scattered readings of James were the only sources he found really useful in preparing his own reading. What he found most useful is Kierkegaard's deployment of Luther's best insights to break down the polarity between faith and works that Luther deployed in his dismissal of the book as a defense of works righteousness. Daily life, Ellul insists, is the irreducible locale for the enactment of faith. Thus, the sign that Christians are enacting wisdom out of their faith in Jesus Christ is that their action is marked by a joyful living that does not need to rely on techniques and powers to secure their fates. Hence the main theme of the book: "Poverty and riches are among the most common tests of our Christian faith."[2]

As a theological ethicist interested in issues of power and money, I find this an arresting volume, more so than the first volume with its emphasis on more universal theological themes. And as one who has also attempted theological exegesis, the density and depth of theological engagement on display in this volume is deeply impressive, especially the treatment of James, which I would rank as one of the best I have read. Ellul takes the words of the text seriously, in their original language and context, and constantly draws the readers' attention to the ways in which these words give life by illuminating the dynamics of our contemporary life. It may not reach the standard of historical critical engagement that biblical scholars have come to expect in the contemporary guild, but Ellul does not bypass historical questions. We may

---

2. Ellul, *On Being Rich and Poor*, 94.

also wonder how closely the text we have was to Ellul's own presentation. But the end result is certainly impressive, and among the many theological commentaries written by Ellul, one of the most winsome and accessible.

Works Cited

Ellul, Jacques. *On Being Rich and Poor: Christianity in a Time of Economic Globalization.* Compiled, edited, and translated by Willem H. Vanderburg. Toronto: University of Toronto Press, 2014.

──────── CHAPTER 19 ────────

Hope and Abandonment in the Bible

Elisabetta Ribet

AMONG MANY DESCRIPTIONS APPLIED to him, Jacques Ellul has been defined as a theologian of hope. *Hope in Time of Abandonment* is not the French scholar's only work analyzing this topic. A long path led him to write this book (which he considered a favorite among his publications), and other writings keep the idea of hope as one of their main roots long after this masterpiece. Hope is at the eschatological foundation of Ellul's entire theological corpus, though it comes through particularly clearly in this book.

In the context of our reflection on Ellul and the Bible, this chapter focuses on the pair of terms *déréliction* and *espérance* (translatable as abandonment and hope), which I develop in three moments: first, a view on how this binomial can be approached according to the dialectical method of the French scholar; second, a reading from a more strict biblical perspective, presenting two aspects; and finally, I will focus on the main biblical characteristics of Ellul's statements about hope, offering remarks on an astonishing silence.

Dialectical Method and Hope: The Relevance of a Binomial

More than the book itself, it is the idea of hope that must be considered as a crucial issue in Ellul's work. Gabriel Vahanian noticed this in 1983,[1] as did other scholars such as Maurice Weyembergh[2] (1989) and Lawrence Terl-

---

1. Vahanian, "Espérer, faute de foi?" In English, cf. Fasching, *Thought of Jacques Ellul*, xv–xxxviii.
2. Weyembergh, "Espoir et espérance chez Jacques Ellul."

izzese[3] (2005). More recently, Christophe Chalamet[4] and Bernard Rordorf[5] have explored the issue more profoundly.

The most important characteristic of Ellul's way of talking about hope is its dialectical construction. In the postmodern world, divided between necessity and freedom, Ellul affirms that there is a gap between history and what may be called *ananké, fatum*, or destiny. As long as humankind obeys the laws of cause and effect which characterize the technological society, there will be no other option but necessity, and no other way to understand history but fate: things *had to* happen like this. As a result, history can only be a history of ongoing consequences. In this binary dynamic, hope represents the unexpected possibility: as Jacob Van Vleet says, hope represents a "dialectical link between the realm of technique and the realm of freedom."[6] What does this mean?

Following the structure of Van Vleet's statement, for Ellul it is not possible to talk about hope without relating it to *déréliction*. From a methodological perspective, the binomial is not made of two terms in opposition, but in relationship to each other: *déréliction* is not the "opposite" of hope. It is hope's "place," the other element which draws hope's boundaries and helps to define it. My own journey to this formulation follows our author's footsteps on a path which leads from his *Presence in the Modern World* (1948), through various minor writings, culminating in the conscious choice of a word: *déréliction*. The first time Ellul explicitly uses this word is in *Prayer and Modern Man* (1970):

Perhaps we are in a time where God 'turns his face away,' the time of [*déréliction*]. This time is described in the apocalyptic passages in the gospels, this moment 'between the times,' in which man no longer discerns any truth, in which power is unleashed, in which there is constant confusion between good and evil ('you will call evil what is good, and good what is evil'), in which man surrenders to his most audacious impulses and experiences every terror imaginable, in which anguish increases to the point of singlehandedly killing those within its grasp.[7]

In this one word, déréliction, Ellul offers then what Rordorf calls "a theological judgement on an historical reality."[8]

---

3. Terlizzese, *Hope in the Thought of Jacques Ellul*.
4. Chalamet, "L'espérance comme provocation et comme invocation."
5. Rordorf, "Jacques Ellul: l'espérance oubliée."
6. Van Vleet, *Dialectical Theology and Jacques Ellul*.
7. Ellul, *L'impossible prière*, in *Le défi et le nouveau*, 727. Translation modified with reference to Hopkin's translation in Ellul, *Prayer and Modern Man*, 140.
8. Rordorf, "Jacques Ellul: l'espérance oubliée," 37.

Several years after the English edition of the book on prayer, *Hope in Time of Abandonment* opens with Ellul mentioning a crisis. This analysis can help us in deeper understanding the idea of the link between hope and abandonment. The postmodern, secularized and technological society at the time of Ellul's writing is also in the midst of a crisis of meaning, deeply analyzed by Ellul not only in the first part of this book, but also in all his sociological works from 1950 to 1970 and beyond. In short, Ellul locates the root of this crisis in a shift in what is considered Sacred in Western society, a shift from Nature to Technique. The postmodern feeling of being abandoned by God and of having lost any connection with a sacred Nature leads humankind towards a process of sacralization of Technique. In this sense, hope is pessimist: the only way to the creation of a "true" hope passes through a process of becoming aware of the reality of *déréliction*. In the technological society, we live in the realm of necessity. As it calls for the possibility to let the Transcendent come back into the human life, Hope is our only guide towards the realm of freedom.

Hope as Foundational for Eschatology

Our second theme concerns the explicitly biblical roots of hope in Ellul's work. Hope is the foundation for Ellul's eschatological perspective. I shall not treat this topic at length; I will only recall some fundamental expressions concerning this theme as found in *Hope in Time of Abandonment*, as well as in Ellul's works on the book of Revelation.

First of all, Ellul's hope finds humans "thrown back upon the eschaton":[9] the clash between necessity and freedom, abandonment and hope, leads the human being to turn towards the eschatological perspective. Hope, Ellul claims, opens a rift in the technological dynamics of a mechanical sequence of cause and effect, showing the "impossible possibility" of the upcoming Kingdom and the accomplishment of God's promises. Consequently, in this situation hope is "the dazzling presence of ultimate realities":[10] eschatological realities are no longer present somewhere in a hoped-for future, but they become present here and now. In this light, hope is defined as the measure of the distance from the Kingdom and the accomplishment of God's promise: "Hope provokes pessimism: for it assigns us our place, *far* from God—so far from God that hope is the only

---

9. "Alors on se trouve rejeté vers l'eschaton, et la théologie de l'espérance devient essentielle . . . l'homme va parler son espérance que le silence de Dieu n'est ni dernier, ni final." Ellul, *L'espérance oubliée*, 173.

10. Ellul, *L'espérance oubliée*, 169.

remaining possibility."[11] In this paradoxical affirmation, Ellul illustrates the path of hope: because hope knows God and his Kingdom, and because hope also knows human beings, it can assign humans their place in relation to God and the Promise. While occupying this place cannot avoid highlighting the distance from the Kingdom, it also simultaneously creates a real awareness of this kingdom in its present dimension.

This is what Ellul calls "the pessimism of hope." As a first remark, we could say that in his analysis of hope and of its action into human life, pessimism and realism need to be very close to each other. The priority of hope is to help the human being looking towards reality without sinking into despair. We need to be aware of the silence of God, and of the *déréliction* we live in, in order to recognize the true hope and live in it.

Here we find a first important link with the thought of André Neher. Two books of the French Jewish theologian are prominent in Ellul's reflections on hope, abandonment and prophecy: *L'exil de la parole. Du silence biblique au silence d'Auschwitz* (Paris, Seuil, 1970, 1996²) and *L'essence du prophétisme*, (Paris, Seuil, 1972; original PUF, 1955). In my doctoral thesis, I have discussed the details of the dialogue between our two authors on three main topics: God's silence—i.e., abandonment; the role of hope; and the role of human words (prayer and prophecy) "in a time of abandonment." These three themes are involved in the movement of what we can call "possibility". One of the most important challenges in postmodern society concerns the importance given and the approach adopted as believers towards what is 'possible,' what 'can be,' and how all of this relates to the power of God and of humankind.

However, our remarks thus far have focused on more of a theological perspective than an explicitly biblical approach.

A Striking Absence: Keywords

Here we find an astonishing silence in the construction of Ellul's thought. Ellul was in close dialogue with André Neher's work throughout *Hope in Time of Abandonment*. It is surprising that he does not make use of another idea from his dialogue with Neher which could have been exploited. A small note concerning the importance of the two biblical terms *nehama* and *azav*, makes us realize that *Hope in time of Abandonment* lacks a treatment of the biblical words used both for abandonment and for hope. Ellul writes:

---

11. Ellul, *L'espérance oubliée*, 222.

In his semantic analysis of the silence of hope, Neher offers the following noteworthy observation: the same word (*nehama*) designates God's *repenting*, his regret, his weariness, the miscarriage of his expectations, and it also means *consolation*, recovery in the face of failure, determination to resume the task, and hope. Likewise, the word *azav* signifies, on the one hand, abandonment, and on the other hand, the fact of being gathered in. 'Abandonment [*déréliction*] and ingathering do not depend on the compensating and healing effect of the passage of time, but on the internal dialectic of their unbreakable relationship.' [cit. Neher, 255]. Thus hope is biblically linked to abandonment."[12] To treat such central vocabulary only in a small footnote is astonishing for Ellul, since we know that he takes the time to deepen other biblical keywords elsewhere: e.g., *hevel* (vanity),[13] the four horsemen,[14] the image of the city,[15] to give only a few examples.

Ellul's note on Neher's exegesis comes in the portion of *L'espérance oubliée* which addresses a silent God, a God who chooses to be silent, and a hope which refuses to accept this choice. This hope steps up, daring even violence and blasphemy to provoke an answer, to break the silence, to pick up the lost trail of the Promise once again.[16] In this part of the book, hope represents the will to make God change, to make God repent of his own choices.[17] The two keywords suggested by Neher and noticed by Ellul are *nehama* and *azav*, "repentance" and "abandonment," as actions coming from God. Let us examine these words more closely.

Nehama comes from the root *nhm* and occurs 119 times in the Bible.[18] Neher reminds that as we affirm that God not only changes his mind, but sometimes repents of his own choices, this "seems so intolerable that this hypothesis is often rejected by the Bible itself (Nb 23:19, 1 Sam 15:29)."[19] This seems to go without saying: repentance comes out from realizing a mistake, a defeat. Thus, the repentance of God speaks about a God doing wrong, a God who is neither perfect nor confident. What Neher points out then is that "the Hebrew word expressing this feeling is *néhama*, and this

---

12. Ellul, *Hope in Time of Abandonment*, 183n6.
13. Ellul, *La raison d'être*, 61–73.
14. Ellul, *L'Apocalypse*, 179–82.
15. Ellul, *Conférence sur l'Apocalypse de Jean*, 89–90; *Sans feu ni lieu*, 45–61.
16. Ellul, *L'espérance oubliée*, 168–87.
17. Ellul, *L'espérance oubliée*, 179.
18. Symian-Yofre, "ṇhm," 9:340–55, 342.
19. Neher, *L'exil de la parole*, 255.

word indicates at the same time repentance but also *consolation*." Through this, the French biblical scholar shows another image of God:

> It is the opposite attitude, the personal recovery in the face of defeat; it is will, energy, putting one's hands back in the dough; it is hope. Therefore, defeat and hope are no longer two separate moments of the divine action . . . and one only word expresses their simultaneity, such that in the biblical text, defeat and hope are read through the same word, are received in the same pivot of the biblical adventure.[20]

Nehama talks about a God who can certainly change his attitude and repent, but also seeks for reconciliation and for building a future of hope again.

According to the *Theological Dictionary of the Old Testament*,

> The only element common to all meanings of *nhm* appears to be the attempt to influence the situation: by changing the course of events, rejecting an obligation, or refraining from an action, when the focus is on the present; by influencing a decision, when the focus is on the future; and by accepting the consequences of an act or helping another accept them, or contrariwise dissociating oneself emotionally from them, when the focus is on the past.[21]

Whether the action aims at the past, present or future, its goal is thus to influence a given situation. Briefly, in interpreting the verbal root *nhm*, there is a clear link with will, freedom and the reasons for choices. This is why I believe it is very important to remember the dual meaning of *nehama* as we talk about hope as God's silence-breaker: it further supports Ellul's thesis. As it fights for God's repentance and return to the creature abandoned in silence, hope acts from the certitude that consolation and healing inhabit that God of whom we see only the back, a consolation destined for the human creature inside its own abandonment.

André Neher also highlights two different readings of the root of abandonment, *azav*: this one, meaning both abandonment and collecting, expresses once again the simultaneity of hope and defeat. "There is no season gap between throwing seeds and the richness of the harvest. The two movements are simultaneous. As the biblical man affirms 'I have been abandoned' he also claims, with the same word, 'I am raised'. Abandonment and harvest are joint together, not by the action of time passing by

---

20. Neher, *L'exil de la parole*, 255.
21. Symian-Yofre, "ṇhm," 342.

and healing, but in the inner dialectic of their unbreakable relation."[22] We meet *azav* in the semantic context including synonymies and antinomies, in spatial, social and emotional perspectives: leaving and staying, going and coming, letting someone go and staying with someone, losing and finding, forgetting and remembering, despising and respecting, and so on.[23] There is no abandonment without a new meeting, no turning back without reconciliation, no *déréliction* without *espérance*.

Conclusions

What, then, shall we say about hope? It is designated by different keywords in the Bible, described by multiple circumlocutions. Ellul chose not to analyze any of them: neither *elpis*, the main greek word used for "hope" in the New Testament, nor *tiqvah* or one of the other, less common words—*seber* and *towchelet*—used in the Old Testament. Yet at the same time, he worked a lot on the difference between *espoir* and *espérance*, a difference we only find in French; another paradoxical attitude.

What we can affirm is that more than deepening the single keywords of the vocabulary of hope and abandonment, Ellul has decided to lean on the biblical narrative's witness of the dialectical movement between the two.

For this reason, I think it is fundamental to keep Ellul's work on hope in close dialogue with other authors and scholars whom he quotes in *Hope in Time of Abandonment* and elsewhere (in particular, Neher, Kierkegaard, Ricoeur, Moltmann, and Vahanian). Through such comparisons, we find the idea of a *Kairos*, a *time*, for hope which comes through strongly. This *Kairos* is found in that break, in that hiatus which is always present between necessity and freedom, between the kingdom of technique and the kingdom of freedom. I am presently reflecting on the idea of an "utopic function of hope", an expression coming from two key dialogues with Paul Ricoeur and Gabriel Vahanian, who invite us to re-appropriate the word utopia and the meaning we can give to this idea. But this is another story to be developed in another chapter.

---

22. Neher, *L'exil de la parole*, 255: "And this simultaneity of defeat and hope in God is found in man, equally marked by the ambivalence of one sole word—*azav*—which means both *abandonment* and *gathering*. There is no interval of time between the throwing of the seeds and gathering the harvest. The two movements are simultaneous. When the biblical man says: 'I am abandoned,' through the intervention of the same word he simultaneously says, 'I am gathered.' The abandonment [*déréliction*] and gathering are held together not by the compensatory effect of passing time which heals, but by the internal dialectic of their unclassifiable relation."

23. Gerstenberger, "'āzaḇ," 10:584–92, 589.

Works Cited

Chalamet, Christophe. "L'espérance comme provocation et comme invocation." In *Jacques Ellul. Une théologie au présent*, edited by Bernard Rordorf et al., 53–73. Le Mont-sur-Lausanne: Ouverture, 2016.

Ellul, Jacques. *Conférence sur l'Apocalypse de Jean*. Nantes: Editions de l'AREFPPI, 1985;

———. *Hope in Time of Abandonment*. Translated by C. Edward Hopkin. New York: Seabury, 1973.

———. *L'Apocalypse. Architecture en mouvement. L'atheisme interrogee*. Paris: Desclee, 1975.

———. *La raison d'etre. Méditation sur l'Ecclésiaste*. Paris: Editions du Seuil, 1987.

———. *Le défi et le nouveau: Oeuvres théologiques 1948–1991*. Paris: La Table Ronde, 2007.

———. *L'espérance oubliée*. Paris: La Table Ronde, 2004.

———. *Prayer and Modern Man*. Translated by C. Edward Hopkin. New York: Seabury, 1970.

Fasching, Darrel J. *The Thought of Jacques Ellul: A Systematic Exposition*. New York: Mellen, 1981.

Gerstenberger, E. "'āzaḆ." In *Theological Dictionary of the Old Testament*, edited by Johannes Botterweck et al., 10:584–92, 589.

Neher, André. *L'exil de la parole. Du silence biblique au silence d'Auschwitz*. 2nd ed. Paris: Seuil, 1996.

Rordorf, Bernard. "Jacques Ellul: l'espérance oubliée." *Perspectives protestantes* 5 (2017) 36–43.

Symian-Yofre, H. "ṇhm." In *Theological Dictionary of the Old Testament*, edited by Johannes Botterweck et al., 9:340–55. Grand Rapids: Eerdmans, 1999.

Terlizzese, Lawrence J. *Hope in the Thought of Jacques Ellul*. Eugene, OR: Cascade, 2005.

Vahanian, Gabriel. "Espérer, faute de foi?" In *Religion, société et politique. Mélanges en hommage à Jacques Ellul*, edited by Etienne Dravasa et al., 153–67. Paris: PUF, 1983.

Van Vleet, Jacob. *Dialectical Theology and Jacques Ellul: An Introductory Exposition*. Minneapolis: Fortress, 2014.

Weyembergh, Maurice. "Espoir et espérance chez Jacques Ellul." In *L'Expérience du temps. Mélanges offerts à Jean Paumen*, edited by Robert Legros et al., 199–226. Bruxelles: Ousia, 1989.

─────── CHAPTER 20 ───────

Ellul on Scripture and Idolatry

Andrew Goddard

ONE OF THE DISTINCTIVE features of Ellul's theological work is his conviction that it is Scripture that enables us to see the world aright.[1] Rather than "demythologizing" the Bible, the Bible is the means by which God "demythologizes" our world. The classic example of this approach is undoubtedly his canonical, Christocentric study of the city in Scripture, *The Meaning of the City*, but the same approach underlies his approach to many other phenomena. This article provides a brief introductory overview of how Ellul's reading of some biblical texts shapes his understanding of idols and idolatry and how, in turn, that understanding leads to a critique of certain attitudes to the Bible and explains the heart of his biblical hermeneutic.[2]

Ellul's biblical discussion of idols and idolatry is not as thorough and focused as his study of the city but it is particularly in *The Ethics of Freedom* and *The Humiliation of the Word* that we find his interpretations of key texts in— as one would expect from Ellul—both Old and New Testaments. Of particular interest is one Pauline text that shapes his account of the idols in relation to the powers.[3] On first glance, we Christians may want to treat idols and powers as synonymous terms and it must be admitted that Ellul himself (here, as in many other areas) is not always consistent and does not always strictly follow

---

1. This chapter is a lightly edited reprint of an article published in *The Ellul Forum* 36 (Fall 2005) 6–8.

2. For a fuller discussion of this, on which this article partially draws, see my article in Stephen Barton, ed., *Idolatry in the Bible, Early Judaism and Christianity* (Edinburgh: T. & T. Clark, 2005).

3. The powers are a subject on which Ellul wrote much more extensively and which, particularly through the work of Marva Dawn, have become prominent in recent Ellul studies.

his own distinctions that he draws from the biblical text. Nevertheless, when he is careful, he does distinguish his understanding of these two phenomena, and he does so because he believes Scripture does so.

The crucial biblical text for Ellul is Paul's discussion of food offered to idols in 1 Corinthians 8, especially verses 4–6. There the apostle writes, "Hence, as to the eating of food offered to idols, we know that 'no idol in the world really exists,' and that 'there is no God but one.' Indeed, even though there may be so-called gods in heaven or on earth—as in fact there are many gods and many lords—yet for us there is one God, the Father, from whom are all things and for whom we exist, and one Lord, Jesus Christ, through whom are all things and through whom we exist."

Ellul takes great care in his analysis of this text, drawing attention to the paradox that Paul here seems to say both (a) that no idol really exists and (b) that there are many gods. Rather than dismiss Paul's statements as incoherent and confused, Ellul seeks to clarify why Paul affirms both these statements. He claims that gods exist in the following sense: "They are part of the powers that claim to be all-powerful or salvific, etc., and that attract people's love and religious belief. They exist. And they pass themselves off as gods."[4] Thus Ellul believes that in order to understand the text and the world we have to see that the language of "gods" is equivalent to (or, perhaps better, a subset of) the category of the powers. As a result, Ellul insists—against the demythologizers and with such writers as Caird, Berkhof, Wink and Stringfellow—that there are real, spiritual powers and forces which influence human lives and societies. These, we learn from Scripture, set themselves up as powerful and redemptive and, by being viewed as such by humans, they stand as a challenge to the one true God.

In his interpretation of Scripture on the powers, Ellul rejects the Bultmannian demythologization project (that dismisses the language of powers as a worldview we must now reject in the light of modern knowledge) but he also refuses to embrace the common popular evangelical and fundamentalist belief in traditional demons that is often understood as the main alternative. Instead he moves between two other ways of interpreting this biblical language of "gods" and "powers." At times he views them as "less precise powers (thrones and dominions) which still have an existence, reality, and . . . objectivity of their own." Here they are seen as authentic, spiritual realities which are independent of human decision and whose power is not constituted by human decision. At other times—particularly in his later writings—the powers are viewed more as "a disposition of man which constitutes this or that human factor a power by exalting it as such" and so

---

4. Ellul, *Humiliation of the Word*, 89.

"not objective realities which influence man from without. They exist only by the determination of man which allows them to exist in their subjugating otherness and transcendence."[5]

Ellul's concern in this understanding is to avoid the idea of powers or demons doing their own work apart from human beings. He therefore stresses that the powers find expression in human works and enterprises. It is this important link between the spiritual powers and the material world, especially of human works, that helps us to understand his view of idols.

> The powers seem to be able to transform a natural, social, intellectual or economic reality into a force which man has no ability either to resist or to control. This force ejects man from his divinely given position as governor of creation. It gives life and autonomy to institutions and structures. It attacks man both inwardly and outwardly by playing on the whole setting of human life. It finally alienates man by bringing him into the possession of objects which would not normally possess him.[6]

These powers are the false gods that Paul says in 1 Corinthians 8 really exist. But what are "idols" and why does Paul say that they do not exist? The key feature of idols—in contrast to the powers to which they are linked—is that they are visible and material entities. Although this would seem to give them a more substantial existence, Ellul argues that idols do not exist because "the visible portrayal of these powers which is perceived by the senses, has no value, no consistency, and no existence."[7] Any idol is really just "a natural, social intellectual or economic reality." It is strictly a material object under human control. Ellul therefore believes that Scripture distinguishes false gods from idols because the latter are simply "a creation of man which he invests with a value and authority they do not have in themselves."[8] Idols, according to Scripture, are simply part of the visible created reality and though linked to the gods or spiritual powers they are to be distinguished from them.

In explaining how it is that, in Paul's words, "no idol in the world really exists," Ellul gives the example of money. He claims that money as a power (Mammon) certainly exists. However, a banknote—the material means by which the power works—strictly does not exist because "it is never anything but a piece of paper."[9] Here we see a central paradox: idols

5. Ellul, *Ethics of Freedom*, 151–52.
6. Ellul, *Ethics of Freedom*, 152–53.
7. Ellul, *Humiliation of the Word*, 89.
8. Ellul, *Ethics of Freedom*, 156.
9. Ellul, *Humiliation of the Word*, 89.

seek to make the invisible false gods and powers visible and concrete but by this very fact of seeking to mediate a spiritual power in the material world they do not themselves exist. We may today think of the Nike Swoop, the McDonalds Golden Arches or other symbols and logos as contemporary idols which on their own are meaningless and powerless but are mediators of some of the global powers of our age.[10]

Faced with them we need to remember that idols are not only part of the ancient biblical world but still a reality in our post-modern "secular" world and to recall Ellul's judgment based on Paul's words: "They exist neither as something visible and concrete (since in this sense they are really nothing) nor as something spiritual . . . (since they cannot reach this level). They have no kind of existence precisely because they have tried to obtain indispensable existence beyond the uncertainty of the word."[11]

Idols, therefore, according to Scripture, lack existence per se and are the attempt by humans to domesticate and bring into the visible, material world the invisible spiritual powers that do exist.

> Idols are indispensable for mankind. We need to see things represented and make the powers enter our domain of reality. It is a sort of kidnapping. False gods are powers of all sorts that human beings discern in the world. The Bible clearly distinguishes these from the idol, which is the visualization of these powers and mysterious forces . . . Things that can be seen and grasped are certain and at our disposition. It is fundamentally unacceptable for us to be at the disposition of these gods ourselves, and unable to have power over them. Prayer or offering cannot satisfy, since they provide no sure domination. If, on the contrary, a person makes his own image and can certify that it is truly the deity, he is no longer afraid. Idols quiet our fears.[12]

This linking of idols to the material or visual, as distinct from the spiritual powers, leads to the second emphasis in Ellul's interpretation of the biblical witness: the priority of listening over seeing.

Ellul reads the narrative of humanity's primal rebellion in Genesis 3 as demonstrating the significance of this—the spoken word is doubted, and visible reality is taken as the source of truth.[13] The same problem is repeated within God's people Israel. Here Ellul's interpretation of the narrative of

10. I am grateful to Alain Coralie for his work on Nike Culture that has helped me make this connection.

11. Ellul, *Humiliation of the Word*, 89.

12. Ellul, *Humiliation of the Word*, 86–87.

13. Cf. Ellul, *Humiliation of the Word*, 97ff.

the golden calf (Exod 32) is of crucial importance. It also illustrates that, although (as in relation to 1 Cor 8) Ellul can take great care and wrestle with the literal or plain sense of the biblical text he is also willing to offer a more spiritual interpretation in order to discern Scripture's message. Thus, drawing on a study of Fernand Ryser (a French translator of two of the great influences on Ellul's theology and biblical interpretation—Barth and Bonhoeffer), he highlights that a source of the gold for the calf is the Israelite's earrings (v2). He quotes Ryser, "Aaron dishonors the ear; it no longer counts; now just the eye matters. Hearing the Word of God no longer matters; now seeing and looking at an image are central. Sight replaces faith."[14] It is this attempt to argue for a biblical basis for the priority of the word and hearing over the material image and sight that is a central theme of *The Humiliation of the Word* as a whole and of its exegesis of key biblical passages.

Finally, Ellul's claim for a biblically based prioritization of hearing over seeing must also be applied to the Bible itself. Although Scripture and biblical interpretation play a central part in Ellul's theology and ethics, he is clear that Scripture, as a permanent, written record has the ambiguity of all written words. Drawing on the biblical narrative of Moses breaking the stone tablets (Exod 32:19), Ellul is adamant that this challenges a common Christian attitude to the Bible for the Bible "is never automatically and in itself the Word of God, but is always capable of becoming that Word—and as a Christian I would add: in a way denied to all other writings."[15]

Rather than treating the Bible as a visible divine word, Ellul insists that

> The destruction of this single, visible, material representation of God ought to remind us continually that the Bible in its materiality is not the Word of God made visible through reading. God . . . has not made his Word visible . . . The Bible is not a sort of visible representation of God . . . God's Word must remain a fleeting spoken Word, inscribed only in the human hear . . . [16]

Of course, as Ellul acknowledges elsewhere, God has in fact made his Word visible, but he has done so uniquely in the person of Jesus Christ and it is, therefore, Christ the incarnate Word who is the key to the Scriptures. Ellul, therefore throughout his interpretation of biblical texts works with a thoroughly theological and Christo-centric hermeneutic and a relative disregard for the tools of historical-critical study.[17]

14. Ellul, *Humiliation of the Word*, 87.
15. Ellul, *Living Faith*, 128.
16. Ellul, *Humiliation of the Word*, 63.
17. For Ellul's fullest account of hermeneutics see his "Innocent Notes on 'The Hermeneutic Question'" in Marva Dawn's translation and commentary on a number of

Ellul's biblical interpretation of some texts relating to idols and idolatry demonstrates that although Scripture plays a central role in his theology, his theological interpretation of those texts also makes him aware of the danger that Scripture may itself become an idol, a means of escaping the spoken Word of the living God. Ellul therefore challenges us to take Scripture seriously but not ultimately seriously, for ultimate seriousness is to be paid to the Word become flesh to whom Scripture—the Word written—bears witness and it is the living Word not the dead letter that is to be our concern. As a result, Christians are called to participate in a believing and attentive listening to hear the Word of God address us in and through the words of Scripture and to be confident that that Word is one which liberates us from the powers and unmasks all our idols as simply "the works of our hands."

Works Cited

Ellul, Jacques. *The Ethics of Freedom*. Translated by Geoffrey W. Bromiley. Grand Rapids: Eerdmans, 1976.

———. *The Humiliation of the Word*. Translated by Joyce Main Hanks. Grand Rapids: Eerdmans, 1985.

———. "Innocent Notes on 'The Hermeneutic Question.'" In *Sources and Trajectories: Eight Early Articles by Jacques Ellul that Set the Stage*, 184–203. Translation and commentary by Marva Dawn. Grand Rapids: Eerdmans, 1997.

———. *Living Faith: Belief and Doubt in a Perilous World*. Translated by Peter Heinegg. San Francisco: Harper & Row, 1983.

Ellul articles, *Sources and Trajectories*, 184–203.

CHAPTER 21

The Tower of Babel and the Hymn of Kenosis

Counterpoint Texts for Ellul

TED LEWIS

EUROPEAN ARTISTS OF PAST centuries who engaged the Tower of Babel story understood well that Babel was as much a spiritual force as it was a physical form.[1] Sir David Lyndsay, in 1554, wrote, "The shadow of that Hyddeous Strength / Sax myle and more it is of length." This line gave C. S. Lewis the perfect springboard for his final, dystopian story in his space trilogy. In *That Hideous Strength*, a techno-scientific attempt to 'improve' England is thwarted by higher powers. In contrast with the nobility of those thwarting higher powers are pretentious powers that indwell human culture. Lewis had no doubt as to how these latter, apparently human powers are larger than their institutional expressions. But Lewis's openly spiritual view is certainly not what we would expect from the more materialist outlook of the modernist suspicion which influenced the course of twentieth century academia. George Orwell, in reviewing Lewis's book in 1945, would have preferred if the "magical element" had been left out. "Unfortunately," he commented, "the supernatural keeps breaking in."[2]

How, then, does one locate the "hideous strengths" of our day, those invisible yet powerful forces that are no less mighty than gravity itself? One year after Orwell's review, Jacques Ellul wrote his seminal article, "Chronicle

---

1. This chapter is an update and adaptation of "Technicity as False Ascendancy: A Review of Ellul's Treatment of the Tower of Babel Narrative," first presented at the Ellul Conference at Wheaton College, 2012.

2. Orwell, "Scientists Take Over," 250.

of the Problems of Civilization," presenting his two-fold track of sociological and theological analysis. "Beyond the social and economic forms, there are forces that condition the life of our time."[3] While the details of Ellul's account of such forces shift over time, these forces were independent of human will, yet never separable from social forms. "We are in an essentially materialist time, or rather, a time of radical separation between two realms, material and spiritual."[4] And if the perennial problems of civilization are found in the combination of social and spiritual factors, the modern separation will lead to an incomplete diagnosis of the problems that threaten the foundations of society. During this post-war period, Ellul keenly recognized the that the right time, the *kairos* moment, had come for Christian scholars to advance this double-analysis of the "principalities and powers" in modern institutional life.[5] For Ellul, any saving hope for "our civilization which is perhaps not far from total collapse" would necessitate this blend of sociological and theological analysis. "We are at an absolutely decisive point," he prophetically announced in 1946.[6] And over the next half-century he spent his career naming the forces for what they are, uncovering the hideous strengths that fuel our technique-driven society.

Unsurprisingly, Ellul made numerous references to the Babel narrative from Genesis 11. He also identified a counter-narrative to Babel: the kenosis hymn of Philippians 2. This deliberate juxtaposition by Ellul will allow us to explore a more comprehensive telling of the Babel narrative that harmonizes with his larger discussion of technological totalism. Given both the centrality of these texts to Ellul's lifelong critique of technique, and the multivalent aspects of Genesis 11 to address linguistic, sociological, technological and spiritual dimensions in an integrated manner, one may wonder why Ellul never wrote a book solely on the Babel text. Nevertheless, important fragments scattered throughout his writings from 1970 to 1990 allow the careful reader to build a more cohesive, composite picture of the Babel archetype which fits into Ellul's larger corpus of writings.

Before we look at references to Babel in Ellul's writings, it is helpful to briefly consider his use of the terms 'sacralization' and 'desacralization.' When *The Secular City* by Harvey Cox came out in 1965, the book had wide sales in France and Ellul was very aware of the book's appeal. Part of the impetus for Ellul's writing of *The New Demons* ten years later was to provide a counterpoint to Cox's thesis of secularization. Ellul notes that where Cox praises

3. Ellul, "Chronicle of the Problems of Civilization," 19.
4. Ellul, "Chronicle of the Problems of Civilization," 20.
5. See the afterword to Jacobs, *Year of Our Lord, 1943*, 196–206.
6. Ellul, "Chronicle of the Problems of Civilization," 15.

science for exorcising the old sacralism away and ushering in the cleaner air of secularism, this house cleaning simply opened the way for seven new demons to take the place of the former one. "Consequent upon this scientific operation, modern man is much more religious, much more dependent, much more sacralized than ever before, and more insidiously so."[7]

Throughout *The New Demons*, Ellul describes how secular society has turned in on itself, preventing outside input, outside questioning—and indeed, outside revelation. The new facts of modern life judge the old sources of authority, rather than vice versa. In this light, Ellul argued that the secular setting cannot even detect how it can (and has) become a new *religious* setting. And since there is supposedly no fundamental difference between Christian religion and Christian revelation—between a human practice and something irreducibly transcendent, or *Wholly Other*—Christianity can blend with anything new, let alone with any other religion. But the greater issue is not how Christianity is compromised or limited in a secular setting. The root issue for Ellul is how modern society becomes re-sacralized in order to maximize the unification of all aspects of societal life. As Lewis portrayed in *That Hideous Strength*, the utopian experiment can only commence when it has a new religious framework that effectively binds everything together into a seamless cultural unity. And because "religious" life provided the loom for the outmoded unity, some new kind of cultural unity must be found, made.

The Secular City, therefore, is essentially a different kind of enslaved Sacred City, whether this slavery is informed by Nazism or Market Mammonism. This city is forever following suit in the pattern of Babylon, the great archetypal city of the Bible. Running through Babylon, of course, is Babel. In short, Babel exemplifies the preservation of a socio-spiritual framework: when an older religious orientation is replaced by a newer and 'better' one, the latter is by no means less religious. In fact, given Ellul's Barthian view of religion—which, in contrast with Cox, does distinguish between 'religion' as human attempts to understand or take hold of God, and 'revelation', i.e., God's self-revelation to humanity—if the new orientation is at odds with God, the new system will be even more religious. Secularization, then, is nothing more than "the enthronement of new religions," the creation of a new social unity.[8] Contrast this utopian drive, if you will, with the self-humbling Jesus's revelatory and desacralizing movement to not count equality with Caesar-aligned gods as something to be grasped. Ultimately, Ellul's treatment of the Babel

---

7. Ellul, *New Demons*, 213.
8. Ellul, *New Demons*, 213.

and kenosis texts prompts us to desacralize all social forms that are at odds with God's creation, revelation, and human freedom.

Ellul's Writings on Babel

In *The Meaning of the City*, Ellul is clear that what is of greater significance in Genesis 11 is not the tower but the city itself. Though its writing began much earlier, this book was published around the same time as *Demons*, providing additional response to Cox's *Secular City*. Human city-making is accompanied by human name-making. Of interest to Ellul is humankind's urge to make things in contrast to receiving things. In "Technique and the Opening Chapters of Genesis," he suggests that "technique was impossible in Eden" and that it is a "phenomenon of the Fall."[9] When the original unity of relationships in Eden is lost, everything in human life becomes an object of potential use. This, for Ellul, brings about the proliferation of means which means that human life becomes populated with intermediaries that could lead to desired ends. To make a city, to make a name, to make an idol, etc., allowed people to distinguish themselves by what they could affect, and this opened the way for greater independence from God. By redefining relationships in terms of objects that could be mastered, people could now become *subjects* like God. The Babel project, then, is not simply a Promethean effort to take over God's power; "it is the desire to exclude God from his creation" so that man could assume God's place.[10]

Babel was therefore "the sign and symbol" of humanity's collective enterprise to build something without the help of God. Babel was a new milieu, "built by man for man," and that is precisely the setting where man, as a mass, could make a name for himself.[11] Ellul reminds us that naming is essentially a spiritual act, establishing at least two important relationships: the relationship between the one naming and the one named, and the relationship between the intrinsic nature of something and its distinctive purpose.[12] Humanity, then redefines its relationship with itself, unaware that the new subject-object configuration will entail new chains requiring the opiates and roses of a man-made religion. Man now controls his own sacrality, having removed the previous Creator-creature relationship, exchanging it for a new glory that promises mastery over anything that humanity can think of doing.

9. Ellul, *Meaning of the City*, 132, 135.
10. Ellul, *Meaning of the City*, 16.
11. Ellul, *Meaning of the City*, 16.
12. Cf. Michael Morelli's essay in this volume.

In summary, we have the roots of Ellul's pessimistic theological view of the city: rooted in the pride of Babel, excluding God, proliferating the technicity of means, taking over nature, birthing greater alienation among people—and all the while, blind to the inevitable consequences of its actions. Man's thirst for technological conquest is tied to his thirst for spiritual conquest. But this will not go unchecked. "Sin always eggs [collective man] on to use things over which he is master in a way conducive to a spiritual destruction that nothing, in the natural order of things, can stop. Such is the city."[13] At this point, however, Ellul notes that God's response is not an iconoclastic smashing of man's enterprise. Rather, God intervenes *before* things get completely bad. In *The Politics of God and the Politics of Man*, Ellul explains how "God permits . . . Babel enterprises because he respects man's freedom and these frenzied methods fall within the perspective of his own design."[14] In other words, God is not responsible for the fallout, but God foresees the fall in relation to the natural order or design of things. What seems to be a harsh judgment is in fact a divine redirection at the best possible time.

Because Ellul sees the problem as a spiritual one (i.e., humanity's making a name for itself without God's involvement), God's response is not to disrupt the form of the city but rather the form of communication required to make a tower. The confusion of language (which provides the etymology for the word Babel) is not an explanation for the birth of languages. Leaving no stone unturned in his biblical exegesis, Ellul keenly spots that the word 'language' is singular, not plural. The Babel builders' dilemma was that they did not understand the *one* language they relied upon. "By confusion of tongues, by non-communication, God keeps man from forming a truth valid for all men, that is, for man as a mass. Henceforth, man's truth will only be partial and contested."[15] What God was thwarting was the nexus of unity for the human race, the point of convergence for human-made truth. What people lost by God's intervention was "the meaning of the city"—that is, the opportunity to find ultimate meaning in human-generated enterprises that left God out of the picture.

In *Perspectives on our Age* (1981), Ellul advances the notion that Babel provides a new type of unity for humankind. Earlier chapters in Genesis set the stage of human tensions: people against God, brother against brother, people against nature, ruler against servant. Without proper relationship to God, all other relationships were marked by conflict and violence. Humanity

---

13. Ellul, *Meaning of the City*, 17.
14. Ellul, *Politics of God and the Politics of Man*, 175.
15. Ellul, *Meaning of the City*, 19.

needed a 'new normal.' The Tower of Babel could offset the harsh realities of destabilized life by offering a new solution to the problems of the day. It offered "the substitution of a cultural unity for God himself."[16] In effect, the tower restored unity in a world of sin and slavery as a way to make life's hardships more bearable. The ultimate questions of life are put to rest because all issues are accounted for within the scope of man's socio-material reality. Religion, namely the cultural unity represented in the ascending tower, gave the glue for unifying everything; the people of Shinar were reconnected to the realm of the gods. But in this unity, every aspect of life must be integrated. Even sin itself is woven into the whole, and thus violence, indulgence and social prestige all have their proper place. This unity also legitimates "the unlimited growth of the means without our being able to guide them toward human ends."[17] Altogether, Ellul recognizes how Babel illustrates the chief values of modern technique: unification and limitlessness.

At the beginning of the 1980s, *The Humiliation of the Word* allowed Ellul to deepen his presentation of Babel's communication dynamics. At the outset he wrote how "sight makes me the center of the world,"[18] whereas the hearing of words places one in relationship to time and others. Next, Ellul associates images with reality and words with truth, then goes a step further by saying that images tend to reinforce conformity; words, however, speak into reality and disturb it. And here is the rub: as people manufacture cultural images which take on the qualities of artifice, images pose as conveyers of truth. This communication environment, where all reality is 'normalized', begins to devalue the capacity for words to truly speak a counterpoint truth that is at variance with 'reality', and eventually words, now humiliated, can only function as images do. "In such a situation, when the word claims to speak only of reality, it is so rapidly outdistanced by the image that the word loses its vitality and gravity. The image is ever so much more efficacious, and the word is stripped of its authenticity."[19]

Ellul thus has much to say about *why* God confused the mono-language of Babel where image trumps word. Making a name is only possible by making an image. As discussed earlier, the rejection of God's name so humanity could make a name for itself amounted to a rejection of the subject-object relationship implied in all naming. To name *oneself* outside of this ordained relationality was a way to assert *autonomy*—that is, etymologically 'apart from the law' or 'a law unto oneself.' If people were to successfully break

16. Ellul, *Perspectives on Our Age*, 130.
17. Ellul, *Perspectives on Our Age*, 87.
18. Ellul, *Humiliation of the Word*, 5.
19. Ellul, *Humiliation of the Word*, 32–33.

away from God, they had to leave the realm of words that define genuine relationships and response-abilities, embracing the realm of images that gave them greater mastery. "Being master of the words about oneself is in reality claiming to be one's own subject and completely autonomous."[20] Consequently, God is turned into an object that can either be used or removed. But this, of course, cannot happen. In the end, God turns the image-soaked language of Babel into a form of non-communication. The former mono-language that rejects external questioning, external truth, due to the fusing of imagery and language which normalizes a human-made reality with no contradictions, cannot continue in a world where God seeks to communicate with people. A similar problem happens with idolatry; further on, we will discuss how the domination of form over content is problematic for a God who reveals true content through form.

Also in the eighties came *Living Faith*, a unique book built on Barth's distinction between religion and revelation. "While religion sacralizes and absolutizes human realities, revelation descralizes and relativizes them."[21] Ellul uses the Babel story to show how people use religious beliefs and activities to hold all aspects of society in unity, all "convergences" for the building of Babel projects. And as the Babel tower goes upward, so "religion goes up; revelation goes down."[22] Religion serves human communities by making them organized, orderly, and sustainable. "All this is fine," says Ellul, "but it is not God; it doesn't bring us any closer to God."[23] The religious impulse is always a matter of 'grasping', as Barth said, and this is illustrated by an upward reach for divinity or higher destiny. In this ascent, wrote Ellul, religion "always expresses itself in a show of power."[24] "People build the tower to climb up and enter into contact with God, to equal him. To get hold of him, and whatever else one can imagine. In the face of this, God proclaims his intention to go down and see." [25] The triple matrix of ascendancy, acquisition and power, all within a religiously-framed context, is essential for Ellul. This is not simply because Christianity or any other traditional religion can be used as the glue for societal integration; it is important because even a so-called post-Christian framework requires a sacralizing 'religion' to hold things together. We will return to the idea later that ascendancy and power-intensification go hand-in-hand.

20. Ellul, *Humiliation of the Word*, 53.
21. Ellul, *Living Faith*, 143.
22. Ellul, *Living Faith*, 129.
23. Ellul, *Living Faith*, 143.
24. Ellul, *Living Faith*, 141.
25. Ellul, *Living Faith*, 137.

The last book to be considered is *What I Believe* (1989). In this book, Ellul significantly added the notion of Babel being a "closed system" that will help us carry the conversation into his broader theory of technique. From the inside, this system had a cultural unity that provided a self-legitimizing aspect to Babel. But no system that is closed or totalistic can exist indefinitely apart from God, for God is the only one who reveals divinity to humanity from the outside.

> Because God reveals himself, the world can never be a closed reality. It cannot find fulfillment in itself or shut itself up in a total system. The technological system comes under the historical law of Babel. This was a city meant to enclose the whole race and its gods. It was a universal city. It had no place for a separate 'transcendent.' The walls of Babel were meant to shut out God, and leave him only a gate.[26]

Therefore God "opens it up from outside." When human evil and human misery reach a feverish frenzy, God comes "down to see" what is happening, leaving his place of rest to intervene. This is important language since the tower image works in the opposite direction. Ellul makes a new comment here: "The building of the city and the tower of Babel is a two-fold offense against God, a repetition of the fall of Adam."[27] Here we see how the clearer demonstration of human hubris in the tower project adds an additional affront to God beyond the city project, and this added enterprise prompts God to come 'down' and thwart the project. This now concludes our review of selected Babel texts from Ellul's writings from 1970 to 1990. With each encounter we see additional layers of commentary that reveal the progression of Ellul's own thinking on this subject.

Ellul's Kenosis Counterpoint Narrative

Five times in books listed above where the Babel story is expounded, Ellul references the kenosis hymn of Philippians 2:5–11. Unlike the common, sermonic juxtaposition of the Babel and Pentecost narratives, Ellul insightfully sees how the real contrast is not about languages and cultural dispersion, but rather about the human capacity to reject God's mode of operation and replace it with an autonomous (and thus oppositional) mode of operation. Again, we note that the story does not move from one language to multiple languages, but rather from a legitimizing, means-intensive language to an

26. Ellul, *What I Believe*, 184–85.
27. Ellul, *What I Believe*, 158.

incoherent, useless language. Ellul rightly aligns the Babel text within the Hebrew polemic against idolatry. And because idolatry is an inversion of divine revelation, Ellul gravitates toward a counter-text that illuminates true revelation. We are dealing here with themes of power and force, where theology and sociology meet and mingle, and Ellul identifies the best New Testament text that illustrates a reversal of Babel ways.

The context for the Philippians hymn has two interrelated sociological layers. First, there are relationships which church members have with one another. The theological hymn emerges out of a discussion of church unity and disunity. Paul's concern is that the Philippians should not be motivated by "rivalry and vain glory" (KJV). These barriers to unity found cultural legitimacy within Roman society where political leaders succeeded by overcoming their rivals, and advanced their status through acceptable displays of *kenodoxia*—literally, 'empty glory.'[28] In sharp contrast, the Philippians are invited to treat each other with humility. Related to interchurch relationships was the second layer, the surrounding citizenry of a Roman colony. Ellul did not present this backdrop, nor did he comment on Paul's usage of *polis* (city) to help his readers think about being an alternative *politaima* (citi-zens).[29] But he was tuned into the power dynamics of Christ's descent. In *Living Faith*, he noted four levels of descent: emptying, taking on human nature, becoming a powerless servant, and dying in humiliation. Nothing could be further from the god-like prestige enjoyed by Caesars than the punishment reserved for rebellious slaves. "And with that we have the capstone on the radical contrast between this God's revelation and all religions."[30]

This counter-matrix of descendancy, non-acquisition, and powerlessness provides not only a new basis for human unity but also a new pattern for how such unity is maintained. Freedom and love, expressed through self-giving action, opens the way for a non-coercive community working together to foster an ethos of descent. When contrasted with Babel, the emptying of Christ is not a giving-up of qualities of God as God really is, but rather of qualities of Greco-Roman deities and rulers, such as status and self-importance. This reading fits best with the earlier usage of *kenodoxia* (empty glory) which sharpens our understanding of genuine *kenosis* (emptying). One moves from pseudo-revelation to authentic revelation. The vital element of revelation is that God speaks, and not only speaks, but comes down into human experience to speak in the best 'language' we can understand. The biblical problem, as noted in *Humiliation*, is when something in

28. Phil 2:3 (KJV rendered the Latin as "vainglory").
29. Phil 1:27; 3:20.
30. Ellul, *Living Faith*, 140.

the realm of the word is reduced to the realm of sight.[31] In Jesus, Ellul sees the "correct equilibrium" or synthesis of the word and image, content and form, whereas in Babel, no less than all idolatry, one finds the domineering role of image over word.

When sight played its role to cause "all humanity and language to swing to its side," and "coveting"—Eden and Babel's primal sin—became the psychological root of all other sins,[32] image-sight laid the foundation for humanity to use anything, including language, to leverage power. For Ellul, Jesus represents the full denial of covetousness; he builds his point in full juxtaposition to the Babel story. "We have the exact antithesis of this attitude in the famous passage in Philippians that describes the decision of the Son to strip himself . . ."[33] This divine downwardness becomes the way for the truth of God's core character to be revealed, establishing Jesus's credentials as the Name above every name. This is the complete opposite of Babel's upwardness that inverts God's 'downward' revelation; Jesus's refusal to grasp his own glory stands apart from all who construct their own name for their own glory. Wherever image and coveting have full sway, truth is obscured in the service of social (and seemingly total) reality. Again, language suffers the greatest casualty. "Because human words are no longer in harmony with the Word of God, languages become separate . . . Once inserted into reality, the word changed to the point where it became incomprehensible language."[34]

Twice in *Perspectives on our Age*, Ellul pairs up the Babel and Pauline narratives. At stake is revelation. In the Babel setting, humanity prefers to "use the divinities." But a God of revelation cannot be used; God will not cater to the ascendancy of religion. "Religion seeks to go from below, where we are, to above, where God is. But the Bible shows us the opposite. I am thinking of that great passage in . . . Philippians . . ."[35] The problem with Christianity is that revelation is continually deformed by the agendas of religion. Ellul is sympathetic with Marx and Feuerbach who critique religion on sociological grounds. But if and when revelation can be held distinct from religion, it then can have a transcendence which even technology, in all its totalism, can never supercede.[36] Only then can technology be critiqued from the outside, and the nature of technique-driven means can be called into question. With this in mind, we can now consider other writings by Ellul that do not mention Babel,

---

31. Ellul, *Humiliation of the Word*, 89.
32. Ellul, *Humiliation of the Word*, 100, 101.
33. Ellul, *Humiliation of the Word*, 101.
34. Ellul, *Humiliation of the Word*, 100.
35. Ellul, *Perspectives on Our Age*, 78.
36. Ellul, *Perspectives on Our Age*, 94, 95.

but nonetheless explore Babel themes. (A chart contrasting all major aspects in Babel's Narrative of Ascent and the Philippian Narrative of Descent can be found at the end of this chapter.)

Babel and Ellul's Critique of Technique

In other writings, Ellul clearly deals with Babel-complexes to account for how technique operates in a totalistic system. References from three books will suffice to represent a much wider array of options. In *The Technological Bluff*, Ellul shows how technology seemingly holds great promise, but never quite delivers the goods in the end. A section on the influence of television and "telematics" concludes with Ellul's prophetic view that "we are in a process of universal transformation without really knowing what is happening. This confirms our older judgment regarding the autonomy and collective supremacy of technique."[37] Just as Babel was a compensation for humanity's dilemma of being spread out, so television, to offset the dispossession and alienation that people feel, is itself "a religion, a kind of God . . . a revelation for humanity."[38] As in modern advertising, there is a fusing of imagery and divinity which sustains an "absolute fascination." Akin to Babel, "television is universal and spectacular; it defies my attempts to master it; it performs what would usually be called miracles; to a large extent it is incomprehensible. It is thus God."[39]

In his discussion on "Technological Morality" in *To Will & To Do*, Ellul describes how this new morality overcomes and absorbs all other moralities. He then speaks of additional "virtues" of technological morality, one of which is a "confidence in the future" to remedy any problem in the present.

> It is the virtue of "Everything is possible," which of course is expressed in large part in the value of the Normal. Everything is possible: not only is there no pre-fixed limit, no moral or spiritual limit to action, but the only recognized barrier is that which is not possible today but will be tomorrow. Nothing is surprising anymore: the disintegration of the atom, Sputnik, all this is completely normal. Tomorrow we will do better. But in reality, above all this virtue expresses a morality of excess, a morality of the unlimited, to which modern man adapts perfectly.[40]

---

37. Ellul, *Technological Bluff*, 346.
38. Ellul, *Technological Bluff*, 346.
39. Ellul, *Technological Bluff*, 346.
40. Ellul, *To Will & To Do*, 1:181.

This morality could rightly be called a Babel morality, for "The excess of means and successes of technique conditions a morality of gigantism and the unlimited. The *Kolossal,* the *Biggest in the World* are expressions of this morality."[41] The totalistic morality prizes the value of 'more-is-better,' where the 'good' is defined by "surpassing limits."[42] Underlying this approach to the good, of course, is a totalitarianism that can never be questioned, which suppresses the virtues of individual or personal morality. Limitlessness leads to the loss of freedom.

In *The Ethics of Freedom*, Ellul begins by describing how technological humankind is more alienated than industrial humankind for two reasons. First, "all the forces and structures of the social order have an unavoidable tendency to expand until they become as total as possible."[43] The second reason is that since all social forces move toward totalism, "they all necessarily take on a spiritual meaning and value."[44] The social form has to become larger than itself to re-present meaning in a world without meaning. Again, the Babel impulse is central: "It cannot in effect be universal unless it ceases to be itself in order to be more than itself by taking on spiritual significance."[45] So first we have an external necessity where all social forces have to converge together, carrying people along with the tide, and then we have what Ellul calls an "internal necessity" which imbues spiritual power upon the social forms, as it happens with idolatry, so that people can retrieve that power for themselves. But at this point the Marxist would rightly ask, "Which people?"

Beyond Babel's city we see how Babel's tower was the ultimate way for spiritual significance and meaning to be given to the urbanizing enterprise. It is one thing to have something made by human hands; it is another for hand-made objects to receive innate powers that exert a social force on society. Here we find a point of convergence for Ellul's intellectual mentors, Karl Marx and Karl Barth. The Marxist sees how social conditions are overlaid with illusions of sacrality to make it more bearable. The Barthian contrasts this upward thrust of religion with humanity's need for God's downward revelation. What revelation is to God, culture-making is to humanity. The problem comes when culture takes on the Babel elements of spiritual significance, and in this idolatry, it becomes an inversion of all aspects of divine

---

41. Ellul, *To Will & To Do*, 1:181. *Kolossal* follows Ellul's spelling, and *Biggest in the World* is in English in the original.
42. Ellul, *To Will & To Do*, 1:181.
43. Ellul, *Ethics of Freedom*, 39.
44. Ellul, *Ethics of Freedom*, 40.
45. Ellul, *Ethics of Freedom*, 40.

revelation. Could it be that by naming the upward Babel force as having spiritual dimensions (while not ceasing to be sociological), Ellul advances on the Marxist critique of religion? Does he not provide a fuller accounting for the *forcefulness* of technique-driven forces that are shaping modern life with their hideous strength?

At this point, our study could go in multiple directions beyond the scope of this chapter. Ellul's listing of attributes in a technique-driven closed system could complete a composite picture of Babel complexes.[46] A deeper study of Ellul's treatment of word and image, truth and reality, as juxtaposed in *Humiliation* would help us better see how Babel forms dominate the role of content. God's effort to frustrate the Babel builders easily leads into a study of Ellul's invitation for people to be response-able through prophetic iconoclasm.[47] Finally, we could note how the divine intervention strikes not at the structure itself, but at the mono-communication ideology that was essentially anti-revelational, leaving no place either for incoming truth or for individual and social diversity.[48]

Altogether, Ellul repeatedly used the Babel narrative as an archetypal source for expounding upon the socio-spiritual forces that shape modern society with totalistic agendas. He also used the kenosis hymn of Philippians 2 as an apt counter-narrative to sharpen the opposition between techno-religious social forms and God's open, invitational, dialogic revelation. This juxtaposition of biblical texts is itself an example of how Ellul used the Bible to create an intra-textual conversation to deepen his own insights. At the same time, biblical texts were not only useful to Ellul pedagogically, but were directive of his very framework. They were *source* as much as they were *reinforcement* of his ideas. For Ellul, a real God does indeed intervene in real human history.

We thus return to the climax of *That Hideous Strength*. Ransom explains to Merlin how the technocrats have over-extended their reach. "Their own strength has betrayed them. They have gone to the gods who would not have come to them, and pulled down Deep Heaven on their heads."[49] By seeking limitlessness, the builders are left with greater limits. Ellul's technological determinism, when viewed as a pessimistic vision in his sociological writings, would suggest there is no other end to the story. For as he wrote in *The Technological Society*, "the technical society must perfect the 'man-machine' complex or risk total collapse"; "There is no

---

46. Ellul, "Search for Ethics in a Technicist Society."
47. Ellul, *New Demons*, 225.
48. Ellul, *Living Faith*, 141.
49. Lewis, *That Hideous Strength*, 294.

other place to go but up."[50] But in his theologically informed writings, we find a balance to this pessimism that speaks of both divine and human responsibility to effect a positive ending to the story. Against the movement of ascent, the movement of descent can make a difference. What remains, then, is if we can act as God acts, refusing to grasp for higher gain, choosing to serve for the sake of freedom.

THEME	BABEL Narrative of Ascent	PHILIPPIANS Narrative of Descent
Attitude	Covetousness institutionalized (pride); grasping mode	Covetousness rejected (relational humility); non-grasping mode
Naming	"Make a name for ourselves" asserts autonomy from God (auto-nomos)	"The Name of names" is not sought but bestowed by God onto Jesus
Form and Content	Form dominates over content after truth is emptied out and grandiose surface image remains	"Form of God" reveals God's true content (nature); grandiosity (a false content) is emptied out
Power	Surface image of tower generates social power through fascination	Image of God, one with divine nature, generates powerlessness
Language	Mono-language controlled by image-intensification and utilitarianism (which devalues words/meaning)	Word of God and Image of God in full synthesis with each other through incarnation and enactment, thus meaning-full
Means	Proliferation of means (any means) to reach desired ends	Integrity of selfless means with selfless ends
Ends	Human-centered exaltation through independency from God; assertion of importance and maintenance of power	Betterment of others through relational interdependencies; relinquishment of importance leads to exaltation of Jesus
Limitations	"Nothing is impossible!" New morality based on what can be done, not what ought to be done	God limits power through vulnerability, accomplishing purposes and expressing morality
Reality	Reality = human-made, cultural fabrications within a closed system, in tension the created order and human freedom; all is contrived by technique	Truth = God's revelation given within an open system (in tension with human-made 'realities') thus inviting dialogue, illuminating what is real; non-contrived

---

50. Ellul, *Technological Society*, 414.

THEME	BABEL Narrative of Ascent	PHILIPPIANS Narrative of Descent
Social Dynamic	Model of centralized mass-man living in conformist and coercive settings; pseudo-independency	Model of diverse individuals living in harmony and freedom; interdependency is normative
Unity	Cultural unity normalizes and legitimizes everything, and is non-dialectical, denying disruptivity and dissent	God's 'yes/no' revelation is disruptive to human life; true unity comes by alignment with God's ways
Spirituality	Sacralization of culture (increase in myth making, promotion of status quo, de-historicization); more religious in broadest sense	Desacralization of culture (true myth rooted in God's work and ways, motivating new change, counterpoint, etc.); less religious

Works Cited

Cox, Harvey. *The Secular City.* New York: Macmillan, 1965.
Ellul, Jacques. "Chronicle of the Problems of Civilization: By Way of a Brief Preface." In *Sources and Trajectories. Eight Early Articles by Jacques Ellul that Set the Stage*, 10–28. Translated and with commentary by Marva Dawn. Grand Rapids: Eerdmans, 1997.
———. *The Ethics of Freedom.* Translated by Geoffrey W. Bromiley. Grand Rapids: Eerdmans, 1976.
———. *The Humiliation of the Word.* Translated by Joyce Main Hanks. Grand Rapids: Eerdmans, 1985.
———. *Living Faith: Belief and Doubt in a Perilous World.* Translated by Peter Heinegg. San Francisco: Random, 1985.
———. *The Meaning of the City.* Translated by Dennis Pardee. Grand Rapids: Eerdmans, 1970.
———. *The New Demons.* Translated by C. Edward Hopkin. New York: Seabury, 1975.
———. *Perspectives on Our Age.* Translated by Joachim Neugroschel. Edited by Willem H. Vanderburg. New York: Seabury, 1981.
———. *The Politics of God and the Politics of Man.* Translated by Geoffrey W. Bromiley. Grand Rapids: Eerdmans, 1972.
———. "The Search for Ethics in a Technicist Society." Translated by Dominique Gillot and Carl Mitcham. *Research in Philosophy and Technology* 9 (1989) 23–36.
———. "Technique and the Opening Chapters of Genesis." In *Theology and Technology: Essays in Christian Analysis and Exegesis*, edited by Carl Mitcham and Jim Grote, 123–37. Lanham, MD: University Press of America, 1984.
———. *The Technological Bluff.* Translated by Geoffrey W. Bromiley. Grand Rapids: Eerdmans, 1990.
———. *The Technological Society.* Translated by John Wilkinson. New York: Knopf, 1964.

———. *To Will & To Do. An Introduction to Christian Ethics*. Translated by Jacob Marques Rollison. Eugene, OR: Cascade, 2020.

———. *What I Believe*. Translated by Geoffrey W. Bromiley. Grand Rapids: Eerdmans, 1989.

Jacobs, Alan. *The Year of Our Lord 1943: Christian Humanism in an Age of Crisis*. Oxford: Oxford University Press, 2018.

Lewis, C. S. *That Hideous Strength*. New York: Macmillan, 1945/1946.

Orwell, George. "The Scientists Take Over (Review of C. S. Lewis' *That Hideous Strength*)." *Manchester Evening News*, 16 August 1945. Reprinted in *The Complete Works of George Orwell*, edited by Peter Davison, No. 2720 (first half), 17:250–51. London: Secker & Warburg, 1998.

─── CHAPTER 22 ───

Ellul's Apocalyptic Understanding of Scripture in *Money and Power*

Declan Kelly

Introduction

"WE MUST NOT LIVE in a dream world." So urges Jacques Ellul as he approaches the conclusion of his 1954 work *L'homme et l'argent* (translated into English as *Money and Power*).[1] But this caution could aptly stand at the head of Ellul's typically perceptive and provocative treatment of what he repeatedly calls "the problem of money." Resistance to life in a dream world is the express aim throughout this text. Ellul's alternative to life in a dream world is life in reality and truth. It is this *reality* that he seeks after in *Money and Power*. And it is this truth that he finds—or rather, that finds him—in the word of God as attested in Holy Scripture.

In this brief chapter I seek to display Ellul's understanding and use of Scripture (with a focus on the New Testament) in *Money and Power*. In particular, part one will demonstrate that Ellul has a distinctively *apocalyptic* account of Scripture, in at least two senses of that freighted term: first, he understands Scripture to accomplish the unveiling of divine and earthly reality; second, his reading of Scripture is everywhere anchored to an understanding of God's saving act in Christ as a victory over the power of Satan. How this apocalyptic account of Scripture shapes his approach to New Testament texts which treat the topic of money is explored in part two.

---

1. Ellul, *L'homme et l'argent*, 123.

I. Scripture as Apocalypse

Apocalyptic as Unveiling

Throughout *Money and Power*, Ellul understands Scripture to have an apocalyptic function in the literal sense of the original Greek word *apocalypsis*: it unveils both divine and earthly realities. It penetrates to the truth of things—in this instance, to the truth of money. To put the matter most forcefully, the whole of Scripture is for Ellul an apocalypse all the way down; it is a revelation of the depths of reality.

When Ellul reads Scripture, he thus does so with the expectancy that the truth of the world—both the truth of its dire situation and the truth of God's will to redeem it—will be revealed. God's revelation, as attested in Scripture, is for him the "illumination that God's word gives the world."[2] Ellul's interest in *Money and Power* is not to find this or that biblical principle that can then be applied to the world as we know it; his interest is in "the reality revealed by the Bible," a reality whose truth we would not know and cannot know apart from God's revelation to faith.[3]

This is not to say that Ellul takes Scripture to be the presentation of an objective "biblical worldview." Crucial for him is that it is God's *word* that illuminates the world. He writes: "When we open the Bible we do not find a philosophy, a political statement, a metaphysic or even a religion. We find instead the promise of dialog, a personal word addressed to me, asking me what I am doing, hoping, fearing—and especially what I am."[4] The unveiling that Scripture offers us takes the form of a dialog, a living, open-ended conversation in which God addresses me and in which I hear and respond in faith.

This "dialogic" grasp of the nature of Scripture's revelatory power has direct implications for how Ellul approaches the problem of money. "All that the Bible has to tell me about money," Ellul insists, "is found in this dialog."[5] And so while Scripture does indeed offer "truth about all things—including money," the character of this truth is neither objective nor subjective. Rather, truth "is found in relationship with God, and nowhere else."[6] This relationship, according to Ellul, is always a relationship of *faith*. "The immense body of revelation," he claims, "does not appeal to reason, evidence or pragmatism." In fact, he is adamant that

---

2. Ellul, *Money and Power*, 118.
3. Ellul, *Money and Power*, 119.
4. Ellul, *Money and Power*, 26.
5. Ellul, *Money and Power*, 26.
6. Ellul, *Money and Power*, 26.

the apocalyptic nature of Scripture "is shut tight against these modes of conviction."[7] Faith in the God who addresses me is the only "mode of conviction" capable of receiving Scripture's illuminating word.

Can the faithful then go about the business of creating a Christian "doctrine of money" on the basis of Scripture? Can they "try to settle definitions, arguments, terms, to come up with a final construction that, intellectually and economically, we can rely on and trust"?[8] Ellul denies such a venture even to faith. He does so because of "the theme of Scripture," because of the very nature of "what Scripture shows."[9] Scripture's theme is a "movement," one that "has the strength and speed of a rushing torrent."[10] And as Ellul reminds us, "We do not build with a torrent."[11] This movement is the activity of God in all its singularity and particularity. The Word of God attested in Scripture, then, is likened by Ellul to a "beam of light from a projector that leaves great areas of darkness in order to focus on the one indispensable point where God's action is concentrated."[12] Being opened to Scripture's revelation in faith, then, we are not opened to a view of the totality. Rather, we are caught up in the movement of God. In this movement it is possible to see the truth of things, including money. But only *in this movement* is such seeing possible.[13] As Ellul writes,

> ... these texts ask us to commit ourselves. They start us down a certain path. They are not providing us with rational options or objective conclusions; the biblical texts never come to conclusions because there is no conclusion apart from the heavenly Jerusalem and our resurrection. The texts are therefore never a 'solution.' To the contrary, they get us started on a journey, and the only answer we can hope to find is the one we ourselves give by our lives as we proceed on that journey.[14]

---

7. Ellul, *Money and Power*, 26.
8. Ellul, *Money and Power*, 31.
9. Ellul, *Money and Power*, 31.
10. Ellul, *Money and Power*, 31.
11. Ellul, *Money and Power*, 31.
12. Ellul, *Money and Power*, 31.
13. On the importance of following the "movement" of the biblical texts themselves, see Ellul, *Apocalypse*, 12. The original title of the book is in fact *L'Apocalypse: architecture en mouvement*.
14. Ellul, *Money and Power*, 26–27.

Apocalyptic as the Triumph of Christ over Satan

Ellul's reference to the dynamic activity of God raises a second sense in which he understands Scripture apocalyptically. Asking how to approach biblical passages concerning money, Ellul urges that we must let these passages "have the character God has given them."[15] According to Ellul, first of all, this means that we understand the fragmentary character of these passages. They are "fragments of the total revelation."[16] That these passages have this character means that they cannot be considered in isolation, but only as part of their wider context. While Ellul's recognition that individual passages have a wider context and should therefore be read with this context in view looks vaguely like what would come to be known as a "canonical" reading of Scripture, the particular context Ellul has in mind is not the totality of Scripture as such but "God's work in Jesus Christ."[17] The content of these individual passages on money always refers to that particular divine work. Ellul thus approaches Scripture in *Money and Power* with what might be called a christological-soteriological hermeneutic, precisely because he takes all of Scripture to be held together by its referral to God's saving work in Christ.

But what makes such an approach to Scripture *apocalyptic*? One might simply claim that Ellul's Christological and soteriological concentration is itself a hallmark of what has come to be known as the "apocalyptic turn" in theology.[18] But there is perhaps a more explicit way in which this approach to Scripture is apocalyptic. For Ellul's understanding of God's work in Christ in *Money and Power* is relentlessly characterized by attention to this work as the dethroning of Satan in the fallen world and God's seizure of power in the person of Christ. All that Ellul has to say about the modern "problem of money" presupposes and explicates this cosmic and spiritual dethroning and seizure of power. His reading of individual biblical passages has this saving event either explicitly or implicitly in view.[19] The difference this makes to Ellul's account of money is considerable and will be pursued below. But for now, it is vital to note that

---

15. Ellul, *Money and Power*, 26.
16. Ellul, *Money and Power*, 26.
17. Ellul, *Money and Power*, 26.

18. On this apocalyptic turn and its consequence for theology see Ziegler, *Militant Grace*. For a set of theses on apocalyptic theology which point to the importance of a christological and soteriological concentration see 26–31, esp. 26–27.

19. On this aspect of apocalyptic theology, see Ziegler's fourth thesis in *Militant Grace*, 28–29.

the particular context of the biblical passages on money is God's redemption of the world from the power of the devil.

To borrow Gustav Aulén's terminology, a *Christus Victor* understanding of the atonement is everywhere assumed in *Money and Power*.[20] "Redemption," Ellul claims, "is very literally the payment of Satan's price in order to free us."[21] *Money and Power* does not present a detailed, systematic account of the atonement along these lines.[22] Ellul's interests lie elsewhere. But as we will see presently, connecting biblical passages about money to God's redemption of the world from the power of Satan is a fundamental aspect of Ellul's engagement with Scripture in this work.

II. Money as Power

We come now to the question of how Ellul's apocalyptic understanding of Scripture is reflected in his handling of those biblical texts that address the topic of money. Money, in fact, has a name: Mammon. This is the name given to it by Jesus in Matt 6:24 and Luke 16:13. Ellul discerns in this language of Jesus a "personification" of money that "reveals something exceptional" about it, something that eludes the calculations and analysis of the economist or politician.[23] Perhaps the central claim of Ellul's book—a claim rooted in his reading of the New Testament—is that money is revealed by Scripture to be a personal power, an agent acting in and upon the world, and ultimately a rival god seeking out worshippers.[24] As Ellul states concerning the words of Christ in Matt 6:24 and Luke 6:13, "What Jesus is revealing is that money is a power. This term should be understood not in its vague meaning, 'force,' but in the specific sense in which it is used in the New Testament. Power is something that acts by itself, is capable of moving other things, is autonomous (or claims to be), is a law unto itself, and presents itself as an active agent.[25]"

And so while many within the world of New Testament studies in the 1950s were ploughing ahead with a program of demythologizing, Ellul finds

---

20. See Aulén, *Christus Victor*.
21. Ellul, *Money and Power*, 87.
22. The closest we get to such an account is Ellul, *Money and Power*, 87–88.
23. Ellul, *Money and Power*, 75.
24. On Ellul's understanding of money as Mammon see Prather, *Christ, Power and Mammon*, 213–16. For a more general and extensive examination of Ellul's account of the "principalities and powers" see Dawn, "Concept of 'The Principalities and Powers' in the Works of Jacques Ellul."
25. Ellul, *Money and Power*, 75–76.

in the apparently "mythological" portrayal of money by Jesus a highly realistic account of its nature and activity.[26] This portrayal is no "rhetorical" gesture on the part of Jesus, insists Ellul, but an acute unveiling of "reality."[27]

But what difference does it make to think of money as a personal power in conflict with the reign of God? For Ellul, the New Testament description of money as a power transports us from a "moral order" to a "spiritual order."[28] To think of money within a moral order to is consider human "behaviour toward an object." But to think of money within a spiritual order is to think of "relating to a power."[29] The difference between these two ways of thinking is the difference between illusion and reality. As Ellul writes,

> ... when we claim to use money, we make a gross error. We can, if we must, use money, but it is really money that uses us and makes us servants by bringing us under its law and subordinating us to its aims. We are not talking only about our inner life; we are observing our total situation. We are not free to direct the use of money one way or another, for we are in the hands ... of this controlling power.[30]

The illusion of the moralist is their misguided sense of autonomy and freedom. The realism of the "spiritualist" (for want of a better term) is their sensitivity to their enslavement and need for liberation.

In Ellul's judgment, the moralistic way of thinking goes hand in hand with a "minimizing of the content of revelation."[31] For Ellul, it is the ongoing temptation of Christians to understand revelation without reference to the spiritual conflict attested there and thus without recourse to talk of "Satan's seduction" and so forth. But Ellul will not countenance this "minimizing," which he takes to be a moralistic strategy leading to a misplaced sense of comfort and ease and serving only to prolong our blindness to the depths of our bonds to powers beyond our control.

If, then, *Money and Power* recommends a kind of "personalising" of the ethical question centred on the commitment and will of the Christian, Ellul's alertness to the spiritual conflict portrayed in the Bible means that this "personalising" does not lead him to recommend techniques and practices of moral improvement as the solution to "the money problem." The power

26. For a classic statement on the program of demythologising Scripture, see Bultmann, "New Testament and Mythology."
27. Ellul, *Money and Power*, 76.
28. Ellul, *Money and Power*, 77.
29. Ellul, *Money and Power*, 77.
30. Ellul, *Money and Power*, 76.
31. Ellul, *Money and Power*, 84.

of money, or rather, the unsettling reality of money as a spiritual power, problematizes such techniques and practices. And so "even if to some extent we are able to master our thoughts and emotions and thus the inclinations which come from our hearts alone, we still cannot dominate the love of money, for this is aroused by a seductive power which is far beyond us, just as it is maintained by a force that is outside us."[32]

Rich Young Ruler

We see Ellul's apocalyptic (in both senses of the term) grasp of Scripture in his reading of the Gospel narrative of the rich young ruler (Matt 19:16–30; Mark 10:17–31; Luke 18:18–30). Within the moral order, the rich young ruler "has no need to feel guilty."[33] His use of money is exemplary. Jesus's command that he sell all he has, give the money to the poor, and come follow him is thus not understood by Ellul to be a command regarding a supremely moral use of money, a command that can then be turned into "a general ethical principle."[34] Jesus's command, rather, is "a judgment, a revelation." It judges and reveals the rich young ruler's "relationship to his money," and more specifically, the fact that "he remains bound to this power."[35] In this way, and only in this way, does Jesus show him "his real situation."[36]

But as noted above, Ellul does not think this passage can be read in isolation from God's redeeming work in Christ. The judgment on the rich young ruler—and on those who read this passage—"is not made in order to damn us, and the command is not given to the young man to show how wicked he is and how right God would be to condemn him."[37] Rather, the purpose of the judgment is its character as a revelation: "its intention is to show that he is weak, a slave; that money is a power; that man's strength is unable to free him; that he needs Jesus's intervention and grace."[38]

---

32. Ellul, *Money and Power*, 84.
33. Ellul, *Money and Power*, 86.
34. Ellul, *Money and Power*, 86.
35. Ellul, *Money and Power*, 86.
36. Ellul, *Money and Power*, 86.
37. Ellul, *Money and Power*, 86.
38. Ellul, *Money and Power*, 86.

The Apocalyptic Paul

Turning briefly to Ellul's reading of Paul in *Money and Power*, we get a glimpse of what it means to live in the light of Jesus's intervention and grace. For Mammon is not only a power. It is amongst those "conquered, deposed powers which Christ, by dying on the cross, has stripped of authority."[39] This is not to say that Mammon is no longer a threat and temptation with which the Christian must wrestle. Ellul finds the apocalyptic conflict between God and Mammon so starkly drawn in the Gospels to be key for a proper understanding of Paul's directives concerning money. Only when we take with full seriousness Christ's claim that we cannot serve God and Mammon (understood as a rival god), argues Ellul, can we understand "why St. Paul says that 'the love of money is the root of all evils' (1 Tim 6:10)."[40] Ellul is adamant that Paul's claim is "not a hackneyed bit of popular morality" but "an accurate summary" of the "conflict" between God and his opponents, a conflict in which one's faith is at stake.[41] Paul's declaration in Eph 6:12 that "we are not contending against flesh and blood, but against the principalities, against the powers, against the world rulers of this present darkness" is thus seamlessly integrated into Ellul's biblically informed description of the problem of money.[42]

But if Mammon remains a power to be fought against, it is not a power that Christians need fear. "Spiritually we can no longer fear money because on the cross Jesus Christ took away its victory and its victims."[43] Decisive for Ellul's account of the Christian life is a soteriological concept deemed by many to be central to Paul's thought: our "association" or "union" with Christ.[44] To be *in Christ*, according to Ellul, is to be "joined to Christ's victory."[45] Now Christ's victory is "an accomplished fact," and "union with Christ by faith is another fact of human life."[46] But recalling the first part of our essay, the truth of these "facts" is neither objective nor subjective but is

---

39. Ellul, *Money and Power*, 85.
40. Ellul, *Money and Power*, 84.
41. Ellul, *Money and Power*, 84.
42. Ellul, *Money and Power*, 84–85.
43. Ellul, *Money and Power*, 134.
44. Albert Schweitzer, who was distinctively attentive to the "apocalyptic" dimensions of the thought of both Jesus and Paul, also made central to the apostle's theology the language of "union" and "participation" in his 1930 work *The Mysticism of Paul the Apostle*. For a recent exploration of the Pauline concept of union with Christ, see Thate et al., *'In Christ' in Paul*.
45. Ellul, *Money and Power*, 135.
46. Ellul, *Money and Power*, 135.

known to us only in a relationship of faith with God, a relationship in which we stand as a dialogue partner addressed by God's present word. And so Ellul, referring to Paul's declaration in Philippians 4 that "I can do all things," writes, "When we are joined to Christ's victory, we must still draw out its implications: this is personal business. We each must learn. The fact that the Holy Spirit is victorious in us does not in any way make apprenticeship unnecessary. Although Paul is truly delivered from the power of money, he must still learn how to live in abundance and in poverty."[47]

In this way, Paul stands for Ellul as the witness to a life that is learning to live into the deliverance from the powers that God in Christ has accomplished. To live such a life is to live in reality and truth. Paul, like Scripture, offers no abstract principles that can foster such a life. As noted at the beginning of this essay, the reality that Scripture unveils is not constituted by an objective set of rules and norms that can be learned and applied like mathematical formulae. For Ellul, reality is ultimately relational and communicative. It is the realty of God's dialogue with us, and it is only as participants in this dialogue (and not, say, by "objective" acts of charity or relinquishment of possessions, nor by the establishment of a Christian economic system) that we can live as those delivered from the power of Satan.

Works Cited

Aulén, Gustaf. *Christus Victor: An Historical Study of the Three Main Types of the Idea of Atonement*. Translated by A. G. Hebert. London: SPCK, 1970.

Bultmann, Rudolf. "New Testament and Mythology: The Problem of Demythologizing the New Testament Proclamation (1941)." In *New Testament and Mythology and Other Basic Writings*, edited and translated by Schubert M. Ogden, 1–43. Philadelphia: Fortress, 1984.

Dawn, Marva J. "The Concept of 'The Principalities and Powers' in the Works of Jacques Ellul." PhD diss., University of Notre Dame, 1992.

Ellul, Jacques. *Apocalypse: The Book of Revelation*. Translated by George W. Schreiner. New York: Seabury, 1977.

———. *L'homme et l'argent*. Neuchâtel: Delachaux et Niestlé, 1954. Translated as *Money and Power*. Translated by LaVonne Neff. Repr. Eugene, OR: Wipf & Stock, 2009.

Prather, Scott. *Christ, Power and Mammon: Karl Barth and John Howard Yoder in Dialogue*. London: T. & T. Clark, 2013.

Schweitzer, Albert. *The Mysticism of Paul the Apostle*. Translated by William Montgomery. 2nd ed. London: A. & C. Black, 1953.

Thate, Michael J., et al., eds. *'In Christ' in Paul: Explorations in Paul's Theology of Union and Participation*. Tübingen: Mohr Siebeck, 2014.

Ziegler, Philip G. *Militant Grace: The Apocalyptic Turn and the Future of Christian Theology*. Grand Rapids: Baker Academic, 2018.

---

47. Ellul, *Money and Power*, 135.

You may be interested in:

Understanding Jacques Ellul

By Jeffrey P. Greenman, Read M. Schuchardt and Noah J. Toly

Jacques Ellul (1912-1994) was one of the world's last great polymaths and one of the most important Christian thinkers of his time, engaging the world with a simplicity, sincerity, courage, and passion that few have matched. However, Ellul is an often misunderstood thinker. As more than fifty books and over one thousand articles bear his name, embarking on a study of Ellul's thought can be daunting.

This book provides an introduction to Ellul's life and work, analysing and assessing his thought across the most important themes of his scholarship. Readers will see that his remarkably broad field of vision, clarity of focus, and boldly prophetic voice make his work worth reading and considering, rereading and discussing.

'This revealing overview of Ellul's life and work enables us to grasp the underlying unity of his principal interests: communication and Christianity' - **Eric Mcluhan,** author of Know Thyself: Action and Perception

Jeffrey P. Greenman is Associate Dean of Biblical and Theological Studies and Professor of Christian Ethics at Wheaton College, Illinois.

Read Mercer Schuchardt is Associate Professor of Communication at Wheaton College, Illinois.

Noah J. Toly is Director of Urban Studies and Associate Professor of Politics and International Relations at Wheaton College, Illinois.

First published by James Clarke & Co. 25 July 2013

Paperback ISBN: 978 0 227 17406 7
PDF ISBN: 978 0 227 90185 4

You may be interested in:

Presence in the Modern World
A New Translation by Lisa Richmond

By Jacques Ellul and Lisa Richmond (translator)

Presence in the Modern World is Jacques Ellul's most foundational book, combining his social analysis with his theological orientation. Appearing first in French in 1948, and later in English as *The Presence of the Kingdom*, it has reached the status of a classic that retains all of its relevance dealing with today's challenges.

How should we respond to such complex forces as technology or the state? How can we communicate with one another, despite the problems inner to modern forms of media? Do we have hope for the future of our civilisation? Ellul responds by describing how a Christian's unique presence in the world can make a difference. Instead of acting as 'sociological beings', we must commit ourselves to the kind of revolution that will occur only when we become radically aware of our present situation and undertake 'a ferocious and passionate destruction of myths'. In this way, states Ellul, we become the medium for God's action in the modern world.

This new edition presents a fresh translation along with new footnotes, an introduction to Ellul's life, and a complete bibliography in both English and French.

Jacques Ellul (1912-94) was a French law professor, social theorist, and lay theologian. In addition to Presence in the Modern World, his best-known works include The Technological Society, Propaganda, The Humiliation of the Word and Hope in Time of Abandonment.

First published by James Clarke & Co. 28 September 2017

Paperback ISBN: 978 0 227 17663 4
PDF ISBN: 978 0 227 90637 8

You may be interested in:

The Gift of the Other
Levinas, Derrida, and a Theology of Hospitality

By Andrew Shepherd

We live in an age of global capitalism and terror. In a climate of consumption and fear, the unknown "Other" is regarded as a threat to our safety, a client to assist, or a competitor to be overcome in the struggle for scarce resources. And yet, the Christian Scriptures explicitly summon us to welcome strangers, to care for the widow and the orphan, and to build relationships with those distant from us. But how, in this world of hostility and commodification, do we practice hospitality? In *The Gift of the Other*, Andrew Shepherd engages deeply with the influential thought of French thinkers Emmanuel Levinas and Jacques Derrida, and argues that a true vision of hospitality is ultimately found not in postmodern philosophies but in the Christian narrative. The book offers a compelling Trinitarian account of the God of hospitality – a God of communion who "makes room" for otherness, who overcomes the hostility of the world through Jesus' life, death, and resurrection, and who, through the work of the Spirit, is forming a new community: the Church – a people of welcome.

> '*The Gift of the Other* provides a salutary perspective on a world in which fear threatens to dominate our lives'
> -**Beth Newman**, Baptist Theological Seminary at Richmond, Virginia

Andrew Shepherd is a researcher and teacher in theology and ethics. He is involved in A Rocha Aotearoa, New Zealand – a Christian conservation movement – and Servants to Asia's Urban Poor.

First published by James Clarke & Co. 27 November 2014

Paperback ISBN: 978 0 227 17484 5
PDF ISBN: 978 0 227 90294 3

You may be interested in:

The Gift of the Other
Levinas, Derrida, and a Theology of Hospitality

By Andrew Shepherd